Oxford Studies in European Law

General Editors: Paul Craig and Gráinne de Búrca

THE LIMITS OF COMPETITION LAW

The Limits of
Competition Law

Markets and Public Services

TONY PROSSER

OXFORD
UNIVERSITY PRESS

*This book has been printed digitally and produced in a standard specification
in order to ensure its continuing availability*

OXFORD
UNIVERSITY PRESS

Great Clarendon Street, Oxford OX2 6DP
Oxford University Press is a department of the University of Oxford.
It furthers the University's objective of excellence in research, scholarship,
and education by publishing worldwide in
Oxford New York

Auckland Cape Town Dar es Salaam Hong Kong Karachi
Kuala Lumpur Madrid Melbourne Mexico City Nairobi
New Delhi Shanghai Taipei Toronto
With offices in
Argentina Austria Brazil Chile Czech Republic France Greece
Guatemala Hungary Italy Japan South Korea Poland Portugal
Singapore Switzerland Thailand Turkey Ukraine Vietnam

Oxford is a registered trade mark of Oxford University Press
in the UK and in certain other countries

Published in the United States
by Oxford University Press Inc., New York

© T. Prosser, 2005

The moral rights of the author have been asserted

Database right Oxford University Press (maker)

Reprinted 2009

ISBN 978-0-19-926669-2

GENERAL EDITORS' PREFACE

Tony Prosser is a recognized authority in the general area of nationalized industry, regulated industry, and privatization. He is therefore especially well-qualified to deal with the subject matter of this book, which concerns the balance between competition law and public service law in the provision of public services. The tension between the two is readily apparent. Competition law is premised on conceptions of economic efficiency, consumer choice and the market. The foundations of public service law by way of contrast are to be found in ideas of citizenship, social and economic rights, and social solidarity. The values that underlie competition law and public service law are explored from a theoretical perspective and this discussion lays the groundwork for the remainder of the work. Prosser argues convincingly that each of these values has validity and importance, and that it is therefore mistaken to see public service simply as a correction for market failure: whether we favour competition law or public service law will depend on the values that we seek to promote in a particular area.

It is a real strength of this book that the interplay between the two is examined from a number of differing perspectives. Thus Prosser analyses the UK approach to competition law and public services, and shows how utility regulators have developed a form of public service law alongside their responsibilities cast in terms of competition. It is however on the Continent, in countries such as France and Italy that a public service law has been most fully articulated. The analysis of the continental approach to public service forms a highly useful counterpoint to the more Anglo-Saxon preoccupation with competition. The focus for the remainder of the book is on the European Union and how the tensions between competition and public service have played out at that level. The discussion ranges over the approach to state monopolies, the way in which the rules of competition have been applied to public undertakings in the context of Article 86, and the application of the rules on state aids to public services. This is followed by in-depth consideration of services of general interest, the approach taken to this topic by the Community institutions, especially the Commission, and the choices embodied in the Constitutional Treaty. The analysis then turns to liberalization and public service obligations in specific sectors, such as telecommunications, energy, postal services, and transport. This is followed by a chapter devoted to the special considerations that apply in public service broadcasting.

This book will be of interest to domestic and EU lawyers alike and also to all those concerned with the values that should underpin the delivery of public services.

Gráinne de Búrca
Paul Craig

PREFACE

This book will examine the role of law in the provision of public services; more precisely, that of two types of law. The first is competition law, increasingly important as the use of competitive markets has grown in public service provision. The second is, to British readers, less familiar; public service law which protects the essentially non-market values associated with public services. Historically, this latter has been a matter for politics rather than law in the UK, but I shall show that in other European countries there is a well-developed body of such law at a high level of principle.

The stark contrast between the 'Anglo-Saxon' and the 'Continental' approaches can also be seen in major tensions within European Community law, where there has for a number of years been an over-riding concern to complete the single internal market, and this has included the introduction of competition to important public services, notably the public utilities of telecommunications, energy supply, and postal services. However, such liberalization has been qualified by the protection of universal service to avoid geographic or social exclusion, and recently there has been a revival in the acknowledgement of the importance of public service values in Community law, seeing them as expressions of citizenship rights which form an essential part of the European model of society. Tensions between competitive markets and public service have existed even more strongly in relation to broadcasting, especially as to the extent to which public service broadcasters should have a distinct role and access to public finance.

I shall describe how each approach is based on distinctive values; competition law on economic concepts of efficiency and on consumer choice, public service on social and economic rights and on social solidarity. A central argument is that each of these values has validity and importance, and that it is a mistake to see public service as simply a correction for market failure. Rather, which approach we choose will depend on the values we need to promote in particular contexts. Where we do not rely on markets and competition law, we need to resolve problems of account-ability in other ways, and this may be done by independent regulation and (much less often) by competitive tendering for service provision. The law and other developments are stated as at the end of July 2004.

As always, a number of institutions and individuals deserve generous acknowledgement in this work. I have benefited from the intellectual stimulation of colleagues in three institutions; first the Centre for Socio-Legal Studies at the University of Sheffield (particularly Douglas Lewis), then the School of Law at the University of Glasgow, and finally the University of Bristol, where the book was actually written. All of them have provided intellectual and social support which has, I hope, resulted in a book which fully incorporates their influence. Some of the work was done, as with my previous work, in Italy, and I am especially grateful to Professor Salvatore Cattaneo, of the Dipartimento di Diritto dell'Economia at the University of Rome 'La Sapienza', for wonderful hospitality during my visits there. I should also like to thank Loredana Giani and Beatrice Locoratolo for guiding me through the labyrinth of the Italian approach to public service.

Finally, as in my earlier work, I must thank above all Charlotte Villiers, not merely for her tolerance of my preoccupations but in suggesting some of the initial ideas for the book. I must now add thanks to Amelia and Laurie, not only for coping with a sometimes distracted father, but for reminding me that there is more to life than just writing books.

Tony Prosser
2004

CONTENTS

TABLE OF CASES

TABLE OF STATUTES

TABLE OF EUROPEAN CASES

TABLE OF EUROPEAN LEGISLATION

Regulations

Directives

Introduction: Setting the Scene

We live in a world of markets and of rights; both have increased enormously in visibility, and in importance, over the last few decades. Alongside markets and rights is a concern with the effects of them both on social solidarity and their possible role in fragmenting the values that hold a society together. One of the most fundamental problems facing modern law is how to attempt to reconcile the values of markets, rights, and social solidarity and how to deal with the tensions between them.

Reconciliation with the market has proved easier in the case of political and civil rights than in the case of social and economic rights, even though the latter are increasingly recognized as fundamental attributes of citizenship in Western societies. It is much easier to conceive of rational economic man as a bearer of political than of social rights. In order to examine the relationship between markets and such rights, this book will concern the development of competitive markets in the provision of public services; their 'marketization', to use an inelegant but useful neologism. Moreover, it is in relation to public services that most claims have been made that delivery through competitive markets contradicts values of social solidarity which are the essence of the public service mission. I shall not approach these questions directly through an economic analysis of the potential role of such markets, but rather examine their legal expression in the twin disciplines of competition law and public service law, the latter a more familiar concept in Continental Europe than in the UK. The adoption of these two legal themes merits a little more introductory explanation.

It is common to find marketization referred to as creating 'free' markets. A moment's thought will show that this phrase is profoundly misleading. Markets are never free, being constructed through, and dependent on, different kinds of legal (and social) structures. Familiar examples would be the allocation of property rights and provision of the tools for creating and enforcing contractual relations. A further legal foundation for the operation of markets is the development of some system of competition law to contribute to *keeping* markets open. As we shall see, the nature and effectiveness of competition law has varied enormously at different times and places, and indeed some market-based societies have managed to do without a formal competition law system. However, marketization has as a central theme a shift to competition law rather than administration or hierarchy as the major organizing principle of a public service; the new law may take the form of the general competition law applicable to other business transactions or, more rarely, of a special regime for a particular sector. In some versions of marketization, competition law is, according to its proponents, the only appropriate discipline for economic regulation; it has a sort of imperialist presence at the expense of other forms of legal relations such as the granting of exclusive or special rights to undertakings providing public services. Thus, in debates about the provision of such services, reliance on competition law is the legal expression of, and surrogate for, the creation and maintenance of open markets. Competition law can also be seen as creating a form of accountability for the exercise of economic power, accountability here to consumers and to shareholders through the marketplace.

By contrast, rights and social solidarity will also find their expression in law. In the UK, legal expression of these values in the economic, as opposed to the civil and political, domain has been limited; their protection has been through political rather than legal means. By contrast, in Continental Europe (especially France) there is a highly developed regime of public service law reflecting both social rights and a concern for social solidarity, and trying to avoid the fragmenting social effects of competitive markets and distributional inequality. Public service law offers a different type of accountability for the exercise of economic power; accountability to citizens through law and through institutional scrutiny by regulators and government. The relationship of this law with competitive markets is a question which has not only arisen in the domestic law of Continental jurisdictions; it has also arisen in an acute way in European Community law and as such has become increasingly relevant to the UK, especially in relation to the public utilities of telecommunications, energy, transport, and postal services.

On the one hand, the 'Anglo-Saxon' argument in Community law debates has been that failure to apply competition law to such enterprises only serves to give them an unfairly protected position and to mask inefficiencies; on the other, the 'Continental' argument (from France in particular) is that the application of competition law without recognizing its limits in relation to public services threatens their very nature by destroying the key values of public service which underlie their distinctive missions. A similar debate has occurred in the context of broadcasting; should we have a protected role for public service broadcasters because of their distinctive contribution to the broadcasting ecology, or instead simply create competitive markets and liberate consumer choice? Not only have these debates taken place at a political level; they have also influenced important amendments to the European Community Treaty and have underlain many decisions of the European courts.

It will be useful for me to mention at this stage two concerns that will be outside the scope of this book, at least as regards their explicit discussion. The first is that of the public service ethic, a concept more familiar in the UK than that of public service law. It has been characterized by a Parliamentary Committee as containing a number of obligations which public servants should meet, especially in the use of public money. These are impartiality, accountability, trust, equity, probity, and service.[1] The public service ethic also denotes the independence and freedom from corruption of public sector institutions and the distinctive culture of the civil service. Though some of these values will be touched on later, this is not the place for a detailed analysis of the public service ethic. The second theme which is outside the scope of this book is the extent to which non-economic factors, such as regional development and employment policies, are taken into account in the decision-making of the ordinary competition authorities, for example in relation to mergers. Again, this will be touched on later, but raises concerns which go well beyond the themes of this book.

Before outlining the scheme to be adopted for my later chapters, I shall describe more fully some of the tensions which can be found between the use of competitive markets and competition law and public services, firstly through looking at the position of some international organizations on this question and then by describing some recent UK examples

---

[1] Public Administration Select Committee, 'The Public Service Ethos', HC 263, 2001–2, para. 12.

of marketizing public services. At this stage it is not necessary to define public service values more precisely as that is a somewhat difficult task which will be addressed in Chapters 2 and 5.

Tensions between Markets and Competition Law and Public Service: The International Dimension

The Organization for Economic Co-Operation and Development (OECD)

According to the influential Report on Regulatory Reform from the OECD, the best approach to the relationship between competition law and public services is a straightforward one; use competition law wherever possible.[2] Included in its recommendations, which are to be applied broadly across sectors and policy areas, is the theme that the scope, effectiveness, and enforcement of competition policy be reviewed and strengthened so as to '[e]liminate sectoral gaps in coverage of competition law, unless evidence suggests that compelling public interests can be served in better ways'. Thus:

Exemptions from national competition laws have accumulated in numerous sectors, including energy and utilities, transport, communications and agriculture. Such exemptions have reduced economic performance by allowing anti-competitive practices – such as abuses of dominant position, cartel conduct, and anti-competitive mergers. An essential reform is to reverse such exemptions and apply the general competition law as widely as possible.[3]

A further recommendation is to '[r]eform economic regulations in all sectors to stimulate competition, and eliminate them except where clear evidence demonstrates that they are the best ways to serve broad public interests'.[4]

There is thus in this case a very strong preference for regulation only through competition law; any exceptions must be justified by 'clear evidence' and 'compelling public interests'. It is interesting to note, however, that in more recent work the OECD has adopted a more sophisticated conception of regulation, emphasizing its interdependence with liberalization and the importance of improving regulatory governance rather than deregulation.[5]

---

[2] OECD (1997) 27–34.   [3] Ibid., 32.   [4] Ibid., 33.   [5] OECD (2002) esp. ch. 2.

The World Trade Organization (WTO) and GATS

The position as regards the WTO and the General Agreement on Trade and Services (GATS) is somewhat different and rather more nuanced. No one disputes in this context that there are limits to competition law in relation to public services; the question is rather how extensive these limits should be and how effectively they can be enforced by national authorities. In the Uruguay Round (concluded in 1994) the relevant dispute centred around the 'cultural exception' for films and broadcasting, and, whilst it was agreed that audiovisual services were in principle covered by the GATS agreement, neither the European Union nor its Member States made any commitments relating to this sector.[6] In the more recent Doha Round (in progress at the time of writing), considerable concern was expressed by supporters of public services about the dangers of opening up trade and markets in relation to them.[7] On the other hand, according to the UK Government, '[t]he EC has said in its requests that it is not seeking the dismantling of public services or state-owned companies . . . Privatisation is not in itself an objective of the GATS, and cannot be forced on any government through the GATS process.'[8] Thus the Community had in the earlier round placed a horizontal limitation on the application of GATS in relation to public utilities, permitting them to be subject to public monopolies or to exclusive rights granted to private operators. It proposed the retention of this exception in the current round, although there have been requests from other countries to lift it. No commitments were made by the Community in health or education; in telecommunications and posts, market opening was expressed to be subject to the retention of universal service safeguards.[9]

Nevertheless, concern continues in two particular areas. The first is that of the unclear and badly drafted provisions of GATS itself relating to public services; thus Article I:3 GATS defines as services within the scope of the agreement services in any sector except services 'supplied in

---

[6] See Footer and Beat Graber (2000).

[7] For a detailed and well-argued statement of the objections see in particular World Development Movement (2002).

[8] Department of Trade and Industry, *Liberalising Trade in Services: A New Consultation on the World Trade Organisation GATS Negotiations* (2002), para. 2.10.

[9] See European Commission, *Summary of the Commission's Proposal for the EU's Services Offer* (2002), at http://europa.eu.int/comm/trade/issues/sectoral/services/docs/servof.pdf (consulted 13 July 2004).

the exercise of governmental authority'; the latter is further defined as 'any service which is supplied neither on a commercial basis, nor in competition with one or more service suppliers'. The Preamble to GATS also includes the words '[r]ecognising the rights of Members to regulate, and to introduce new regulations, on the supply of services within their territories in order to meet national policy objectives...'. According to the UK Government, this makes it clear that under GATS 'national governments retain the right, and the ability, to regulate services in order to meet national policy objectives, such as universal service, affordable prices etc'.[10] Others are less sanguine, pointing to the possibility of a narrow definition of Article I:3 by WTO Dispute Panels, especially since many public services are no longer supplied directly by governmental bodies and, as we shall see, a degree of competition exists in markets where special provisions relating to public services nevertheless remain of the utmost importance, for example in the health sector.

A second concern relates to Article VI:4 of GATS setting out a work programme which appears to apply to all sectors, not just those in which Members have made specific commitments. It commits Members to 'disciplines' on domestic regulation, including licensing requirements, which

shall aim to ensure that such requirements are, inter alia:
a) based on objective and transparent criteria, such as competence and the ability to supply the service;
b) not more burdensome than necesary to ensure the quality of the service;
c) in the case of licensing procedures, not in themselves a restriction on the supply of the service.

Once more the UK Government is sanguine; '[s]ome commentators have argued that...WTO dispute settlement will, in effect have power of veto over whether or not a national regulatory measure is necessary at all or more burdensome or trade restrictive than necessary. While it is recognised that this is something to guard against, this claim has been exaggerated and there is no intention by WTO Members to prevent each other from regulating for domestic policy objectives.'[11] Again, others do not agree; as the World Development Movement puts it, in relation to whether regulations are 'burdensome' or 'necessary', '[s]uch judgments

---

[10] Department of Trade and Industry, *Liberalising Trade in Services*..., para. 6.28.
[11] Department of Trade and Industry, *Liberalising Trade in Services*..., para. 5.15.

are inherently political and should not be left to a small body of trade lawyers in Geneva'.[12]

This debate is more directly concerned with liberalization and lifting regulatory burdens than with competition law, but of course such reforms do imply a move to competition law as the new regulatory principle instead of less competition-based forms of regulation. There is a clear tension between this and public service values; the opposition to GATS during the Doha Round suggests that anxiety about the future of such values has appealed to wider social concerns.

The European Union

In the GATS context there is a sense that the debate on liberalization on public services is only just beginning, and much depends on what concessions are made in a revived Doha Round of negotiations. In the European Union, by contrast, controversy on the limits on the application of competition law to public services is well established, both in its politics and its law. Indeed, it is so well established that three chapters of this book (Chapters 6–8) will be devoted to it, and it is just necessary to point out here that the debates have concerned both the extent to which public services are economic activities and so caught by competition law, and, if they are, whether they can be protected by special provisions in the Treaty which provide a highly qualified exception for 'services of general economic interest'. Another current concern is the extent to which Member States can fund such services through state aid, and the procedures (such as competitive tendering) necessary to select service providers. All these issues will be discussed in detail in the later chapters.

Tensions between Competitive Markets and Public Service: Some UK Examples

The Health Service

The provision of a public health service is the quintessential public service, perhaps particularly so in the UK given the symbolic importance of the National Health Service (NHS). Nevertheless, whilst the service has not been made subject overall to a general or special competition law

---

[12] World Development Movement (2002) 16.

regime, important steps have been taken by governments of both political complexions to introduce market mechanisms within it. The most celebrated example was the Conservatives' internal market implemented by the National Health Service and Community Care Act 1990.[13] In brief, the earlier hierarchical organization of the health service was replaced by a division between purchasers and providers within it. They were linked by contract, in the case of private providers in the ordinary private law form, but within the Service they took the form of 'NHS Contracts'.[14] According to the legislation, such a contract 'shall not be regarded for any purpose as giving rise to contractual rights or liabilities'.[15] Instead a system of internal arbitration was provided to handle contractual (and pre-contractual) disputes, although this was rarely used.

It is no longer controversial to suggest that the internal market was a failure. Reasons for this included limited real competition and restricted opportunities for exit by dissatisfied parties.[16] The incoming Labour Government acted quickly to reform the system; it stated that, whilst there would be no return to a centralized command and control system, 'nor will there be a continuation of the divisive internal market of the 1990s. That approach which was intended to make the NHS more efficient ended up fragmenting decision-making and distorting incentives to such an extent that unfairness and bureaucracy became its defining features.'[17] The reforms nevertheless retained important elements of the internal market, notably the purchaser/provider split, although the emphasis was now placed more on longer-term contracts, planning health needs, and audit of clinical care.[18]

In later reforms, even under a Labour Government, we have seen the use of further market-based mechanisms within the health service, alongside continuing rhetoric which is critical of competition. Thus the *NHS Plan* of 2000 once more criticized the internal market as 'the market ethos undermined teamwork between professionals and organisations vital to patient-centred care. And it hampered planning across the NHS as a whole, leading to cuts in nurse training and a stalled hospital building programme.' By contrast the new model would strengthen the unique

---

[13] For a detailed and excellent account of the reforms see Davies (2001).
[14] Harden (1992) 42–3.
[15] National Health Service and Community Care Act 1990 s. 4(3).
[16] See Davies (2001) 164–7.
[17] Department of Health, *The New NHS – Modern, Dependable*, Cm 3807 (1998).
[18] For which see Davies (2000). The reforms were implemented by the Health Act 1999.

public service ethic of the NHS.[19] Yet a more detailed document two years later concerning implementation of the plan emphasized themes of payment by results and money following patients; 'perverse incentives need to be replaced with a new system that rewards good performers with more resources for appropriate treatment of more patients to higher standards'. Thus in future, instead of hospitals being given block contracts they would be paid for the activity they undertake; in 2004 a standard tariff was introduced for gradual phasing in to introduce competition on the basis of quality (but not of price), and greater choice was to be permitted between alternative providers, public or private.[20]

Most controversially of all, in 2003 legislation was passed for the introduction of Foundation Hospital Trusts.[21] The Trusts are not subject to direction by the Secretary of State and permission for their establishment is given by an independent regulator, who will also monitor their performance. They have greater financial and management freedoms including freedoms to retain surpluses and to invest in the delivery of new services, as well as to make extra payments to staff. They are responsible to locally elected Boards of Governors. These provisions of the Act were only passed on the last possible day before the dissolution of Parliament, with a Government majority of only 35. The reasons for the opposition to them have been examined by the Health Committee of the House of Commons; the objections are that competition between the trusts would corrode co-operation in the health service, that they could engage in 'cream-skimming' of the most 'profitable' patients, that they would drag resources away from poorer-performing hospitals, that staffing freedoms would lead to inequities and that inequitable access to resources would compound health inequalities.[22]

It is clearly apparent that there are unresolved tensions here between a universalist model of health service emphasizing the principles of equal access and equal treatment of patients, and a market-driven model emphasizing efficiency, innovation, and patient choice. In this case competition law has not been the means of regulating the embryonic internal markets; however, as we shall see in Chapters 2 and 6 below, both domestic and Community competition law are beginning to affect

---

[19] Department of Health, *The NHS Plan*, Cm 4818 (2000), paras. 6.3, 6.5.

[20] Department of Health, *Delivering the NHS Plan*, Cm 5503 (2002), paras. 4.6, 4.10, 5.3. For progress see Department of Health, *The NHS Improvement Plan*, Cm 6268 (2004) esp. ch. 8.

[21] Health and Social Care (Community Health and Standards) Act 2003, Part 1.

[22] Health Committee, 'Foundation Trusts', HC 385, 2002–3.

some important aspects of health service contracting with the private sector, though the extent to which they do so remains controversial.

Compulsory Competitive Tendering of Local Authority Services

A further example of marketization undertaken by the Conservative Governments of the 1980s and 1990s was to require the compulsory competitive tendering of local authority services.[23] Once more a key element of this was a purchaser/provider split, with councils required to bid through separate direct service organizations in competition with the private sector. Here a special, and complex, competition law regime was created. Thus the 1988 Act required that a local authority 'in reaching the decision that they should carry out the work and in doing anything else . . . in connection with the work before reaching the decision, did not act in a manner having the effect or intended or likely to have the effect of restricting, distorting or preventing competition'.[24] This was supplemented under the 1992 Act with a power for the Secretary of State to specify conduct to be regarded as having such an effect.[25] Regulations were used to do so in considerable detail, including matters such as the relationship between the direct service organization and the purchasing authority; further detailed guidance was also issued.[26] Enforcement was for the Secretary of State through the issue of a notice requesting further information, or a direction depriving the authority of the power to provide the service or imposing conditions; for example, in 1995 he served twelve notices and issued seven directions to local authorities because of anti-competitive behaviour, in most cases requiring re-tendering of work and requiring his consent for it to be awarded to the direct service organization.[27]

The compulsory competitive tendering regime created serious problems.[28] Thus ' "[h]ard" quasi-market structures have tended to undermine the trusting, co-operative relationships necessary for efficient contracting. Excessive separation of interests is accompanied by

---

[23] The legislation was the Local Government, Planning and Land Act 1980 Part III, the Local Government Act 1988, and the Local Government Act 1992 Part I.   [24] S. 7(7).

[25] S. 9.

[26] The Local Government (Direct Service Organisations) (Competition) Regulations 1993, SI 1993/848; Department of the Environment, *Competition in the Provision of Local Authority Services*, Departmental Circular 5/96.

[27] Vincent-Jones (2000) 92, and see the Local Government Act 1988 ss. 13–14.

[28] See e.g. Vincent-Jones (1997).

communication and information flow problems, and by increased risk of opportunism by one or both sides ... The result has been a tendency to relatively high levels of conflict expressed in defaults, penalties and disputes.'[29] Instead, it was suggested that '[t]he paramount concern of the authority should be the subordination of client and contractor interests to a public service ethos'.[30] A further concern was that the overriding concentration on cost of services led to a neglect of service quality.

These problems led to reform under the Labour Government, with the replacement of compulsory competitive tendering by 'best value' under the Local Government Act 1999.[31] The new system was intended to provide greater flexibility and discretion for local authorities in meeting the duty of best value, defined as making arrangements 'to secure continuous improvement in the way in which its functions are exercised, having regard to a combination of economy, efficiency and effectiveness'.[32] However, competition for service provision is still strongly encouraged; according to the White Paper preceding the legislation 'retaining work in-house without subjecting it to real competitive pressure can rarely be justified', and government guidance indicates that '[w]hile authorities have discretion over how individual services are provided, the highest standards of service provision are more likely to be achieved where there is genuine competition, choice for service users and a mixed economy rather than where any one supplier dominates the provision of services'.[33] Monitoring is for the Audit Commission with the Secretary of State having extensive powers of direction in relation to failing authorities; however the complex competition regime for compulsory competitive tendering no longer exists.[34]

We also see here an example of the introduction of competitive markets into the provision of public services, again accompanied by some uncertainty as to the most effective mechanisms to make them workable and to respect the particular values of public service. In this case, unlike in the case of health, a special competition law regime was created but rapidly proved unwieldy, and has now been replaced by more flexible

---

[29] Vincent-Jones (1997) 154.   [30] Ibid., 163.
[31] See generally Vincent-Jones (2000).   [32] Local Government Act 1999, s. 3(1).
[33] Department of the Environment, Transport and the Regions, *Modern Local Government: In Touch with the People*, Cm 4014 (1998) para. 7.28; Office of the Deputy Prime Minister, *Local Government Act 1999: Part 1 Best Value and Performance Improvement*, Departmental Circular 03/2003.   [34] Local Government Act 1999, ss. 10–15.

arrangements whilst keeping competition as an element in the broader best value regime.

Bus Services

A further example of a move from a highly regulated public service to a competitive market was that of bus services.[35] The Transport Act 1985 abolished the long-established requirement for route licensing outside London; instead only notice of the intention to run a service needed to be given by operators. Financial support for unprofitable services had to be awarded by a system of competitive tendering. The result was extensive competition through new entry, although the sector has more recently consolidated considerably. The market was policed by the general competition authorities, and very soon they became heavily involved; between 1987 and the end of 1994 the Office of Fair Trading received 541 complaints alleging anti-competitive conduct by bus operators and fifteen references were made to the then Monopolies and Mergers Commission. Many of the complaints concerned seriously anti-competitive behaviour.

The competition authorities expressed considerable concern about the high level of their involvement in the industry, the Director General of Fair Trading pointing to a continuing problem of securing effective and sustained competition in the bus industry, and the Commission calling for a general review of the industry, with the possibility of establishing a specialist regulator.[36] Governments of both political complexions have refused to establish such a regulator; however action has been taken to qualify the effect of general competition law in certain respects. Thus a block exemption under the Competition Act 1998 has been issued to permit collaboration between operators in relation to certain ticketing schemes, notably multi-operator travel cards and through tickets. A special competition test has also been laid down in relation to quality partnerships implementing local authority bus strategies; both these provisions will be discussed in more detail in Chapter 3 below. It should be noted, however, that, as we shall see in the next chapter, the House of Commons Transport Committee has been highly critical of the

---

[35] For a more detailed examination see Prosser (1997) 200–12.

[36] Director General of Fair Trading, *Annual Report 1993*, HC 551, 1993–4; Monopolies and Mergers Commission, *The Supply of Bus Services in Mid and West Kent*, Cm 2309 (1993), paras. 6.85–7.

application of competition law as a limit on collaboration in the public interest between bus operators.

The Public Utilities

In many ways the most important example of the introduction of competitive markets to public services is that of the public utilities of telecommunications, electricity, gas, water, rail, and posts. The privatization of the former monopoly utilities has, in the telecommunications and energy sectors, been accompanied by a massive increase in the role of competitive markets; in telecommunications there is no longer any requirement of a licence to provide services and in gas and electricity supply markets have been fully liberalized. This has raised major public service concerns, notably in relation to the adoption of cost-based pricing ending cross-subsidy to household consumers and in relation to policies on disconnection of supply. In this case the enterprises are subject to general competition law but also to a special regulatory regime in each sector. The regulators have powers to apply general competition law but are also subject to certain social duties, and since the 1997 change of government their social role has increased, for example as a result of new provisions empowering ministers to issue guidance to them on social policies.

The liberalization of utility markets is clearly of enormous importance, both because the changes are well established and highly unlikely to be reversed, and because they show very clearly the interaction of competition law and public service values. For this reason they are discussed in detail later in this book, with the competition law powers of the regulators described in Chapter 3 and the whole of Chapter 4 being devoted to the development of public service law and policy by the regulators themselves. Thus further discussion can be postponed until those chapters.

Broadcasting

The final example of the introduction of competitive markets in a public service is that of broadcasting. Although commercial broadcasting alongside the BBC has a fairly long history in the UK, it has been highly regulated to protect public service broadcasting values. However, recent years have seen a considerable growth in the number of broadcasters, and the fuller development of digital broadcasting permitting a far greater profusion of channels is taking this much further. The Government's response has been in the form of the Communications Act 2003.

On the one hand this opens markets further by abolishing restrictions on ownership of UK broadcasters by non-European Economic Area concerns and has lifted restrictions on cross-media ownership and concentration of broadcasting ownership. This liberalization caused considerable concern as potentially limiting media pluralism, and a special 'plurality test' may now apply to some media mergers to address these issues. On the other hand, the Act sets out a definition of public service broadcasting in the round for the first time, and the new regulatory body is responsible for reviewing periodically the extent to which the public service remit is met. This is accompanied by moves towards co-regulation with monitoring of the achievement of each public service broadcaster's remit being initially a matter for the broadcaster itself, with reserve sanctioning powers for inadequate performance being retained by the regulator.

Once more, this raises important issues of the relationship between opening markets and public service, some of which are specific to broadcasting. This sector will be discussed in detail in Chapter 9 below, so once more fuller discussion can be postponed until then.

It is thus clear that in a considerable number of important public services there are, at best, strong tensions between competitive markets and competition law on the one hand, and public service values on the other; at worst the two types of regime may seem incompatible. Where reconciliation of the two approaches is possible this gives an important role to law, including the decisions of competition and regulatory authorities. We shall see that very different approaches to this task have been adopted in the UK, in Continental Europe, and in European Community law. Before moving on to discuss them, it will be helpful to summarize the structure to be adopted.

The Scheme of the Book

After this introduction, Chapter 2 examines the theoretical and philosophical background to tensions between competition law and public service values. It will examine the bases and purposes of competition law, and will contrast these with those of public service based on social rights and social solidarity. Thus equipped with appropriate analytical tools, it is then possible to tackle the actual legal position in more detail. Chapter 3 will summarize the major relevant aspects of UK competition law, emphasizing the recent shift away from a 'public interest' test to one based on maximizing competition, and describing the concurrent powers of the utility regulators to apply the law in their sectors. It will also consider the scope of competition law and the extent to which it applies to public services. Chapter 4 will examine the work of the utility regulators in more detail, concentrating on how they have, in conjunction with government, developed a form of public service law alongside their economic and competition responsibilities. This new law is, however, somewhat inconsistent and uncoordinated.

By way of contrast, Chapter 5 will consider public service law in France and Italy, covering both their constitutional and their administrative law. It will suggest that, particularly in France, public service law has developed at a high level of principle and has more recently been adapted for the application to liberalized markets. In Italy a similar process has taken place, and there in particular independent regulatory authorities have assumed considerable importance in the reconciliation of competitive markets and public service values.

Chapter 6 is the first of three considering European Community law and policy. In this context the tensions between competitive markets and public service are well recognized and are considered in an extensive body of legal materials, albeit legal materials that leave doubts as to the correct answers to some important questions. It will be suggested that the approach of the European courts has changed, from treating public services (or 'services of general interest') as unwelcome impediments to completing a single internal market to seeing them instead as independently valuable expressions of citizenship rights. This is now recognized by such services being granted a form of constitutional status in amendments to the European Community Treaty. There will also be an examination of important recent decisions in relation to state aids, which also raises the question of the extent to which competitive tendering is necessary to assign public service tasks. A similar theme underlies Chapter 7, covering the political background to the treatment of public services by the Community and the various statements of principle from the European Commission relating to them. Chapter 8 will look at the liberalized sectors of telecommunications, energy, postal services, and transport, highlighting the public service obligations which have gone alongside market liberalization, and the creation of independent regulatory authorities to monitor their implementation amongst other tasks, including policing competition. Finally Chapter 9 will examine broadcasting, looking at public service broadcasting in both Community and UK domestic law and highlighting the special position of public service values in this sector, where particularly serious tensions exist between the established role of public service broadcasters and rapidly changing markets and technology. Chapter 10 will draw the work together by providing some general conclusions and recommendations for future development of public service law within the context of competitive markets.

Conclusions

It should already be apparent that there are a number of important questions raised by the introduction of competition to public services. Should regulation be left only to general competition law, or should there be special protection for public service values? If so, what is the most appropriate form of such legal protection, which can range from the constitutional recognition of these values to their inclusion only in soft law? What are the best institutional arrangements for implementing public service values; for example, what is the most appropriate role for independent regulatory authorities, and to what extent should competitive tendering be required before granting state aid to bodies carrying out public service activities? Are the UK and Continental European approaches to public service incompatible, or can they be synthesized, perhaps through the further development of European Community law? In order to seek answers to these questions, it is necessary to begin by examining the underlying theoretical and philosophical issues, and these will be the subject of the following chapter.

2

Competition Law, Citizenship Rights, and Social Solidarity

The preceding chapter has suggested that there is at minimum a tension between the application of competition law to key public services, such as the public utilities, and the principles underlying the distinctive nature of these services. In this chapter I shall address the question in greater depth, commencing with a description of the generally accepted justifications for, and objectives of, competition law and comparing them with the social rights which form one basis for the distinctive nature of public services. I shall also discuss the tradition of public service derived from social solidarity, and the concept of the state as the protector of public service values. This should prepare us for proper critical assessment in the following chapters of the more detailed legal questions that have arisen in the UK, in France and Italy, and in European Community law.

The Justifications for Competition Law

The main justification of competition law is, obviously enough, that it removes unnecessary restrictions on competition. It is also closely linked to the advantages of the market as a means of allocating goods and services; competition law is the means by which markets are kept open and competitive. Much of the discussion in this book will indirectly concern the question of the extent to which markets are an appropriate means of delivering public services. However, a general analysis of the role of markets will be outside its scope; rather I shall concentrate on the legal structuring of markets through competition law as their major regulatory principle.

Such a justification for competition law of course begs the question of why competition is desirable, and it is through this aspect of economic theory that the ultimate justification of this area of law can be found. The chief, and, according to many commentators, the only justification for competition law is the promotion of consumer welfare through maximizing efficiency. This has been particularly pronounced in relation to the influential work of the Chicago School; in the words of one of its leading proponents, '[e]fficiency is the ultimate goal of antitrust [that is competition law in European terminology], but competition a mediate goal that will often be close enough to the ultimate goal to allow the courts to look no further'.[1] Another influential commentator has summarized this view as 'efficiency is the sole objective of antitrust law, and that what is to be understood as efficient and hence consistent with consumer welfare is any conduct or situation that transfers to the consumer's benefit qualitative improvements in manufacture or in cost reduction, without giving anyone room to "restrict" the market...'.[2]

The Chicago view is of course merely one (albeit influential) approach to competition law, and other approaches have included objectives other than efficiency maximization (although it has often proved difficult to identify just what those other objectives may be). As we shall see below, recent moves in UK competition law (whilst not adopting the full rigours of the Chicago approach) have been away from an assessment of whether potentially anti-competitive conduct is in the public interest to a more focussed competition-based test (to be discussed more fully below and in Chapter 3), administered by specialist authorities rather than ministers. Excluded by this approach would be social goals, for example the protection of small businesses or the distribution of wealth.[3] Thus even in the UK we have moved much closer to an efficiency-based system of competition law.

The concept of efficiency is in this context a technical one which often bears little resemblance to popular usage. It can be divided into at least

---

[1] Posner (2001) 29.

[2] Amato (1997) 21–2. The literature of the Chicago School is vast but for a useful summary see Foster (1992) 369–73. An influential statement of themes which came to be adopted by the School is Bork (1993); see esp. 81–9 though note that this is predominantly directed to the capacities of the courts as antitrust authorities, whereas this book will be more closely concerned with the European arrangements where responsibility is more often that of legislatures and administrative authorities.

[3] For the development of US antitrust law towards an efficiency-maximization goal see Eisner (1991).

two and possibly three different senses; allocative efficiency, productive efficiency, and dynamic efficiency.[4] They can be defined more clearly as follows.[5] After setting out definitions some applications of these concepts to public services will be suggested as these are not immediately obvious from the concepts themselves, which are highly theoretical.

Allocative efficiency refers to the situation where, in conditions of perfect competition, goods and services are allocated between consumers according to the price they are prepared to pay and price never rises above the marginal cost of production.[6] 'Everyone who values the produce at its cost of production will, therefore, be able to purchase it. The supplier will not make more, but neither, if it is acting rationally to maximize profits, will it make less.'[7] Allocative efficiency is closely related to the concept of Pareto efficiency, under which an allocation of resources is efficient when it is impossible to make any one individual better off without, at the same time, making someone else worse off.[8] The chief implication in this area of study is that prices should be closely aligned to costs and that there should be no deliberate cross-subsidies on social or other grounds. Whether this is desirable is of the utmost importance in the context of the provision of services by public utilities.

Productive efficiency is closer to everyday uses of the term 'efficiency'. It means that as little of society's wealth is expended in the production of goods as necessary, so goods are produced at the lowest possible cost.[9] Lack of productive efficiency is also referred to as X-inefficiency. The emphasis here is thus on the internal management of an enterprise and in the effects of, for example, the market for corporate control in removing inefficient management. Finally, and closely related to productive efficiency, dynamic efficiency is the incentive to innovate provided by constant exposure to consumer demands; the market acts as a form of discovery process.[10]

It should be stressed that competition, and competition law, also find justification from a direction different from that of economic theory. They can be justified as maximizing consumer choice, not merely because through open markets this leads to an efficient distribution of goods, but

---

[4] Dynamic efficiency may also be considered as one type of productive efficiency.
[5] Whish (2001) 2–4 provides a useful summary, and see also Jones and Sufrin (2001) 8–12. For fuller definitions of types of efficiency see Bork (1993) 91–106.   [6] Whish (2001) 3.
[7] Jones and Sufrin (2001) 9.   [8] Ogus (1994) 24.
[9] Whish (2001) 3; Jones and Sufrin (2004) 8–10.   [10] Whish (2001) 4.

because it is a good in itself.[11] Competitive markets thus promote consumer sovereignty (although it should be noted that this is a very different type of freedom from that implied in political theories of democratic self-government).[12] Thus they are justified not on efficiency but on libertarian grounds.[13] Consumer sovereignty through choice in competitive markets is particularly relevant to some public services as it has provided a major justification for their liberalization and in several cases, for example UK telecommunications and energy supply markets, there has been a dramatic increase in such choice since privatization. However, it has also been suggested that in certain circumstances liberalization may restrict choice through ending cross-subsidies which have supported uneconomic services, or through resulting in a geographic concentration of services in the most profitable locations whilst neglecting less profitable locations such as rural and inner-city areas. As we shall see Chapter 3, this latter argument has been used, for example, to justify entry restrictions into the provision of pharmacy services.

Competitive Markets and Public Services

During the 1980s and 1990s there was, as we saw in Chapter 1, extensive use of competitive markets in the delivery of public services, both through contracting out and the opening up of utility markets. The principles described above which justify the use of competitive markets, and the use of competition law to ensure that they remain competitive, have considerable implications for the provision of utility services in particular.

The theoretical concept of allocative efficiency appears at first sight of limited relevance to the provision of public services. However, the concept is of enormous importance as its implementation threatens to undermine the traditional means by which many such services had been delivered. This is because of its insistence on cost-based pricing. Previously such pricing had been departed from in relation to public services in important ways and major elements of cross-subsidy existed by which some consumers subsidized others. Thus business customers often subsidized domestic consumers, notably in telecommunications; rural

---

[11] See Lewis (1996) esp. 111–19.   [12] See Sunstein (1997) 344.
[13] Jones and Sufrin (2004) 16.

customers were subsidized by urban customers, and, for example in transport, little-used services were subsidized by users of popular services in times of peak demand. In particular, there was a history of what is sometimes referred to as 'postal stamp' pricing; the adoption of a standard price for the service irrespective of costs. The most noteworthy example is that of the postal service itself, where a single letter rate is paid irrespective of the distance and costs of delivery; telecommunications charges were also geographically averaged and energy prices were not fully cost-reflective. As we shall see later in this chapter, these special pricing principles were justified by social rights to utility services and by social solidarity through preventing disadvantages to rural or poor consumers. In all these cases, competition and moves towards greater allocative efficiency through cost-reflective pricing threatens to result in a major redistribution of costs between different groups of consumers and to fragment cost structures. Indeed, the implications go beyond this, for certain services, for example in rural areas or to inner-city households, could become so uneconomic without supporting cross-subsidy that they could no longer be provided. This would undermine the concept of universal service which had previously been one of the central characteristics of utility provision, as will be described in later chapters.

Productive efficiency has been one of the major justifications given for privatization, especially where competitive markets have been created as well as enterprises sold to the private sector, and where regulators act as surrogates for market forces in the remaining monopoly areas.[14] There is no doubt that this process has resulted in some major efficiency improvements; for example, costs have been reduced substantially in the privatized energy markets and some of these reductions have been passed on to consumers; between 1995 and 1999 (the period of the final liberalization of domestic energy markets) domestic electricity prices fell by over 20% and gas prices by 15%.[15] Similarly, opening up telecommunications markets has encouraged innovation and a much wider choice of product and of services than was previously available, thus contributing to the process of increasing dynamic efficiency.

---

[14] For an early discussion of privatization and productive efficiency see Vickers and Yarrow (1988).

[15] Department of Trade and Industry, *Energy Report 2000* (nd), Appendix A, para. A3.4–5, at http://www.dti.gov.uk/energy/bluebook/pdf/appendix3.pdf (consulted 13 July 2004).

Despite these major achievements, there have been criticisms of the use of privatization and markets to increase productive efficiency in provision of public services. One has been that pressure to meet demanding efficiency standards set by regulators leads to a squeezing of investment in the search for short-term efficiency gains, putting longer-term security of supply at risk; this has particularly concerned the remaining areas of regulated infrastructure where the regulator acts as a surrogate for market forces. Thus the Trade and Industry Committee of the House of Commons has concluded that *'the Regulator's policy to date of both tightly limiting capital expenditure for replacement and continuing the pressure to reduce operational expenditure on maintenance is incompatible with the long-term stability of the electricity network'*.[16]

There have been similar criticisms that an emphasis on productive efficiency may threaten safety through cutting resources devoted to the maintenance of safety standards. Such criticisms have occurred in the energy industries, notably in relation to gas transportation, but the major area in which safety concerns have been expressed is in relation to rail, where, after a series of serious accidents, the privatized Railtrack was accused of neglecting safety and of failing to control and supervise properly its contracted-out maintenance functions. Here, however, there is nothing in the inherent nature of public services which leads to a potential conflict between maximizing shareholder value and safe operation; it exists equally in more competitive markets, for example the food industry.

There is a further criticism of the use of competitive markets policed by competition law in this context, and this relates to both types of efficiency. It is that competitive pressures prevent useful collaboration between enterprises providing public services. For example, a former president of the French railways has suggested that the future of European rail transport can be best protected through co-operation between operators rather than further European Union steps to increase competition.[17] Closer to home, as mentioned in the previous chapter, the House of Commons Transport Committee has strongly criticized the effects of competition law, as applied by the Office of Fair Trading, on the bus industry. According to the Committee, the prohibition of anti-competitive agreements prevents both the co-ordination of services

---

[16] Trade and Industry Committee, 'Resilience of the National Electricity Network', HC 69, 2003–4, para. 103 (emphasis retained).   [17] Fournier (2000) esp. at 292.

between operators to enable the services to be regularly spaced and collaboration on joint ticketing (although travelcards and some other ticket types have been granted a block exemption from the prohibition). The Committee concluded that 'The Office of Fair Trading's position . . . is a case of theory running riot over common sense . . . The concerns that the Office of Fair Trading has about a loss of consumer benefit that co-ordinated timetables, fares and frequencies will bring are largely unfounded . . . *The Office of Fair Trading must allow services to be co-ordinated. If the application of the Competition Act to the current de-regulated regime does not permit this then it is clearly at odds with the Government's aim of providing a truly integrated transport system.*'[18] Thus here a prohibition on agreements between undertakings, intended to promote both forms of efficiency, has, it is alleged, the effect of lowering the quality of service offered.

It should finally be mentioned that governments have sometimes attempted to limit the operation of the market for corporate control, itself a key means of promoting productive efficiency through the threat of take-over, by various devices (most famously, 'golden shares') aimed at preventing changes of control of former public enterprises, including those providing public services.[19] These have had limited effect, are few in number in the UK, and are now severely restricted by Community law.

Thus, overall, there are concerns about the stress on productive efficiency brought about by competition in public services, especially in relation to long-term investment and co-operation, but these are relatively minor compared to those relating to allocative efficiency and the effects of this approach to pricing. The justifications underlying competition law create some distinctive problems in relation to public services and may need to be qualified by other goals. However, it could be suggested that the model of competition law put forward here is misleading because it takes the Chicago view of competition law more seriously than is justified by the law's actual operation.

[18] Transport, Local Government and the Regions Committee, 'The Bus Industry', HC 828, 2001–2, paras. 27–41 (emphasis retained). This is not the only example of conflict between the Committee and the Office; see also the successor Transport Committee's report 'The Regulation of Taxis and Private Hire Vehicle Services in the UK', HC 251, 2003–4, para. 60, which describes a study by the Office as 'partial, doctrinaire, sloppily conducted and does not provide sufficient evidence to support any change in the law . . .'.

[19] For the origins see Graham and Prosser (1988) and for the position in Community law, Fleischer (2003).

Thus it could be argued that, in practice, competition law itself, rather than being concerned with the pure pursuit of consumer welfare through efficiency maximization, has weighed competing values and is perfectly capable of factoring into its own operation the distinctive needs of public services. I shall assess this argument in the following section.

Can Competition Law Internalize Public Service Values?

Is the version of competition law described above an unduly restrictive and dogmatic one? In practice competition law in the past has reflected values other than maximization of consumer welfare through the pursuit of economic efficiency.[20] Thus the protection of competitors was also a major theme in early US antitrust law, often in the form of the protection of small businesses against larger enterprises; '[b]y maintaining open markets and a deconcentration of economic power, antitrust could promote individual economic opportunities that might otherwise be foreclosed, preserve small business and local ownership, and protect individual property rights'.[21] In the European Union, a very different concern has been to promote and protect the growth of national champions able to compete for Europe on an international stage (although this is more often seen as imposing limits on competition law, particularly the law on mergers, than as a goal of competition law itself).[22] Linked to the protection of small businesses, competition law has also been seen as having certain redistributive goals, and it is precisely distributive concerns which form the basis for special rights of access to public services. Thus '[a]ggregations of resources in the hands of monopolists, multinational corporations or conglomerates could be considered a threat to the very notion of democracy, individual freedom of choice and economic opportunity'.[23]

This role of competition law as a means of combating social and political power is usually attributed to early US antitrust law. However, it also had a place to play in the origins of European competition law through the strong influence of the German Ordoliberals, who in addition to seeking the efficient allocation of resources were concerned with

---

[20] Jones and Sufrin (2004) 15–17.   [21] Eisner (1991) 2; see also 49–50.

[22] For this and other public policy goals, see Monti (2002).

[23] Whish (2001) 17; see also Jones and Sufrin (2004) 16–17.

the political power of large companies.[24] Indeed, '[a]lready aware of the economic efficiency grounds to be found in various restrictions on competition (monopoly, they even said, is not necessarily inefficient), the ordoliberals set the reasons for antitrust law almost entirely in the area of the illegitimacy of private economic power and of the devastating effects it can produce'.[25] The resulting conflict between this goal and that of economic efficiency has led to considerable debate about the extent to which European competition law should incorporate values other than those of welfare maximization discussed in the first part of this chapter.[26]

Indeed, the model of a flexible competition law with multiple goals found its apogee in the post-war system adopted in the UK. Quite apart from the fact that it had only very restricted application to public services (to be discussed in Chapter 3 below), the test adopted as the basis for this law was not based around economic efficiency, was not even primarily competition-based, and was highly discretionary, based instead on an assessment of whether restrictions on competition were contrary to 'the public interest'.[27] This enabled a wide range of matters to be considered in reaching a judgment on whether a restriction on competition should be struck down; the statute required the Monopolies and Mergers Commission to take into account 'all matters which appear to them in the particular circumstances to be relevant'; matters specified included 'maintaining and promoting the balanced distribution of industry and employment in the United Kingdom', thereby incorporating regional policy.[28] The very breadth of the public interest test might therefore have permitted some reference to social considerations to permit practices which would otherwise have been condemned as anti-competitive. Moreover, the ultimate decision-maker was the Secretary of State, not the specialist competition authorities, thereby creating further opportunities for non-economic principles to shape decisions.

This public interest-based competition law is, however, no longer the dominant one even in the UK, let alone Europe or the United States. The use of non-economic considerations in competition policy has been faced with a barrage of criticism. In its most extreme form this has come from the Chicago School which has indeed gone further, through

---

[24] See Rodger (2000) esp. 292–4, 304; Jones and Sufrin (2004) 30–2.
[25] Amato (1997) 99.   [26] See Gerber (1998) esp. 419–20; Monti (2002).
[27] See notably the Fair Trading Act 1973, ss. 69 and 84. A fascinating account of the development of the test in practice by the former Monopolies and Mergers Commission is to be found in Wilks (1999).   [28] Fair Trading Act 1973 s. 84.

adopting a narrower conception of efficiency, in limiting the range of economic considerations which, it maintains, should be taken into account. This narrowing of relevant factors for decision-making has been expressed forcefully by Bork: '[a] different line of attack comes from those who observe, quite correctly, that people value things other than consumer welfare, and, therefore, quite incorrectly, that antitrust ought not be confined to advancing that goal. As non sequiturs go, that one is world class.'[29] The Chicago arguments have had considerable impact in the United States.[30] Even in the UK since the election of the New Labour Government in 1997 we have seen fundamental reform of competition law which has replaced the public interest test with a competition test derived directly from European Community law. This is not to say that the Chicago model has been adopted; whereas most Chicago School members have criticized much competition law as an intrusion into a potentially self-regulating market, the UK reforms have aimed to strengthen the law, notably through the introduction of criminal penalties and of stronger investigatory powers for the competition authorities. However, under the new model the scope for the use of non-competition, public interest-based arguments has been radically restricted.

Thus the Competition Act 1998 introduced prohibitions on anti-competitive agreements and of abuse of a dominant position; for monopolies public interest investigations were retained along with the new prohibitions, but have in turn now been replaced under the Enterprise Act 2002 with a competition-based test; a similar test has also been introduced by that Act in the case of mergers. The ultimate decision-makers are now the competition authorities themselves, not the Secretary of State. As we shall see in Chapter 3, the 1998 Act contains a very limited exemption from its provisions for public services, again based on Community law.[31] The Enterprise Act also contains powers for the Secretary of State to issue a notice that a merger or a market investigation raises public interest considerations, which then makes the minister rather than the Competition Commission the prime decision-maker, and she may take account of the public interest consideration.[32] It is however envisaged that this power will be used extremely infrequently, with the only category of public interest considerations included in the Act being those

---

[29] Bork (1993) 428.

[30] For the gradual move of US antitrust law towards a Chicago-based approach see Eisner (1991) esp. chs. 5–8.   [31] Sch. 3 para 4.

[32] Ss. 42–70, 139–53.

relating to the interests of national security.[33] Special provision is also made by the Communications Act 2003 for media mergers; these will be discussed in Chapter 9 below.

Thus UK competition law has now reached the end of a process of change from a regime in which the public interest is built into the basic test used by the competition authorities, and in which the minister has a central role, to one in which the test is wholly competition-based subject to very limited exceptions for public interest considerations, and is applied by independent competition authorities. To a considerable degree this follows European Community competition law; although considerations other than efficiency maximization have played an important role in decision-making by European Community institutions, the tests set out in the Treaty are competition-based. The goal of market integration is however of central importance in Community law, and in addition the tests are subject to limited exceptions which may permit the consideration of broader considerations.[34] Thus Article 81(3) relating to anti-competitive agreements permits the granting of exemptions for such agreements on certain limited grounds; these are not however broad enough to encompass general public interest considerations or special concerns relating to public services. More important in this context is the provision relating to services of general economic interest, where the application of the rules of competition law must not obstruct the performance of the tasks assigned to them.[35] This complex provision and others related to it will be discussed in detail in Chapter 6 below; for the moment it is enough to stress that it does not provide any sort of discretionary and general public-interest-based regime such as characterized the former UK law.

A regime in which a discretionary system of competition law could balance within its own tests the demands of efficiency against the special tasks of public services has now ended even in the UK; instead competition law is to concentrate on maximizing consumer welfare through minimizing impediments to competition, with public interest considerations playing a role only through limited exceptions to the general law. This reflects the European approach, and makes it far more necessary to determine which special considerations may limit the application of competition law fully to public services. To accept that such

---

[33] S. 58.   [34] See Jones and Sufrin (2004) 35–40; Monti (2002).
[35] EC Treaty Art. 86(2).

considerations may exist is, however, to beg the question of what values may justify such restrictions on the normal operation of competition law. This will be the subject of the remainder of this chapter.

Citizenship Rights and Public Services

Returning to the consumer-welfare-based model of competition law discussed at the beginning of this chapter, it will be useful to commence by asking why the type of economic efficiency on which it is based is seen as a desirable goal. In the case of productive efficiency this appears straightforward; the production of the maximum outputs from the minimum inputs, thereby increasing society's overall wealth.[36] For allocative efficiency (which raises particularly strong difficulties for public services) the justification is more complex, but is basically that this principle allocates goods to those who value them most. Underlying this may be, on one interpretation at least, a constitutional assumption to the effect that this approach treats members of the society as equals because competitive markets ensure that they each take responsibility for the true costs of their actions; '[s]omeone who abstains from some act on the ground that it would cost his neighbour more than it would benefit him takes his neighbour's welfare into account on equal terms with his own; a duty to act in that way might be thought to rest on some egalitarian basis'.[37] Thus we can see the efficiency goals of economics as reflecting an underlying citizenship right of equal treatment without at the same time imposing any substantive goals on citizens, who are treated as sovereign consumers. It is this which provides a constitutional case for preferring the values of markets maintained through competition law as the central means for allocating goods and services to meet consumer preferences.

There are however some serious limitations to this market model for treating citizens as equals. It views citizens solely in their capacity as consumers. Thus Mark Freedland has pointed to a 'contestation' between two rival types of citizenship, constitutional citizenship on the one hand and market citizenship on the other. Recent neo-liberal thought, he argues, has stressed the latter and has reconceptualized the

---

[36] But cf. Dworkin (1985) chs. 12–13.
[37] Dworkin (1986) 295, and see generally ch. 8. See also Dworkin (2000) 66–71, 149–52.

citizen as primarily an economic rather than a social or political actor.[38] Governments

have experienced and responded to incentives to identify and interpret the citizen, not just as a market citizen, but more particularly as a consumer citizen. That is to say, the citizen is especially valued as the maker of choices about consumption of goods and services by which alone the market economy can be disciplined into the condition of 'efficiency' which is necessary to its prosperity in an internationally competitive environment. Emphasis is placed on the role of the citizen as the discriminating purchaser of goods and services, as the maker and enforcer of economically sound and rational consumer contracts.[39]

Moreover, the consumerist view of citizenship is non-egalitarian; although consumer groups may have some egalitarian aims, consumerism is essentially about the conditions of participation in markets, not the overall distribution of wealth.

Most importantly, the consumerist version of citizenship may come into conflict with other types of citizenship rights. This is obvious at the simplest level in the fact that we do not consider market exchange appropriate for important types of political action; for example, selecting governments, where more democratic procedures in the form of one person one vote are a more effective way of recognizing equal citizenship. In other respects, behaviour as a citizen is radically different from behaving as a market actor; for example 'the difference is connected to the fact that a citizen is helping to make a judgment not simply for himself but for a collectivity. In this sense, there are important contextual differences between market behaviour and voting behaviour . . . the role of citizen is accompanied by norms that can discourage selfishness and encourage attention to the public good.'[40]

Above all, markets are seriously inadequate means of protecting rights to equal citizenship because we do not come to markets as equals. Our market power as consumers is determined by the existing distribution of wealth in which we are placed, and this determines our ability to satisfy our preferences in a market system. In the absence of a Dworkinian redistribution to ensure equality of resources,[41] competitive markets are likely to defeat the equal allocation of rights because of the radically unequal power of different market actors.

---

[38] Freedland (1988) 6–11.   [39] Freedland (1988) 10.   [40] Sunstein (1997) 44–5.
[41] See Dworkin (2000) ch. 2.

This is of course why we have accepted that market mechanisms are not the best means of allocating rights where equality is particularly important, for example the right to vote. As Dworkin has put it (writing in the different context of the role of the market under equality of resources), the market

enters because it is endorsed by the concept of equality, as the best means of enforcing, at least up to a point, the fundamental requirement that only an equal share of social resources be devoted to the lives of each of its members, as measured by the opportunity cost of such resources to others. But the value of actual market transactions ends at just that point, and the market must be abandoned or constrained when analysis shows, from any direction, that it has failed in this task, or that an entirely different theoretical or institutional device would do better.[42]

The point has also been put eloquently by Sunstein:

A system is efficient if entitlements have been allocated so as to 'maximise value,' with reference to private willingness to pay. For believers in a democratic system, however, this criterion is inadequate in two different ways. First, a democracy system operates on the principle of one person, one vote. By contrast, a market allocates 'votes' in accordance with how much people are willing to pay for things. Since willingness to pay is a function of ability to pay, wealthy people will be willing to pay far more than poor ones. Indeed the indigent will be able to pay nothing at all. The principle of political equality, so central to democratic theory, is violated by the efficiency criterion.[43]

A move away from market allocation also implies a move away from the use of competition law, and it is this move that is justified by the radically unequal distribution of resources giving access to markets. Indeed, one sees acceptance of this point even in the most radical advocates of an efficiency-based consumer law; according to Bork '[a]ntitrust thus has a built-in preference for material prosperity, but it has nothing to say about the ways prosperity is distributed or used. Those are matters for other laws.'[44] Thus rights, which are to be enjoyed equally, trump the outcomes of markets, and in doing so imply the setting of limits to competition law where such rights come into play. What however is missing from Bork's statement is an appreciation that the values underlying the 'other laws' may come into conflict with those of competition law. Thus '[t]he justification of public action that these

---

[42] Dworkin (2000) 112.   [43] Sunstein (1997) 344; see also 75, 225.
[44] Bork (1993) 90; see also 111–12.

values, principles and rights constitute are not a matter of pure political discourse; they provide a resource to restrict or contest the influence of "market" mechanisms, in other words the dynamic of competition law, in its broadest sense'.[45]

The examples referred to above relate primarily to the more traditional political and civil rights such as the right to vote and freedom of expression. However, in the context of this work I am more concerned with social and economic rights; indeed, when I come to discuss public service broadcasting in Chapter 9 I shall touch on cultural rights as well. Here we may appear to face a difficulty. Although the concept of civil and political rights is well accepted (though there may be disagreement on their content and on the best means of protecting them), social and economic rights remain more controversial. More particularly, in the UK we do not have any form of incorporation of these rights into domestic law such as was implemented for civil and political rights by the Human Rights Act 1998. This implies that we need to address three questions at this stage: whether such rights can find theoretical justification, whether they can be found in existing international obligations of the UK, and what their content is.[46]

The first point, of the theoretical justifications for social and economic rights, cannot be fully rehearsed here, especially bearing in mind the very extensive discussion which already exists in the literature.[47] As in the case of market allocations discussed earlier, these rights draw their basis from the principle of equal citizenship.[48] However, the emphasis is different, being placed on access to the means for basic social well-being. In this sense they are positive rights to active assistance rather than negative rights to be left alone.[49] At an abstract level there is considerable academic support for such rights and indeed for their constitutionalization.[50] As for content, Fabre has argued that principled social rights should include the right to a minimum income, a right to housing, a right to education, and a right to health care.[51]

There is still debate on the extent to which such rights should be constitutionalized,[52] but even if they are not, they may still perform

---

[45] Lyon-Caen (2002) 187.   [46] For a general survey see Fredman (2004).

[47] Notable examples include Gewirth (1996), Fabre (2000), and, more closely concerned with the current UK situation, Ewing (2001).   [48] Gewirth (1996) 72–5; Ewing (2001) 300–1.

[49] Gewirth (1996) ch. 2, which defends positive rights against more traditional liberal individualistic claims for negative rights alone. See also Fabre (2000) ch. 2.

[50] See in particular Fabre (2000) ch. 3.   [51] Fabre (2000) 33–9, 107–8.

[52] Cf. Fabre (2000) and Hare (2002).

important roles in the orientation and interpretation of other legal norms, including those of competition law.[53] What is important to note is that, despite these disagreements, there is a growing acceptance of the importance of such social rights; Hepple has referred to 'a rebirth of social and labour rights in the global economy' and to a 'new dawn of social and labour rights'.[54] Indeed, a number of important social and economic rights are already recognized in international instruments to which the UK is a party.[55] Not only does this impose international obligations which the UK Government is required to observe, it can also be argued that the especial nature of human rights implies an obligation on government to recognize them in domestic law.[56] The most important of these is the Council of Europe's European Social Charter of 1961.[57] Of particular relevance in the Charter are Article 16, which provides a right of the family to social, legal, and economic protection and Article 11 providing a right to the protection of health.

None of the theoretical justifications for social and economic rights nor the international legal instruments referred to above suggests a direct right of access to public services, though this could be inferred from, for example, rights to health care or to social and economic protection for the family. Moreover, such a right is potentially more complex than other social and economic rights in that, rather than mandating direct provision by public authorities, it relies on regulation to affect the behaviour of both public and private suppliers, for example by providing a duty on such a supplier to connect a client on demand and by limiting price differentials that a supplier can charge. However, the fact that services are privately provided does not prevent the existence of duties applying to the state to ensure that rights are respected in their provision:

[t]he state through its democratically based laws must require the various institutions and policies of what I have called the "economic constitution" to provide for the fulfillment of the economic and social rights, including welfare, education, employment, and so forth. Whether the constitutional and legislative requirements themselves are to be laid down cannot be left open as a function of

---

[53] See Lyon-Caen (2002).   [54] Hepple (2002) 14–15.   [55] See Fredman (2004).
[56] See Gewirth (1996) xiii, 29–30 referring to the UN Universal Declaration of Human Rights. For details of the argument see Beyleveld (1995) and Beyleveld and Villiers (1997).
[57] See Ewing (2001) 305–8; Lewis and Seneviratne (1992); Prouvez (1997).

privatization: neither the market nor private charity is to be entrusted with decisions concerning whether the requirements are to be set.[58]

It is when we move to law of the European Union we find a much more direct reference to rights of access to public services. In addition, given the incorporation of norms of Community law, we also have a more immediate basis for the claim that rights must be recognized in the UK legal system; even provisions that are not directly effective of course have a much more influential role in domestic law than do other international instruments.[59]

There will be detailed coverage in Chapters 6 to 8 below of the Community law applicable to public services. However, two provisions deserve mention here as they bring our discussion of international obligations directly to rights of access to such services. The first is the new Article 16 added to the EC Treaty by the Treaty of Amsterdam. This relates to services of general interest (which broadly correspond to our concepts of public services and public utilities); it states that, subject to other provisions,

given the place occupied by services of general economic interest in the shared values of the Union as well as their role in promoting social and territorial cohesion, the Community and the Member States, each within their respective powers and within the scope of application of this Treaty, shall take care that such services operate on the basis of principles and conditions which enable them to fulfil their missions.

Given the requirement to 'take care', it is doubtful that this provision is directly effective and its meaning is highly contested.[60] One possible interpretation is however that, whilst not providing directly effective rights, the provision provides a means for further development of notions of Community citizenship through elevating the values represented by services of general interest into at least a 'minimum overlapping Union consensus' entrenched as a set of Community values. It thus represents 'a critical step in the concretising of non-market (or post-market) concerns in both the psyche and legal hierarchy of Union development'.[61]

---

[58] Gewirth (1996) 328. Of course other more familiar social rights will also be implemented in part through regulatory requirements applying to private providers; for example housing and medical care. But cf. *R (on the Application of Heather) v. Leonard Cheshire Foundation* [2001] EWHC Admin 429.

[59] See for example, in the context of an unimplemented directive, Case C-106/89 *Marleasing SA v. La Comercial Internacionale de Alimentacion SA* [1990] ECR I-4135.

[60] See Ross (2000) esp. 28–38; cf. Buendia Sierra (1999) 329–36.   [61] Ross (2000) 34.

Further development in this respect can be found in the EU Charter of Fundamental Rights adopted at the Nice Summit in December 2000. Article 36 of the Charter is entitled 'Access to Services of General Economic Interest' and provides that:

The Union recognises and respects access to services of general economic interest as provided for in national laws and practices, in accordance with the Treaty establishing the European Community, in order to promote the social and territorial cohesion of the Union.

Article 35 also provides a right of access to health care and to medical treatment.

Whilst there are limitations on the legal enforceability of the Charter,[62] it does represent a further recognition of the role of access to public services as an important Community principle. Finally, the Constitutional Treaty drawn up by the Convention in 2003 and adopted, subject to national ratification, in 2004, repeats these provisions with only minor amendments.

I have now been able to suggest that there are certain values in the form of social and economic rights that will trump competition law and so require limitations to be placed on its application to public services. These arise from inequalities in distribution which make equal treatment of citizens unachievable simply through the use of competitive markets. However, a further argument must be considered. Even if we accept rights to the provision of public services, rather than requiring limitations on markets and competition law instead the tax and social security systems should be used to deal with the problems at their base, through direct correction of inequalities. This would then permit reliance on an efficiency-based competition law without the need to impose limits which may imperil the application of its values in important areas, and would secure a much tidier division between the application of efficiency-based competition law and distributive interventions through fiscal means and direct subsidy. The simple answer to this is that redistribution on this scale and the adoption of such a strict distinction between types of intervention is highly unlikely. In the UK currently the Government does not even publish the levels of assistance provided in income support to pay for utility bills.[63] However, to respond to this argument in more sophisticated terms I must now examine different conceptions of the role and responsibilities of the state.

---

[62] See Ewing (2001) 320–3.   [63] Klein (2003) 57.

Social Solidarity and the Role of the State

When we come to examine, in Chapter 5 below, the approach to public service taken in Continental Europe, we shall discover a central theme that is radically different from the consumerist model underlying competition law. This is the theme of social solidarity; the idea that the state has duties to ensure equal treatment of citizens irrespective of their economic resources. The concept underlies much of the special public service law which has developed in France, and indeed has now found its way into European Community law via the new Article 16 and the Charter of Fundamental Rights mentioned above with their references to 'promoting social and territorial cohesion'.

This is somewhat different from the language of rights considered in the previous section. As one commentator has put it, this 'inclusive' view of citizenship implies that '[c]itizenship and membership of the community are seen as permanent attributes, not to be forfeited by misfortune or failure. The duty to conform to society's or the community's standards is matched by the community's own obligation to support its vulnerable and disadvantaged members.'[64] Rather than starting from individual rights this view starts from the duties of the community to secure such inclusiveness, resting both on a moral sense of equal citizenship and a more prudential goal of minimizing social fragmentation.[65] Indeed, the major theorist in this tradition, Leon Duguit, denied the existence of rights as opposed to duties and social functions.[66] It may however be compatible with the rights-based approach to citizenship outlined in the previous section; Gewirth for example argues for rights as entailing 'a mutualist and egalitarian universality: each human must respect the rights of all others while having his rights respected by all the others, so that there must be a mutual sharing of the benefits of rights and the burdens of duties'.[67] The concept of social solidarity is not however compatible with a market-based view of citizenship underlying the full application of competition law to public services. On this latter view

[h]ealth, education, employment, and housing are treated as commodities to be purchased and traded on the most competitive available terms, not as obligations to be undertaken, and still less rights to be protected, by the State,

---

[64] Faulkner (1998) 39. [65] Cf. Bork (1993) 112.
[66] Duguit (1970) xx (translator's introduction by Harold Laski). [67] Gewirth (1996) 6.

provided by public services, and enjoyed by the citizen. Citizens are defined as individual consumers of public services, rather than as people who share a sense of common interest or identity or who are joined by any sense of mutual obligation or trust.[68]

The work of Duguit was particularly influential in developing the concept of public service founded on the older concept of social solidarity derived from the work of Durkheim.[69] Thus he saw public service as a replacement for a discredited theory of sovereignty as the basis for public law. Public service was defined as follows: '[a]ny activity that has to be governmentally regulated and controlled because it is indispensable to the realisation and development of social solidarity is a public service so long as it is of such a nature that it cannot be assured except by governmental intervention'.[70] This would apply both to services supplied directly by government and those supplied by private enterprise under concession. The social function of public law was to ensure the performance of public service tasks without interruption, through the mass of rules governing the organization of public utilities, notably communications, transport, and electricity.

A fuller discussion of the implications of this work for the French law of public service will follow in Chapter 5. However, an important point must be made now; the public service approach is intimately connected to a strong concept and tradition of the state characteristic of France but markedly lacking in the UK.[71] As I have suggested (with a colleague) elsewhere, the concept of the state as the means for 'the rationalist pursuit of order (in its broadest sense) in a society subject to ceaseless change' has been absent from the English political and legal traditions.[72] In France, by contrast, one finds more use of the concept of the state as a moral unifier standing above the struggles of civil society. This even influenced attitudes to the privatization process in France; the right-wing prime minister, Jacques Chirac, in charge of the first major privatization programme emphasized that privatization did not mean the suppression of the state but enabled it to concentrate on its missions of ensuring a fair distribution of the fruits of economic growth and that the development of competitive markets and private enterprise must take place without risk to the national interest.[73]

---

[68] Faulkner (1998) 43. [69] See Loughlin (1992) 106–13. [70] Duguit (1970) 48.
[71] See Dyson (1980). [72] Graham and Prosser (1991) 35, quoting Dyson (1980) 7.
[73] Graham and Prosser (1991) 36.

Through the state tradition the values of social solidarity have also entered French law; to quote Carol Harlow, 'the idea of public service imbues public law with a strong set of values and morals. These ideas differ from those familiar to common lawyers, for whom the values of administrative law tend to be, on the one hand, individualistic and, on the other hand, procedural.'[74] Thus in Chapter 5 I shall outline a well-established body of public service law reflecting these values.

The implication of this concern with social solidarity and with the state and law as bearers of these values is to make it much more difficult to adopt the particular solution mentioned above to the problems discussed in this chapter; that of using the social security and taxation systems to adjust initial distributions and then to leave the market and competition law to operate unhindered. In the French tradition, markets tend to be distrusted as inherently fragmenting the values of social solidarity which the state should protect, and this has indeed formed a major part of the strong French criticisms of the liberalization of public services in the European Union, as we shall see in Chapter 7. Rather than simply setting the initial conditions for markets to operate, the state has the role of intervening continually to maintain the conditions for social solidarity, and this involves protecting access to public services. It would be far too grand an oversimplification to suggest that on the French view markets have traditionally been the servants of the state's values; but in relation to public service there is a grain of truth in this, despite the developed French privatization programme and the major steps taken to open up competitive markets in important parts of the French economy. As we shall see in later chapters, this French view has also had profound effect on the European process of liberalization of public services.

Conclusion

The argument in this chapter, then, has been that both competition law and the competitive markets which it protects are primarily justified by values of efficiency. One justification for this is that of citizens' rights to equal treatment, requiring that they bear their own costs. Another basis for competition law is that of individual choice and freedom through consumer sovereignty. However, rights to equal treatment, in a society of

---

[74] Harlow (1998) 51. See also Amato (1998), and more generally Allison (2000) esp. chs. 3–4.

unequal distribution, also require other values to be respected which may conflict with those of competition law. This has been implemented in the past through restricting the application of competition law to public services and, at least in the UK, through adopting a broad 'public interest' test which includes space within competition law itself for values other than those of economic efficiency and the maximization of competition. However, this approach is now rapidly changing with the creation of competitive markets in public services and the development of a new form of competition law far removed from the older public interest model. A more explicit recognition of the limits to competition law has become necessary. These can partly be found in the concept of rights to public services which are increasingly recognized as part of new social and economic rights and can be drawn from international obligations; recent developments in the European Union have been particularly important in this regard. One response would be to provide redistribution through tax and social security measures whilst leaving markets and competition law to operate fully in relation to public services. However, a concern for social solidarity, and the role of a state tradition as bearer of this principle, are also of importance in suggesting limits to liberalization of public services and to the use of competition law as their regulatory principle.

A further implication is that it is misleading to suggest that interventions by public authorities are only justified when they correct market failures, for this would be to give an unjustified primacy to the market as the first-choice distributor of goods and services. In fact, different mechanisms for allocation may be justified by different values, and whether we choose markets, a rights-based approach, or one based on social solidarity will depend on which values we wish to promote in a particular context and, for example, which types of rights are involved.

These arguments have been at a high level of abstraction. In the following three chapters I shall compare more concretely the different ways in which public service and rights of access to utility services have been protected in the UK and in France and Italy.

3

The UK Approach to Competition Law and Public Services

In this chapter I shall outline the relationship between competition law and public service in the UK, starting with a brief discussion of the common law position and then covering that under nationalization which existed during much of the twentieth century. We shall see that both public service and competition came to be protected by essentially political means rather than through directly enforceable rules of law. This will be contrasted with the new approach to competition policy and law ushered in by the Competition Act 1998 and the Enterprise Act 2002, and there will be an examination of the application of this law to public services, including its application by the sectoral utility regulators. In Chapter 4 the ways in which the regulators have attempted to protect public service goals will be examined in detail.

The Common Law

At common law, a number of cases suggested that there were limits to the use of private property which can be seen as inspired both by the public service goals of public access to important facilities and by the avoidance of unfair competition on the part of such facility owners.[1] The most celebrated is *Allnutt v. Inglis*[2] in which it was held that a statutory dock monopoly was created for the benefit of the public as well as that of the monopolist, and so the latter was not free to impose unreasonable charges that would prevent public access to his facilities. Similar

---

[1] For full discussion of these see Craig (1991) and Taggart (1994).
[2] (1810) 12 East 527.

principles were applied to other 'common callings' and indeed to early public utilities, and in Scots law such principles existed in relation to ports, harbours, and ferries.[3] One interpretation of these cases is as precursors of the modern 'essential facilities' doctrine through the imposition of rules limiting attempts by the owners of the monopoly facilities to restrict output.[4] Another is, however, to see them as an expression of a socially based right of public access to scarce resources, and this latter approach is more in line with the actual phraseology of the opinions in the cases. For example, in *Allnutt* Le Blanc J. considered that 'where private property is affected with a public interest, it ceases to be juris privati only; and in cases of its dedication to such a purpose as this, the owners cannot take arbitrary and excessive dues, but the duties must be reasonable'.[5] Similarly, in one of the Scottish cases, the Lord Ordinary (Robertson) decided that:

[r]ights of ferry are not only important to the party in whom they are vested, but are beneficial to the public interest. They impose on the parties possessing such rights a corresponding duty to accommodate the public, which private speculators, where their interests do not prompt them (as for example in plying the ferry in the winter season), are under no obligation to perform.[6]

The position has been well characterized by Craig as determining forms of public property rights triggered by the potential of the owner to limit access to privately owned services that are in some sense essential for users.[7]

These cases went on to play an important role in the development of the US constitutional jurisprudence on regulation, but were neglected in the UK. There were several reasons for this neglect. The first, as we shall see, is the development of statutory provisions providing equivalent protections for user rights in relation to the public utilities. The second, and more important, was a marked tendency to replace legal controls with political controls through the nationalization of the industries. The third was an attenuation of public service concerns in the common law itself, with preference given instead to an absolutist conception of property rights to be employed as the owner wished. The high point in this was *The Mayor, Aldermen and Burgesses of Bradford v. Pickles*.[8] The House of Lords held that there was nothing in law to prevent

---

[3] See e.g. *Aiton v. Stephen* (1876) 3 R (HL).

[4] For the essential facilities doctrine, see Downie and Macgregor (2000).

[5] At 542.   [6] *Magistrates of Kirkaldy v. Greig* (1846) 8 D 1247, at 1248.

[7] Craig (1991) 54.

[8] [1895] AC 587. The case has recently been analysed in gripping fashion in Taggart (2000).

interference by a neighbouring landowner with percolating water necessary to supply a municipal water utility, even if the interference was actuated by malice, and the court refused to employ arguments which in civil law systems formed the basis for the doctrine of abuse of rights. It should be noted that this was not a competition case as the landowner was in no sense a competitor to the municipal water utility. However, at almost the same time the judiciary was also in the process of limiting the potential use of the economic torts as a means of policing unfair competition, notably in the decision in *Mogul Steamship v. McGregor*[9] where it was held that it was legitimate to conspire to engage in predatory pricing to drive out a new market entrant. Fry LJ commented in his opinion that 'to draw a line between fair and unfair competition ... passes the power of the court'.[10] Henceforth the common law was to have very little role in both the protection of public service principles (in marked contrast to the role of case law in France) and in developing the modern law of unfair competition.

Public Ownership

For the public utilities the next phase represents a near-total rejection of competition law and instead the implementation of public service goals through political rather than legal means, which is not to say that there were no legal requirements to implement particular aspects of those goals. Such requirements indeed pre-date the major nationalizations of the 1940s and formed part of what were often very elaborate structures for the regulation before the Second World War of mixed nationalized, municipally owned, and private utilities. For example, in the case of electricity, a duty to supply customers on demand was contained in the Electric Lighting (Clauses) Act 1899 and incorporated into the Electricity Act 1947; the Electric Lighting Act 1882 made arrangements to regulate the disconnection of supplies, reinforced by the Electric Lighting Act 1909, which limited disconnection to cases where there was no *bona fide* dispute.[11] In addition to the legal requirements, the development of universal service through rural electrification and the development of a properly co-ordinated transmission and distribution

---

[9] (1889) 23 QBD 598, (CA).
[10] At 625. For fuller analysis of this area see Furse (2002) ch. 17 and Carty (2001).
[11] See McAuslan and McEldowney (1988) 178–82.

system were central goals of reform of the industry and of nationalization itself.[12] Indeed, it could be argued that the creation of such a
technological basis for universal service was the major success of public
ownership.[13]

After nationalization, the major means for protecting public service
goals was to be political rather than legal. This could take several forms,
including through the role of the minister, through the ability of the
board of the industry, no longer distracted by the profit motive, to devote
itself to implementation of the public interest, and through the representation of consumers by consumer councils and consultative mechanisms.[14] These mechanisms proved in practice remarkably ineffective and
did not produce any clear public service principles to guide the industries;
indeed, they were incapable of resisting attempts to make the industries
behave like ordinary capitalist firms in the latter days of nationalization
when, for example, disconnection rates for energy supply were high.

The political mechanisms were accompanied by legal provisions in the
nationalization statutes protecting particular aspects of public service,
often simply taken from earlier pre-nationalization law, as in the case of
electricity; examples would be those requiring supply to be made available on demand and prohibiting undue discrimination against particular users or undue preference in favour of others.[15] However, these
provisions were limited in two ways. They were in themselves deeply
ambiguous. They can be seen either as a means of requiring universal
service of a type that would not be provided by an unregulated firm free
to choose its customers, but could also be interpreted as essentially based
on pro-competitive concerns of preventing abuse of a dominant position,
and even as limiting the ability of the enterprises to adopt socially based
policies benefiting particular types of consumers.[16] Secondly, each legal
provision existed in isolation and certainly did not form the basis for
any coherent set of principles of public service law. The legal provisions
applying after nationalization did not provide the basis for any
overarching conception of public service.

---

[12] And see s. 1(6)(b) of the Electricity Act 1947 imposing a duty to secure so far as practicable
the development and extension to rural areas of supplies of electricity.

[13] For the case of electricity see e.g. Robson (1962) 35–7, 403.

[14] For a detailed account see Prosser (1986) esp. chs. 2, 8–10.

[15] For details see Daintith (1974); Sharpe (1992).

[16] See Prosser (1997) 20–4, and for the problems of interpretation raised by such clauses *South
of Scotland Electricity Board v. British Oxygen Co.* [1956] 3 All ER 199 (HL).

The role of competition law was also extremely limited. As the official history of the Monopolies and Mergers Commission has put it, '[p]rior to 1980, the nationalised industries had largely kept the competition authorities off their patch. Their statutory monopoly effectively made them immune from restrictive practices legislation and it would have been illogical for ministers to refer a nationalised industry to the Commission.'[17] Indeed, the Fair Trading Act 1973 excluded from the scope of monopoly references by the Director General of Fair Trading gas, electricity, rail or road transport, posts, telecommunications, and water amongst other categories of goods and services; in these cases references could only be made by ministers.[18] In addition, it was agreed that the Director General would not refer the activities of the industries outside the areas excluded by the Act.[19] It is notable that the exclusion in the 1973 Act went so far as to include road transport thus preventing references by the Director General relating to the regulated and largely municipally owned bus industry, which became a major source of references after liberalization in the 1980s.

It might at first appear that the effective exemption of the nationalized industries from ordinary competition law ended with the passing of the Competition Act 1980. The Act provided that the minister was able to refer to the Monopolies and Mergers Commission questions relating to the efficiency and costs of the service provided by a nationalized industry, or a possible abuse of a monopoly position; this might include the question of whether it was pursuing a course of conduct that operated against the public interest.[20] However, rather than representing an application of general competition law this represented a new form of efficiency audit of the nationalized industries, albeit audit that was limited in scope and which was dependent on the discretion of the minister for its initiation and terms of reference.[21] Although a considerable number of references under this section took place (thirty-five reports were produced between 1980 and 1993) they certainly did not represent any application of the general norms of competition law to the enterprises.

In conclusion, then, the protection of the principles of public service during the period of public ownership was political and discretionary; it

[17] Wilks (1999) 244.   [18] S. 50(2), schs. 5 and 7.   [19] Wilks (1999) 185.

[20] S. 11.

[21] For a critical account of the operation of this provision see Prosser (1986) 212–18; cf. Wilks (1999) 246–52.

formed part of an ill-defined concept of the public interest to be protected through nationalization rather than a set of specific norms susceptible to legal enforcement. Perhaps more surprisingly, the same is true of competition law; even apart from the broad exclusions of the goods and services offered by nationalized industries from monopoly references by the Director General of Fair Trading, the law itself was highly discretionary, based on a public interest test, and largely implemented by ministers. Before discussing this in detail, however, we need to look at the process of privatization which was to change both approaches in fundamental ways.

Privatization and Regulation

The massive privatization programme of the 1980s and 1990s was of crucial importance both for the protection of public service goals and for competition law and policy. This has had effects throughout the field of public services, in particular through the adoption of market-based approaches and contracting out in health, social services, and many areas of local government.[22] Some of the implications of these approaches will be will discussed later when I consider general competition law; however, the arrangements adopted for the regulation of the public utilities have been of particular importance as they have involved both the special application of competition law and the implementation of social values.

At first sight it might appear that privatization, almost by definition, would reduce the role of public service by increasing that of competitive markets and limiting public interventions. However, somewhat reluctantly, the Government created new regulatory authorities for each of the public utility sectors, initially with the aim of restraining monopoly until it could be replaced by competition.[23] The system first adopted was that of vesting regulatory powers in a Director, such as the Director General of Telecommunications, assisted by an office such as the Office of Telecommunications or Oftel, the latter taking the form of a non-ministerial government department similar to that of the Office of Fair Trading. Apart from this example, similar arrangements were adopted for water (the Office of Water Services or Ofwat), gas (the Office of Gas Supply or Ofgas), electricity (the Office of Electricity Regulation or Offer) and the

---

[22] See e.g. Harden (1992), Davies (2001).   [23] See notably Littlechild (1984).

railways (the Office of the Rail Regulator or ORR).[24] The system evolved after the 1997 change of government into a somewhat different one with a regulatory commission being adopted for gas and electricity markets, regulated together by a new Gas and Electricity Markets Authority assisted by the Office of Gas and Electricity Markets (Ofgem); the Communications Act 2003 merges Oftel into a new Office of Communications (Ofcom) in the form of a regulatory commission, and legislation also changed the rail and water regulators into commissions.[25] In the case of buses, no new regulator was created and instead the ordinary competition authorities were responsible for what quickly became a massive amount of work applying competition law to this complex sector.[26] Finally, a new regulator in the form of the Postal Services Commission (Postcomm) was created by the Postal Services Act 2000 for a sector dominated by a single enterprise, the Royal Mail, which remained in public ownership.

The work of the utility regulators has been extensively discussed elsewhere, and in the following chapter I shall describe in detail their work in implementing public service goals. At this stage I shall merely note that they were also given important responsibilities for policing competition in relation to the public utilities; indeed their work to some extent prefigured the reforms of competition law implemented by the Labour Governments in power from 1997 and to be considered below. This in itself raised issues of the relationship between the application of competition law and the special values appropriate to the role of public utilities. Some brief examples will illustrate this.

On the first point, that of the prefiguring of later competition law reform, the most striking example is that of the telecommunications fair trading condition. Statutes and licences covering the regulated enterprises often included goals of promoting competition and prohibited particular anti-competitive practices. These were, however, difficult and cumbersome to enforce and in 1995 Oftel announced that it proposed to take a new approach through a licence condition dealing with anti-competitive behaviour in general. The new condition was modeled on what are now Articles 81 and 82 of the EC Treaty, prohibiting anti-competitive agreements between undertakings materially affecting

[24] For a more comprehensive account of the regulatory structures see Prosser (1997).
[25] Railways and Transport Safety Act 2002, ss. 15–17; Water Act 2003, ss. 34–8.
[26] See Prosser (1997) 206–12.

competition in the UK telecommunications market and abuse of a dominant position so as unfairly to exclude or limit competition.[27] After surviving a legal challenge by British Telecom,[28] the new condition came into effect at the end of 1996 and within a year was included in the licences of over 350 companies. It was enforceable by the regulator who could take action for breach of any licence condition, and formed a precursor of the concurrent powers of the regulators to be discussed below.

The fair trading condition did not in itself cause any particular problems relating to public service. However, as we shall see in the following chapter, the disconnection of utility services for non-payment of bills had been a perennial problem from the time of privatization (and indeed earlier) and restrictions on disconnection could come into conflict with a more commercial approach. A most striking clash of values appeared with the liberalization of gas and electricity markets and in particular its extension to domestic (household) as well as industrial consumers, a process completed in 1998 for gas and in 1999 for electricity. The first concern here related to fears of 'cream-skimming' or 'cherry-picking'. By definition, opening up the market signalled an end to universal tariffs (which had never fully applied to the energy markets in the UK anyway). The fear was that new entrants would offer service only to the most profitable customers, assumed to be the larger and more wealthy consumers, leaving the poor as an unprofitable rump retained by the former monopoly supplier. The second concern was that social obligations retained by monopoly suppliers would not apply to competing new entrants. How these problems were addressed by government and regulator will be one subject of the next chapter; it is enough simply to note here that liberalization involved a potential tension between the values of competitive markets and those of public service. Similar problems can also be seen in posts where the regulator was made subject to a primary duty to ensure the provision of a universal postal service but also to a secondary duty to promote effective competition.[29] Perhaps the tension was strongest in the transport field; in rail the scope of competition was severely limited to preserve a network of services and to make the industry saleable. In the case of buses, application of ordinary

---

[27] Oftel, *Effective Competition: Framework for Action* (London: Oftel, 1995).

[28] *R v. Director General of Telecommunications, ex parte British Telecommunications plc* [1997] CLY 4844 (QBD), noted by C. Scott at (1997) 8(4) *Utilities Law Review* 120.

[29] Postal Services Act 2000, ss. 3(1) and 5(1).

competition law by the competition authorities raised major difficulties and, as we saw in the preceding chapter, integration of bus services has been restricted by the application of competition law.

In the case of the public utilities we can see a new dimension to the resolving of the tensions; the creation of regulatory bodies at arms-length from government with responsibilities for devising regulatory solutions, whereas under public ownership these responsibilities had been lost in the general sponsoring role of government departments for their industries. As we shall see, this led to a more open style of grappling with the problems together with a greater use of formal legal norms in statutes and licences to protect public service goals.

The effects of privatization and liberalization were not of course confined to the public utilities; they have had an important role to play in health and social services through contracting-out and other market-based reforms. To understand fully the context it is necessary to examine a further change whose effects are likely to be as great as the move from public ownership to regulation; the new general system of competition law introduced by the Competition Act 1998 and the Enterprise Act 2002. As we shall see, apart from its application by the utility regulators, this has already been tested in the health and social services sector.

The New Competition Law

The 'Juridification' of Competition Law

UK competition law until the coming into effect of the Competition Act 1998 in 2000 had a distinctive character all of its own, and one which is remarkably similar to the approach adopted for the protection of public service goals. Thus its major characteristics were discretion based around a public interest test for monopolies and mergers, central political input through the role of the minister in key stages of decision-making, and a reluctance to use detailed rules of law or decisions of the courts to resolve disputes. The exception to this was the control of restrictive agreements which were subject to control which was both formal and ineffective by the Restrictive Practices Court under the Restrictive Trade Practices Act 1976. However, monopolies and mergers were examined on the basis of the test laid out in section 84 of the Fair Trading Act 1973; rather than requiring any economic approach to be taken in assessing the effect of the contested behaviour on competition, the Monopolies and Mergers

Commission was required to consider whether the public interest was being harmed. In doing so the Commission was required to 'take into account all matters which appear to them in the particular circumstances to be relevant'; among other things, the Commission was to have regard to the promotion of effective competition, promoting the interests of consumers, promoting cost reduction and the entry of new competitors, 'maintaining and promoting the balanced distribution of industry and employment in the United Kingdom', and promoting exports.[30]

In addition to the sheer breadth of the public interest test, the Secretary of State played a prominent role in the process. Thus in the case of monopoly references, although most references were made by the Director General of Fair Trading, the minister also had power to refer and indeed sole power to do so in certain cases, including the activities of the nationalized utilities referred to above.[31] All merger references were made by the Secretary of State. Once the Monopolies and Mergers Commission had reported, if a detriment to the public interest had been found the Secretary of State had a discretion whether or not to take action, and as to what action should be taken. Indeed, the courts decided that the minister had an 'unfettered discretion' in deciding whether or not to follow the views of the Commission in a merger case, and that, in deciding whether or not to refer a case to the Commission, he was under no duty to give reasons.[32] As a leading writer put it, '[t]he Secretary of State for Trade and Industry is the sun around which British competition policy orbits'.[33]

Finally, there was only limited use of formal legal rules or resort to the courts. Thus the Monopolies and Mergers Commission had not developed a rule-based system as the basis for its decisions and, although a number of judicial review actions were brought against it, the Commission did not lose any case until 2001.[34]

The cumulative effect of these factors was that there was very little need to create specific exceptions for, or limitations to, the application of competition law to public services. As we saw above, in many cases public services were effectively exempt from the application of competition law; however, even where they were not, ministerial discretion allowed

---

[30] Fair Trading Act 1973, s. 84.   [31] Fair Trading Act 1973, schs. 5 and 7.

[32] *R v. Secretary of State for Trade, ex parte Anderson Strathclyde* [1983] 2 All ER 233 (QBD); *R v. Secretary of State for Trade and Industry, ex parte Lonrho* [1989] 1 WLR 525 (HL).

[33] Wilks (1996) 150.

[34] For the relationship between the Commission and legal controls see Craig (1987).

control of the application of the law to take place at the political level. Even where competition law did apply, the breadth of the public interest test would allow public interest factors to be internalized as part of competition law itself.

The system was changed fundamentally by the Competition Act 1998 and the Enterprise Act 2002.[35] The 1998 Act, in brief, introduced new prohibitions based on Articles 81 and 82 of the EC Treaty; they thus prohibited agreements which may affect trade in the UK and which have as their object or effect the prevention, restriction or distortion of competition (the Chapter I prohibition), and abuse of a dominant position (the Chapter II prohibition). These prohibitions replaced the use of the public interest-based test in earlier law for the control of monopolies. Although the public interest test was briefly retained for use in special cases, it was in turn abolished by the Enterprise Act 2002 which introduces instead a system of market investigation references by the Office of Fair Trading to the Competition Commission; the test applied is whether features of the market referred prevent, restrict or distort competition.[36] A similar test is adopted in place of the public interest test for mergers, where it has to be determined whether the merger would result in a substantial lessening of competition.[37] Thus the broad discretion and the wide range of factors which could be considered under the old law have been replaced by more focussed tests based around the effect of disputed conduct on competition in the UK. Importantly, the 1998 Act also requires the competition authorities to ensure that questions are dealt with in a manner consistent with treatment in Community competition law, thus opening up the jurisprudence to be considered in Chapter 6 below.[38]

The administrative machinery has also been changed in major respects by the legislation of 1998 and 2002. The central role of the Secretary of State has effectively been ended, although she does retain some powers, notably adopting block exemptions under the Chapter I prohibition and deciding on special categories of monopolies and mergers raising public interest concerns (see the discussion later in this chapter). The enforcement mechanism now however lies with the corporate Office of Fair Trading, which may fine undertakings up to 10% of UK turnover for

---

[35] For a useful introduction to the former see Maher (2000); for more detail see Rodger and MacCulloch (2000).   [36] Enterprise Act 2002, s. 134.
[37] Enterprise Act 2002, ss. 35–6.   [38] Competition Act 1998, s. 60(1–2).

breach of the 1998 Act's prohibitions and may also issue directions to end an infringement and interim relief. Appeal lies from its decision to the Competition Appeal Tribunal and thence on point of law to the Court of Appeal. In addition, private law actions may be brought to obtain damages for breach of the prohibitions, initially in the courts but, from the coming into effect of the Enterprise Act, in the Competition Appeal Tribunal itself. Not only will this depoliticize the enforcement process, it will also increase the substantive reliance on detailed legal rules rather than discretion and will increase the use of legal proceedings; indeed, the appeal tribunal has already produced important case law on the 1998 Act, some of which will be considered shortly. As one writer on the 1998 Act put it, 'reform can properly be seen as a seismic shift in the regulation of competition within the UK leading to a juridification and codification of competition policy backed by a system of sanctions'.[39]

The Case of Pharmacies

The potential effect of this depoliticization of competition law can be detected in an important case involving health care, that of entry restrictions for retail pharmacy services in the UK. It must be stressed that this was a case that would not be affected directly by the new law. The Office of Fair Trading here undertook a market study under the Fair Trading Act 1973 s. 2; although this provision is now repealed by the Enterprise Act 2002, similar studies can be undertaken under provisions of the new legislation, and indeed the Office of Fair Trading is continuing to do so.[40] Moreover, the studies are not limited by a competition-based approach and, in this case, took the form of advice to government on the reform of regulations, thereby placing the ultimate decision in the latter's hands. Nevertheless the study resulted in an interesting difference in viewpoint between the competition authorities and the Government.

The Office of Fair Trading stated that it was 'guided by the principle that competitive markets to which there are no barriers to entry generally serve best the interests of consumers'. However, it had 'remained mindful of the public policy objectives of health departments in the UK'.[41] It

---

[39] Maher (2002) 544.

[40] Enterprise Act 2002, ss. 5–7; Office of Fair Trading, *Annual Report 2002–3*, HC 906, 2002–3, 18–21.

[41] Office of Fair Trading, *The Control of Entry Regulations and Retail Pharmacy Services in the UK*, OFT 609 (January 2003).

concluded that all control of entry regulations for retail pharmacies should be abolished because the benefits of increased competition for prices and service quality would not be countered by substantial net exit of pharmacies and reduced public access.[42] The Health Select Committee of the House of Commons issued a highly critical report on the proposals, claiming *inter alia* that the Office had 'singularly failed' to take into account the bigger picture of the NHS and the country's health needs.[43] The Government did not fully accept the Office of Fair Trading's report, because the Government 'must take into account wider NHS policy objectives, and the impact of changes in regulations on NHS services and patients. That was not part of the OFT's remit but its recommendations must be seen within that broader picture.'[44] Thus '[w]e do not believe that simple deregulation is the best way to achieve our aims ... the Government does not believe that this is the time to move to a fully deregulated system. It therefore intends to move cautiously in the direction recommended by the OFT.'[45] Reasons underlying the decision not to implement the report in full were the current shortage of pharmacists, the need to give a strong role to pharmacies in the NHS, and the need to avoid undermining the market available to smaller community pharmacies. Thus only limited exceptions to the control of entry requirements would be granted to raise standards 'without jeopardising the vital role played by community pharmacies particularly in poorer and rural areas'.[46] The Government then proceeded by issuing a consultation document and establishing an advisory group on implementation of the changes. As a result, liberalization was further restricted, a decision heavily criticized by the Office of Fair Trading as a missed opportunity.

Although it must be stressed once more that the particular issue of a market study into the operation of regulations is not affected by the recent changes in competition law, nevertheless the case of pharmacies is revealing in showing a contrast between the competition-based approach of the Office of Fair Trading and a response by Government more open to social goals. This brings us to the central question of how the recent developments in competition law will affect its application in relation to

---

[42] Ibid., ch. 5.

[43] 'The Control of Entry Regulations and Retail Pharmacy Services in the UK', HC 571, 2002-3, para. 57.

[44] Department of Health, *Proposals to Reform and Modernise the NHS (Pharmaceutical Services) Regulations 1992* (2003), 42.   [45] Ibid., 43.

[46] Ibid., 44.

public services and their underlying values? The less discretionary and less politicized nature of the new law creates a need for some more explicit treatment of any exceptions or limits to competition law rather than relying on ministerial discretion and the public interest test, and these exceptions will be considered in the following section. However, there are two other preliminary issues for discussion; the special arrangements for enforcement of the new law by the utilities regulators and the degree to which it applies to the activities of public bodies at all.

The Regulators' Concurrent Powers[47]

We have already seen how the utility regulators had used their powers to enforce licence conditions as a way of policing competition by the public utilities. The Competition Act 1998 went further by conferring powers to enforce the Act's prohibitions on the Directors General of Telecommunications, of Electricity Supply, of Water Services, and of Gas Supply, and on the Rail Regulator; the Civil Aviation Authority later acquired concurrent powers in relation to air traffic control services.[48] More recently, the Communications Act 2003 has conferred similar powers on the new Ofcom covering both telecommunications and broadcasting.[49]

The concurrent powers permit these regulators to enforce the prohibitions in their own sectors; the sectors are widely defined; for example 'commercial activities connected with the generation, transmission or supply of electricity'.[50] The regulators acquire for this purpose wider powers of investigation given to the Office of Fair Trading under the 1998 Act, and they are also given much wider remedial powers than they previously possessed, including the imposition of interim measures, the granting of exemptions to the Chapter I prohibition, and the power to impose financial penalties and to issue directions to bring an infringement to an end. Their decisions taken under these powers are appealable to the Competition Appeal Tribunal in the same way as those of the Office of Fair Trading. Regulations have been put in place to co-ordinate the work of the regulators and of the Office, for example allowing exchange of information between them, setting out procedures

---

[47] For more details see Prosser (2000), and Office of Fair Trading, *Concurrent Application to Regulated Industries* (OFT 405, 2001).

[48] S. 54 and Sch. 10; Transport Act 2000, sch. 8 para. 14.

[49] Communications Act 2003, s. 369.   [50] Competition Act 1998, sch. 10 para. 4(5).

for determining which should act in a particular case and preventing simultaneous investigation by more than one authority.[51] In addition, a Concurrency Working Party has been established including a repres- entative of each of the authorities to ensure co-ordination between them, to ensure that no case is investigated by more than one authority and to secure consistency of approach.

The scheme of the Act is that the prohibitions should be applied in the same way by the regulators as by the Office of Fair Trading, rather than being shaped by the different context of utility services. Thus the Act (through a tortuous process of drafting) amends the statutes creating special duties applying to each regulator (for example, duties to secure universal service or that the provider of a service can finance them) so that they do not apply in relation to Competition Act functions of the regu- lator. Each regulator may however have regard to the matters covered by the sectoral duties insofar as they are matters which could be considered by the Office of Fair Trading in exercising its powers under the Act.[52]

In addition to the powers to apply the Competition Act 1998, the regulators have also been given the power under the Enterprise Act 2002 to undertake market investigations under its provisions, as well as con- current powers to apply for director disqualification and to investigate 'super-complaints' by designated consumer bodies.[53]

Several of the sectoral regulators have issued guidance on the application of the Act in their sectors.[54] These again confirm that the regulators will apply the prohibitions in the same way as the Office of Fair Trading rather than taking a different general approach because of the nature of utility industries. They are generally concerned with the familiar competition law questions of market definition, assessment of market power, and so on in the particular context of the industries rather than with public service concerns; insofar as they do make reference to the special position of utilities as services of general economic interest,

---

[51] Competition Act 1998 (Concurrency) Regulations 2004, SI 2004/1077.

[52] See Prosser (2000) 235–6 and Sch. 10 of the 1998 Act.

[53] Enterprise Act 2000, ss. 204–5, Sch. 9, Pt. 2; the Enterprise Act 2002 (Super-complaints to Regulators) Order 2003, SI 2003/1368.

[54] The guidelines are published on behalf of the regulators by the Office of Fair Trading: *Competition Act 1998: The Application in the Telecommunications Sector* OFT 417 (nd), *Competition Act 1998: Application in the Water and Sewerage Sectors* OFT 422 (nd), *Competition Act 1998: The Application in the Energy Sector* OFT 428 (2001), *The Competition Act 1998: Application to Services Relating to Railways* OFT 430 (2002), *The Competition Act 1998: Application to the Northern Ireland Energy Sectors* OFT 437 (2001).

this will be referred to in discussion of the qualifications to the full application of competition law to them later in this chapter.

The concurrent powers are thus of very great importance, but do not reflect a major acceptance that utility industries are different from others because of their public service role. Rather they can be justified by the informational advantages a regulator with an intimate knowledge of an industry will possess over a generalist fair trading authority in applying ordinary competition law. However, there are certain qualifications to the Competition Act prohibitions which do suggest that in some circumstances public services require special treatment. But first it is necessary to consider whether competition law applies at all.

The *BetterCare* Decision[55]

In many cases, notably the public utilities, it is clear that the new law will apply subject to any specific exceptions to be considered below. However, in another area of public service some important issues were raised in one of the early decisions of the appeal tribunal; the second *BetterCare* case.[56] BetterCare ran private care homes and complained to the Office of Fair Trading that the local health and social services trust, its main customer, was abusing a dominant position. It was alleged that the trust, which as well as purchasing care from private concerns also provided its own care directly, offered unfairly low prices and unfair terms in its purchases from BetterCare of residential and nursing care. The Director General rejected the complaint on the ground that the trust when purchasing care for the disadvantaged, using money raised from taxation, was not acting as an undertaking. Therefore it was not covered by the 1998 Act which only prohibits abuse of a dominant position on the part of one or more undertakings.[57] If this decision were to be upheld, it would clearly limit considerably the applicability of competition law to public bodies providing public services.

The appeal tribunal allowed the appeal, dealing at considerable length with the arguments about the extent to which the Act applies to public bodies acting as such and rejecting a number of arguments made by the

---

[55] For discussion of this case see Bright and Currie (2003) and Rodger (2003).

[56] *BetterCare Ltd v. Director General of Fair Trading* [2002] CAT 7. The first case had concerned the earlier question of whether the Director General had made an appealable decision.

[57] S. 18 (1).

Director General of Fair Trading. Thus the fact that the trust was carrying out social functions or allocating state funds between social welfare priorities was not relevant to its position as an undertaking, this being distinguished from, for example, the registration of a residential home. The situation was not one of regulatory or administrative decisions normally classified by the European Court as 'the exercise of official authority'.[58]

The Director General had also argued that the functions of the trust were based on the principle of 'solidarity' and so were not economic in nature; this was also rejected by the tribunal, holding that:

in focussing exclusively on the 'social' dimension of [the trust's] activities, the Director's argument overlooks what we have described as 'the business dimension'. Thus, although the *funding* which [the trust] provides has a social purpose, the way in which [the trust] carries out or *delivers* its functions is *by using business methods*. Thus, looking at the matter from the point of view of Bettercare and other independent providers dealing with ... NHS trusts, and local authorities, the independent providers are entering into commercial transactions ... In our view the contracts in question take place within a business setting and are as much commercial transactions from [the trust's] point of view as they are from the point of view of the independent providers.[59]

European cases concerned with solidarity as differentiated from economic activity were distinguished as only referring to 'internal' solidarity between participants in pension, insurance, and sickness schemes, rather than 'external' solidarity such as that between the trust and its independent providers.[60] Finally, it was argued by the Director General that application of the competition rules would interfere with the state's ability to distinguish between its social priorities. The tribunal stressed that the existence of an undertaking was distinct from the question of whether a dominant position was being abused, or whether the action fell within the special provisions to be discussed below relating to services of general economic interest. Without fully examining the question, the tribunal was of the view that the latter exception would give the trust 'considerable scope for demonstrating that the adoption of alternative pricing policies would substantially interfere with the performance of its statutory functions' and so the full competition rules would not

---

[58] [2002] CAT 7, paras. 49, 60, 171, 175, 224–6.   [59] Para. 234 (emphasis retained).
[60] Paras. 227–43.

necessarily apply.[61] Nevertheless, the trust was in principle subject to the competition rules as an undertaking.

The Director General decided not to appeal the tribunal's decision to the Court of Appeal on the ground that 'the OFT agrees with the view that, with more public services being provided by the market, the disciplines of the market place, including competition law, should apply. The OFT's role is to make markets work well for consumers and that includes markets that involve public services.'[62] The decision of the tribunal on the definition of an undertaking appears clearly right on the facts.[63] However, there are some doubts as to whether it is compatible with more recent developments in Community law, to be considered in Chapter 6 below, although it may be possible to distinguish the more recent case law.[64]

The *BetterCare* decision is of considerable importance for emphasizing two points. The first is that the new competition law will apply to a wide range of bodies exercising public functions; not just the obvious trading bodies such as the public utilities, but others performing more directly social roles insofar as they conduct activity within a marketplace, even if that marketplace is highly regulated, as was the case in *BetterCare*. This is particularly so in the health and social services sector where there has been extensive contracting-out coupled with the retention of some direct provision. Indeed, at first sight it is difficult to think of any public institution, apart from one which is limited to policy-making, that would not fall under the new law in relation to at least some of its functions. However, the ultimate outcome of the case illustrates that there are still limits to the application of competition law here. The Office of Fair Trading determined that there had been no breach of competition law as the trust in question did not actually set the prices paid to BetterCare. These were instead set by the relevant health board and Northern Ireland government department. These latter were not undertakings because they did not carry out economic activities through offering goods and services on a market; rather they allocated public funds in order to discharge social functions.[65]

---

[61] Paras. 209–220, 265–7. The quotation is from 214.

[62] Office of Fair Trading Press Release, 2 September 2002, 'OFT not to Appeal BetterCare Legal Ruling'.   [63] And see Rodger (2003) 9.

[64] See Case T-319/99 *FENIN v. Commission* [2003] ECR II-357 and Rodger (2003) 6–9; Cases C-264/01, C-3-6/01, C-354/01, and C-355/01 *AOK Bundesverband* OJ [2004] C94/2.

[65] Office of Fair Trading, *BetterCare Group Ltd/North & West Belfast Health and Social Services Trust (Remitted Case)* Decision CA98/09/2003, esp. at paras. 37–9.

The second important point is that the general applicability of the competition rules does not mean that there are no modifications or exceptions which may apply. Indeed, the case has suggested that the most appropriate procedure is to accept a broad definition of an undertaking and then to apply the exceptions to it.[66] It will thus be necessary to examine the exceptions to general competition law which may apply to public services in considerable detail. As we shall see, the most important of these closely follows European Community law, to be examined fully in Chapter 6 below. At this stage I shall limit myself to discussion of the UK provisions, although it should always be borne in mind that they are situated in, and derived from, an important European context.

Special Treatment for Public Services

Public Policy

The first special provision relevant to public services in the Competition Act is of very little practical importance. This is paragraph 7 of Schedule 3 to the Act, which permits the Secretary of State to exclude application of the prohibitions where he is satisfied that there are 'exceptional and compelling reasons of public policy' for doing so. No orders have been issued under this provision, which, given the strictness of its conditions, appears more likely to be applicable in national emergencies or defence than in the everyday utility or health services.[67]

Block and Individual Exemptions

In relation to breaches of the Chapter I prohibition only, sections 4–9 of the Act permit block and individual exemptions to be granted by the Secretary of State and the Director General. At first sight these appear to have very limited relevance to public services; the criteria are that the exemption contributes to improving production or distribution or promotes technical or economic progress, subject to further conditions to ensure their proportionality.[68] However, equivalent provisions have been of considerable importance in European Community competition law.[69] Moreover, the domestic provisions have been used in one

---

[66] And see Rodger (2003) 9–16.

[67] See Whish (2001) 305–6. It was noted in the *BetterCare* decision that no such order had been made in the case; para. 217.   [68] S. 9.

[69] Monti (2002).

situation referred to earlier, that of public transport. A block exemption has been granted to certain ticketing schemes, notably multi-operator travelcards and through tickets as these are seen as producing consumer benefits and improvements in the efficient use of resources.[70] It is however subject to strict conditions and applies only to local public transport services; as we saw in the previous chapter, the way in which competition law is applied to bus services has been severely criticized by a parliamentary committee, despite the existence of the exemption. Of course this type of exemption will not apply to abuse of a dominant position and the Chapter II prohibition. Similarly, there is some scope for agreements otherwise in breach of the Chapter I prohibition to benefit from a parallel exemption on the basis that they benefit from an exemption at the European level.[71] This may have some limited effect in the rail sector where the European Commission may grant an individual exemption to improve the quality of transport services or to promote their continuity or stability where supply and demand are subject to considerable temporal fluctuations.[72]

Complying with a Legal Requirement

Of more apparent importance is another provision in Schedule 3 to the 1998 Act. This provides that neither prohibition applies to an agreement or to conduct to the extent to which it is made or engaged in to comply with a legal requirement.[73] A legal requirement is defined as a requirement 'imposed by or under any enactment in force in the United Kingdom', or by directly effective Community law. This would seem to offer considerable scope for the restriction of the application of the Act in regulated industries, for, as was made clear in the Parliamentary debates, it would apply where a licence condition of a utility company required it to act in a certain way.[74] An obvious example would be where a licence, either in its original form as determined by the Secretary of State or, as is more likely at this stage, as amended by the regulator, imposes a price cap. Other examples would be where the Rail Regulator issues directions

---

[70] The Competition Act 1998 (Public Transport Ticketing Schemes Block Exemption) Order 2001, SI 2001/319 and *Public Transport Ticketing Schemes Block Exemption*, OFT 439 (2002).   [71] S. 10.

[72] *Application to Services Relating to Railways*, op. cit., paras. 4.14–4.22 and Reg. (EEC) 1017/68 applying rules of competition to transport by rail, road, and inland waterway OJ L175, 23 July 1968, 1.   [73] Para. 5(1–2).

[74] See 583 HL Debs. 13 November 1997, cols. 332–6.

under the Railways Act to require companies to enter into or to amend access agreements in relation to their facilities.[75]

Some degree of the complexity of the issues involved can be seen in the context of the bus industry, where legislation passed after the 1998 Act has imposed a special competition test when the Office of Fair Trading investigates a local authority's quality partnership, ticketing scheme, or tenders for services in the bus industry. It is of special interest as an attempt to balance public interest factors and competition in a more explicit way than is done elsewhere. A quality partnership scheme is an agreement to implement a local bus strategy in which the local authority agrees to provide facilities such as bus lanes; any bus operator wishing to use these facilities must agree to meet quality standards. Ticketing schemes will include, for example, multi-operator travelcards and tendering will take place where a local authority seeks to subsidize services. The basis of the special competition test is whether the scheme would have a significantly adverse effect on competition, but it can still pass the test if it nevertheless secures improvements in the quality of vehicles or facilities used, or other improvements of sub-stantial benefit to users of local services, or it reduces or limits traffic congestion, noise, or air pollution. The effect on competition must also be proportionate to the benefits.[76] At first sight, the test is a good example of a statutory requirement which would prevail over the ordinary application of the Competition Act. On closer examination, however, it is in fact a supplement to the Competition Act test rather than replacing it. Thus, according to the guidance on the test, it is doubtful whether a local authority in these circumstances is an under-taking and therefore covered by the Competition Act.[77] Therefore the new test alone will apply to making or varying of schemes by the authority itself. However, agreements between bus undertakings implementing the scheme would be caught by the Competition Act unless they fall within the block exemption referred to earlier or are required by law by a local authority, in which latter case they would be considered under the special test in the transport legislation rather than

[75] See the Railways Act 1993, ss. 16A, 17–19A, 22A, and 22C.

[76] Transport Act 2000, sch. 10; Transport (Scotland) Act 2001, s. 37; see also *The Transport Act 2000 and the Transport (Scotland) Act 2001: Guidance on the Competition Test*, OFT 393 (2003).

[77] Cf. the *BetterCare* decision above, although given the ultimate decision of the Office of Fair Trading the guidance is probably still accurate.

under the Competition Act by virtue of the exclusion now being discussed.

There could be scope, using the legal requirement exclusion from the Competition Act, for a clear division of labour between government and regulators on the one hand and the competition authorities on the other, with the former imposing public service obligations through licences thus providing a framework within which the latter could police fair competition. This would seem a promising and transparent structure; however, it must be seen as subject to two major qualifications. The first is that the exclusion only applies where the agreement or conduct is actually required to comply with the legal requirement; it does not apply where the enterprise itself has a degree of discretion, as was made clear in the parliamentary debates; an example of this would be the setting of particular prices within an overall price cap.[78] As we shall see in the next chapter, the style of regulation adopted in the UK has tended to proceed by giving enterprises considerable discretion in the means adopted to implement social goals, with the exception of some aspects of price control and some particular legal requirements such as the prohibition on water disconnections in the Water Industry Act 1999.[79] The exclusion does not permit any balancing of social goals against competition goals in the exercise of that discretion. Secondly, the Appeal Tribunal pointed out in the *BetterCare* decision that there is no direct counterpart of this provision in Community law.[80] This may be questionable,[81] but, as we shall see in Chapter 6 below, European Community competition law is addressed not merely to enterprises but to Member States themselves.[82] Thus even if a requirement is imposed by law, it will not be immune from challenge under Community competition law in the increasing number of public utility sectors where there is a Community dimension.

Services of General Economic Interest

The final exclusion from the scope of the prohibitions in the Competition Act would appear to be of the greatest importance, derived as it is

---

[78] See Lord Simon at 583 HL Debs. 13 November 1997, col. 335.

[79] S. 1. It is of course unlikely that a policy of not disconnecting for failure to pay a bill could in any event constitute abuse of a dominant position.   [80] At para. 288.

[81] See Rodger (2003) 14.

[82] See Art. 86(1) of the EC Treaty, which has no counterpart in domestic legislation.

from the major Community law provision of this kind. It is in paragraph 4 of Schedule 3 to the Act and provides that:

Neither the Chapter I prohibition nor the Chapter II prohibition applies to an undertaking entrusted with the operation of services of general economic interest or having the character of a revenue-producing monopoly in so far as the prohibition would obstruct the performance, in law or in fact, of the particular tasks assigned to that undertaking.

It is modelled closely on Article 86(2) of the EC Treaty and so the jurisprudence of the European Court on this provision, and indeed the new Article 16 of the Treaty itself, are to be taken into account by the UK authorities as a result of section 60, as mentioned above. However, it should be noted that there are minor differences in wording and important differences in context between the domestic and European provisions, and this may limit the extent to which they are to be interpreted uniformly.[83]

The Office of Fair Trading has issued a consultation draft of guidance on the interpretation of paragraph 4. It stresses that '[t]he Director General of Fair Trading will interpret the exclusion strictly, with undertakings seeking to benefit from the exclusion having to meet all the requirements of the exclusion'.[84] Whilst accepting the application of the obligation to avoid inconsistency with Community competition law under section 60, according to the guidance 'due to the extent of deregulation and liberalisation of the economy that has occurred in the United Kingdom compared to other parts of the EU, it is unlikely that there will be a significant number of cases in which previous European Commission decisions will be relevant when considering whether the exclusion applies in the United Kingdom'.[85] Moreover, '[w]hile the Director General of Fair Trading recognises the need to ensure the provision of certain services, he considers that, in the majority of cases in the United Kingdom, the free operation of the market will be best able to provide services of general interest, to meet the needs of consumers'.[86] Finally, the Director General 'does not consider it likely that many undertakings in the United Kingdom will meet all the criteria set out in the Act in order to benefit from the services of general economic interest

---

[83] Freeman and Whish (1999) para. 7.20; Rodger (2003) 12.

[84] *The Competition Act 1998: Services of General Economic Interest Exclusion (Formal Consultation Draft)*, OFT 421 (2001), para. 1.6. [85] Ibid., para. 1.9.

[86] Ibid., para. 2.20; see also 3.8.

exclusion . . . ' and he then casts doubt on its applicability in the energy, postal services, air traffic control, telecommunications, and rail sectors, whilst accepting that it may apply to some aspects of water services.[87]

The doubts as to the applicability of paragraph 4 appear to be shared by the sectoral regulators. The general guidance on the concurrent powers does envisage that paragraph 4 may mean that the Act does not apply to certain activities of regulated businesses, though the regulators will still be able to use their sectoral powers to ensure that services are available throughout the UK on reasonable terms in these cases. However, in their guidelines on the applicability of the Act referred to above, there is only minimal reference to paragraph 4. In the case of telecommunications, amongst the detailed discussion of the application of ordinary competition law principles, there is no discussion of this exclusion from the Act with only passing reference to the requirement of geographically averaged prices in the context of market definition; the implications of the exclusion was dealt with more explicitly in the consultation draft of the guidance, which stated that it was unlikely to apply to any telecommunications companies.[88] The guidance on water is a little more explicit, noting that water and sewerage undertakings may fall within the concept of undertakings entrusted with the operation of a service of general economic interest, but that the exclusion would be unlikely to apply to many aspects of their conduct.[89] For energy too a restrictive approach is taken; the exclusion's application is 'particularly narrow'.[90] In the rail guidance this exception is not discussed, with exclusions from the Act based on other grounds instead, for example the legal requirements exclusion where access agreements are entered into as a result of directions by the Rail Regulator under the Railways Act, as noted above.[91]

It could be argued that these interpretations of the exclusion are too narrow. As we shall see in Chapter 6 below, the jurisprudence of the European courts has become considerably more liberal recently as regards the special position of services of general economic interest. Moreover, there have been major reforms, in particular the new Article 16

---

[87] *The Competition Act 1998: Services of General Economic Interest Exclusion (Formal Consultation Draft)*, OFT 421 (2001), paras. 3.9–17.

[88] *The Application in the Telecommunications Sector*, para. 5.12; cf. Oftel, *Draft Guidelines on the Application of the Competition Act in the Telecommunications Sector – Consultation* (1999), para. 7.15.

[89] *Application in the Water and Sewerage Sectors*, para. 3.14.

[90] *The Application in the Energy Sector*, para. 3.36; the Northern Ireland guidance is virtually identical; *Application to the Northern Ireland Energy Sectors*, paras. 3.35–37.

[91] *Application to Services Relating to Railways*, paras. 2.11–12.

of the Treaty, which can be interpreted as creating a new duty to facilitate the achievement of public service missions, and this has had an important effect in producing a more positive approach towards them on the part of the Commission.[92] These developments in turn may have an important effect on the UK authorities as a result of the requirement under section 60 of the Competition Act to avoid inconsistency between principles laid down by the Treaty and decisions of the European Court on the one hand and domestic decisions on the other. It is interesting in this context to note that, in the *BetterCare* case, the appeal tribunal appeared to take a more liberal approach than that in the draft guidance to the interpretation of paragraph 4, noting *obiter* that it seemed to give the trust 'considerable scope for demonstrating that the adoption of alternative pricing policies would substantially interfere with the performance of its statutory functions'.[93] Meanwhile, issuing of final guidance was considerably delayed by the need to await the Commission's Green Paper on services of general interest, published in May 2003; new guidance was promised by the Office of Fair Trading for early 2004, but in fact all that was produced was a new consultation draft as part of the process of modernization of competition law through national enforcement of Community obligations.[94] This has few differences from the earlier draft, the only material one being that it does not deal explicitly with each of the regulated sectors.

Public Interest Cases under the Enterprise Act

Discussion so far has concerned the special provision for public services under the Competition Act 1998; however, there are also some limited opportunities for special treatment under the Enterprise Act 1998. Firstly, in the case of mergers the Act provides for the Secretary of State to intervene where she considers that a specified public interest consideration is relevant. This means that she then has the power to decide whether a reference should be made to the Competition Commission, and on action to be taken in relation to a public interest consideration after it has reported.[95] The Commission itself is also empowered to consider whether the merger would operate against the public interest in

---

[92] See Ross (2000).   [93] *BetterCare*, para. 214.

[94] Office of Fair Trading, *Services of General Economic Interest Exclusion: Draft Competition Law Guideline for Consultation*, OFT 421a (2004).   [95] Ss. 42–58.

relation to the notified consideration.[96] Similar provisions also apply in relation to market investigation references to the Competition Commission.[97]

These provisions would appear to be of considerable importance for the purposes of this analysis, but this is in fact not the case because of the narrow definition of a public interest consideration. The only such consideration set out in the Act is the interests of national security.[98] Additional public interest considerations may be added by order, but according to the Government during the passage of the legislation 'we have no plans to specify new public interest considerations'.[99] Thus the special provisions under the Enterprise Act appear to have no relevance to public services.

There are also special provisions in the Enterprise Act relating to water mergers, but these do not provide for special treatment on public service grounds, most importantly bringing the existing regime into line with the general mergers regime under the Enterprise Act.[100] More important are changes made by the Communications Act 2003. As envisaged for some time, they reform the position in relation to newspaper mergers and, after considerable controversy about the liberalization of media ownership under the bill, they permit the Secretary of State to notify specified media public interest considerations in relation to media mergers, with a special advisory role for Ofcom.[101] This raises important issues concerned with public service broadcasting which will be considered in Chapter 9 below; once more, however, the scope of ministerial intervention is limited in such as way as not to be applicable to public services in general.

Conclusions

We have seen in this chapter that, after some early moves to protect access to public services through the common law, public service values were implemented in the UK through political means, especially through nationalization, rather than through any distinct body of public service law. Until recently, the workings of UK competition law were rather similar, with a public interest test and a central role for ministerial

---

[96] S. 47(2), (5).   [97] Ss. 139–153.   [98] Ss. 58(1), 153(1).
[99] Miss Johnson, Standing Committee B, Ninth Sitting, 30 April 2002, col. 343.
[100] S. 70.   [101] Ss. 375–389.

discretion. However, from 1998 onwards the latter has been subject to major reform replacing the public interest test with more clearly legally defined competition-based tests and a much greater role for the legal authorities in decision-making. In addition, Community law principles and decisions have also been incorporated into the relevant materials for decision-makers via section 60 of the Competition Act, which will increase the relevance of the discussion in Chapter 6 below of the Community approach. It is quite clear, especially from the *BetterCare* decision and the role of the utility regulators under the 1998 Act, that these new legal principles will have a potentially important effect on the ways in which public services are delivered.

By contrast, there appears to have been little development of principles relating to the special needs of public services. The exceptions to the application of the Competition Act prohibitions have hardly been worked out in practice, and all the indications so far are that they will be interpreted in an extremely narrow way by the competition authorities, although, as we shall see, this may be questionable given recent developments in Community law. For public service, though not for competition law, the British tradition that the goals are to be implemented through political rather than legal means has been retained. There is, for example, no attempt to codify the special requirements of public service where they may conflict with the values of competition law.

Perhaps this is inevitable; it could be argued that competition principles lend themselves more easily to clearly defined legal rules than do the inherently vague and highly politicized principles of public service. However, some of the duties applying to the utility regulators do import public service principles into their decision-making, and it may be that, alongside applying competition law in their own sectors, they are able to develop a new system of public service law in conjunction with government; the extent to which they are doing so will be the subject of the following chapter. Then I shall look at two other European legal systems which have attempted to develop legal principles of public service and shall assess whether they can teach us any useful lessons. This will be followed by analysis of the hugely important body of European Community law on these matters to assess how the relationship between competition and public service has been approached there.

4

Regulation and the New UK Public Service Law

Introduction

In the previous chapter, I described the competition law of the UK in its application to public services, and we saw that the nature of that law has changed radically in recent years. From being discretionary, political, and public interest-based, it has moved to being more 'juridified' and has acquired a much stronger orientation towards 'pure' competition-based analysis. As regards public service, although there had been some protections as part of the common law, with nationalization public service had become a matter of politics rather than of law, and enforcement of public service goals was entrusted to ministers and to (weak) consumer councils.

However, from the early 1980s there has been a major growth of new regulatory institutions in many areas. Thus one could point to well-established bodies such as the Health and Safety Executive and the Health and Safety Commission, or to a large number of recently established bodies in the health and social services field; an example of the latter would be the National Care Standards Commission, which now regulates care homes, children's homes, private hospitals, and other similar institutions.[1] The list of such bodies seems ever-increasing; legislation has recently added a Commission for Healthcare Audit and Inspection and a Commission for Social Care Inspection.[2]

---

[1] Established by the Care Standards Act 2000.
[2] The Health and Social Care (Community Health and Standards) Act 2003.

These are, however, social regulators; their duties are to implement purely social goals such as the adequacy of care provision (although, as we saw in the previous chapter, competition issues may arise even in these sectors for resolution by the general competition authorities). Much more important for this book will be the work of those regulatory bodies which combine economic regulation, including the application of competition law, with social duties. Thus in this chapter I shall concentrate on the regulators established for the public utilities in telecommunications, energy, water, postal services, and transport. Not only are the public utilities themselves of particular importance for the focus of this work as regulated suppliers of essential services, but their regulation is now well established and we can see in some detail the development of special principles and practices of regulation relating to public service, alongside the regulators' competition law responsibilities described in the preceding chapter. In brief, my argument will be that, through the work of the regulators, a body of public service law has been established, mainly in the form of conditions contained in the licences under which the regulated enterprises operate. However, this body of law is highly pragmatic, lacks general principle and is not consistent, although we have seen some improvements in the latter respect since 1998.[3] This will involve analysing two aspects of utility regulation; first the statutory duties applying to the regulators to establish the extent to which they are required to adopt public service values, and second the extent to which action has been taken in practice which can be interpreted as based on such values.

The Regulators' Statutory Duties

The Original Model

It has to be said that, at the time of the privatization programme and the creation of the regulatory bodies, the UK Government had no intention of embodying principles of public service in law; indeed, it was determined to avoid legal controls on the utilities as much as possible.[4] Law

---

[3] For a more detailed examination making similar points see Klein (2003).

[4] The seminal statement of regulatory principle can be found in the first Littlechild Report, Littlechild (1984), in which neither social regulation nor law played any great role; see also, for an insider's view, Foster (1992), esp. chs. 9 and 12.

was perceived as encouraging meddling by the courts, as well as creating an unnecessary recourse to legal rights where market solutions would be more appropriate. Nevertheless, as mentioned in the preceding chapter, regulators were established for the telecommunications, gas, electricity, water, and rail sectors, initially with the aim of restraining monopoly until it could be replaced by competition. In this process political compromises had to be made, and the legislation setting out the duties of the regulators and those of ministers in relation to these sectors contained a number of duties mixing economic and social rationales. I shall now consider these in a little more detail, before moving on to consider changes made by the Labour Governments from 1997 onwards; it should be noted that the initial duties described below have now been largely replaced or face imminent replacement.[5]

The duties were contained in the statutes and in the licences under which the regulated enterprises operate; the latter have been amended considerably since their initial issue. The first of the regulators to be established was the Director General of Telecommunications, assisted by the Office of Telecommunications (Oftel). The Telecommunications Act 1984 imposed two primary duties on the regulator (and on the Secretary of State). The first was to ensure that, so far as practicable, telecommunications services were provided throughout the UK which satisfied all reasonable demands, including in particular emergency services, public call-box services, directory inquiries, maritime services, and services in rural areas.[6] I have argued elsewhere that this is best interpreted in a broad social sense indicating the principle of a universal right of access to telecommunications services.[7] The second primary duty was to ensure that providers of telecommunications services were able to finance them.[8] Rather surprisingly in an industry where competition developed very quickly, the maintenance and promotion of effective competition and the promotion of the interests of consumers and users were only secondary duties expressly made subject to the primary ones; they were not made overriding regulatory goals. Particular attention was to be paid to the interests of consumers who were disabled or of pensionable age.[9] It thus appears that universal access to telecommunications services was set as an important regulatory goal; as we shall see below,

---

[5] For a more detailed analysis of the original duties see Prosser (1997) 15–24, which this section updates.   [6] S. 3(1)(a).

[7] Prosser (1997) 17.   [8] S. 3(1)(b).   [9] S. 3(2)(a–b).

this has indeed characterized the regulatory regime in practice, alongside the major goal of promoting competition.

In the next chronological example, gas, somewhat different considerations applied given the prohibitive cost of extending gas supplies to some rural areas; thus the original Gas Act 1986 included a duty to secure that all reasonable demands were met but only 'so far as it is economical to do so'.[10] This was however supplemented by requirements to provide gas to premises close to a gas main and the licence (here termed authorization) granted to British Gas contained detailed conditions aimed at limiting disconnections of supply. Further changes were made by the Gas Act 1995 in preparation for the liberalization of retail markets. These included adding a primary duty to secure effective competition and replacing the duty to supply in the statute with a duty limited to connection by a public gas transporter.[11] The secondary duty of protecting the interests of consumers was once again applied in particular to those who were disabled or of pensionable age; the 1995 Act added those who were chronically sick.[12] Licence conditions also imposed other social obligations on licensed companies.[13] Again, we see here a mixture of social and pro-competition duties. In the case of electricity, the primary duties included a duty to promote competition, although even here we find amongst the secondary duties protection for the interests of consumers in rural areas in pricing matters, and for the disabled and pensioners on quality matters; for the north of Scotland there was also a unique primary duty to avoid a distinction between tariffs for urban and for rural areas.[14]

In the case of the water industry in England and Wales, the Water Industry Act 1991 imposed primary duties of ensuring that the functions of water and sewerage undertakers were properly carried out in every area together with the financing duty, here specifying the securing of a reasonable return on capital. Secondary duties included the protection of the interests of consumers, especially in rural areas, and of pensioners, and facilitating competition; these were supplemented by general environmental and recreational duties.[15] Finally, in the case of railways, given the very distinct nature of the industry a different pattern of duties was imposed, but these included the protection of the interests of users of rail

---

[10] S. 4(1)(a).   [11] S. 1 and sch. 3 para. 4.   [12] Gas Act 1986, s. 4(3); Gas Act 1995, s. 1.
[13] Prosser (1997) 93–4.   [14] Electricity Act 1989, s. 3(4–5), 3(2)(a).
[15] Water Industry Act 1991, ss. 2(4), 3–5.

services and the promotion of the use of the rail network to the greatest extent that the regulator considered economically practicable.[16] The legislation also contained detailed provisions for the regulation and restriction of the withdrawal of rail passenger services.[17]

This list of statutory duties makes for tedious reading, but two important points can be gathered from it. The first is that the privatized utility enterprises were not expected to behave simply as ordinary profit-maximizing companies; there were important regulatory requirements that were based on social goals, notably the provision of universal service.[18] The second point is that no coherent approach had been taken to the setting of such goals; the statutory provisions were a mishmash with few discernible underlying principles. This lack of coherence was to change, at least in part, after the election of a Labour Government in 1997 with the imposition of new statutory duties.

Statutory Duties: The New Model

The new Labour Government was more sympathetic to the need for social regulation than had been its predecessors: '[e]nsuring that the services provided by [the utilities] are available to all members of society, including the most vulnerable, on fair terms, is important to the Government's wider objective of creating a fairer society'.[19] In 1998 the Government organized a major review of utility regulation which was to result in the Utilities Act 2000 and other later statutes.[20] The review concluded that 'the Government, not regulators, should determine the social objectives of regulation'[21] and proposed a new approach under which it would issue statutory guidance to regulators in each sector; this will be discussed further below. However, the review also proposed that the incoherent statutory duties described above should be replaced by a new primary duty to protect the interests of consumers, wherever possible through promoting competition.[22] This would continue to be supplemented by secondary duties

---

[16] Railways Act 1993, s. 4(1).   [17] Ss. 37–50.

[18] Cf. Ernst (1994), discussed in Prosser (1997) 20–23.

[19] Department of Trade and Industry, A *Fair Deal for Consumers: The Response to Consultation* (DTI, 1998), para. 10.

[20] Department of Trade and Industry, *A Fair Deal for Consumers: Modernising the Framework for Utility Regulation* (Cm 3898, 1998); the conclusions were set out in the *Response to Consultation*, (above n. 19).

[21] *A Fair Deal for Consumers: Modernising the Framework for Utility Regulation*, para. 5.4.

[22] *Response to Consultation*, para. 16.

including those of a social nature, which would be extended to cover low-income consumers and the chronically sick.[23]

This standardizing approach was however initially limited by a decision, taken during the passage of the Utilities Bill through Committee in the House of Commons, to limit its application to the energy utilities; telecommunications and water were to wait for future reform (which has now been implemented).[24] Thus the Utilities Act 2000 was limited to creating a new regulatory authority for gas and electricity, the Gas and Electricity Markets Authority (in practice referred to under its previous administrative title as Ofgem, the Office of Gas and Electricity Markets) and providing it with new statutory duties. The new overriding duty was as follows: 'to protect the interests of consumers . . . , wherever appropriate by promoting effective competition'.[25] The regulatory authority is also required to have regard to securing that all reasonable demands for energy are met, ensuring that licence-holders are able to finance their activities, and to the interests of the disabled, chronically sick, pensioners, individuals on low incomes, and individuals in rural areas.[26] Thus, although the importance of competition is explicitly addressed, the other matters mentioned also explicitly require social considerations to be taken into account, a requirement backed up by the social guidance to be considered below.

A similar approach is now being implemented for water under the Water Act 2003. The Act will establish a Water Services Regulation Authority from 2005, whose primary duties will be to protect the interests of consumers, wherever appropriate by promoting effective competition, to secure that licensed companies can finance their functions through a reasonable return on capital, and to secure that the functions of water and sewerage undertakings are properly carried out. Secondary duties will include having regard to particular groups of vulnerable consumers, as in the case of energy.[27]

Of the major utilities, this does not cover telecommunications. Here the approach is necessarily different given European liberalization of

---

[23] Ibid., para. 13.

[24] See the Secretary of State for Trade and Industry, 345 HC Debs, 2 March 2000, cols. 555–60.

[25] Utilities Act 2000, s. 9 (gas), adding a new s. 4(AA)(1) to the Gas Act 1986; s. 13 (electricity) adding a new s. 3(A)(1) to the Electricity Act 1989.

[26] Ss. 9 and 13, adding new ss. 4(AA)(2–3) and 3(A)(2–3).

[27] Water Act 2003, s. 39, amending s. 2 of the Water Industry Act 1991.

telecommunications markets, to be discussed in Chapter 8 below. The Communications Act 2003 creates a new single regulator covering tele-communications and broadcasting; this new Office of Communications (Ofcom) is under the now standard principal duty to further the interests of consumers, but also under a second principal duty to further the interests of citizens in relation to communications matters.[28] It must secure, *inter alia*, the availability of a wide range of electronic commun-ications services throughout the UK and must have regard to the needs of persons with disabilities, the elderly, and those on low incomes as well as the different interests of those in rural and urban areas. It also has a duty to promote media literacy.[29] The new regime in telecommunica-tions introduced by European law implemented by the Act, however, gives responsibility to the Secretary of State for determining the content of universal service requirements, which are then applied by Ofcom.[30] In relation to broadcasting, the new regulator will of course have extensive public service duties, including administering and enforcing a new public service remit; this will be discussed in detail in Chapter 9 below on public service broadcasting.

In relation to the privatized utilities, then, we now have a more clearly presented set of statutory duties which include both competition and social requirements. This is also the case for one sector where the major enterprise has not been privatized but where nevertheless independent regulation has been established and some liberalization has taken place; that of postal services. An independent regulatory commission was set up in the form of the Postal Services Commission (Postcomm) by the Postal Services Act 2000.[31] The statutory duties here are radically different from those discussed above in that Postcomm has been given a single over-riding statutory duty; to ensure the provision of a universal postal service.[32] Such a service is defined as requiring at least one delivery to each home and one collection from each access point per day and a service of delivering letters and small parcels at 'affordable prices determined in accordance with a public tariff which is uniform throughout the United Kingdom'. A registered postal service is also required at such prices.[33] Other duties of Postcomm are expressly made subject to the universal service duty; they include the duty to exercise its

---

[28] S. 3(1).   [29] Ss. 3(2)(b), 3(4)(i), 3(4)(l), 11.   [30] Ss. 65–72.
[31] For further details see Prosser (2001) 506–14.   [32] Postal Services Act 2000, s. 3(1).
[33] S. 4(1).

functions in the manner which it considers best calculated to further the interests of users of postal services; it must have particular regard to the interests of the disabled and chronically sick, pensioners, those on low incomes, and those living in rural areas.[34] A further important social duty, which will be examined in more detail below, is to provide advice and information to the Secretary of State about the number and location of public post offices and their accessibility to users.[35]

Finally, a little needs to be said about transport and, in particular, rail. The Labour Government undertook reforms to the arrangements for the regulation of the privatized system, notably replacing the Office of the Franchising Director, which had been responsible for issuing and monitoring operating franchises, with the new Strategic Rail Authority.[36] The Authority remains however very different from other regulatory bodies, being in effect an arm of government; one of its major tasks is dispensing public funds to operators and it is subject to both directions and guidance from the Secretary of State.[37] It was announced in July 2004 that the Authority will be abolished, its functions being divided between the Department for Transport and Network Rail, the infrastructure operator. The same legislation also made amendments to the objectives of the Rail Regulator, adding duties to facilitate the furtherance of the Authority's strategies, to contribute to the development of an integrated system for the transport of passengers and goods, and to contribute to the achievement of sustainable development. The promotion of competition is now also expressed to be 'for the benefit of users of railway services'.[38] Once more we see a greater prominence being given to social objectives, although the particular position of rail with its requirement of massive continuing subsidies from government has made both the structure of the privatized industry and the role of the regulatory bodies very different from those in other sectors.

Generally, however, the clarification of the statutory objectives of the utility regulators has come closer to a standard pattern, and one which makes it clear that, although delivering competition is an important goal, it is not the only way in which benefits for consumers can be achieved and that more directly social objectives are also important. This theme is reinforced by a further reform; the provision for the issuing of social and environmental guidance by ministers.

---

[34] S. 5(1–2).   [35] S. 42.   [36] Transport Act 2000, Part IV.
[37] Ibid., s. 207(5).   [38] Ibid., s. 224.

Social and Environmental Guidance and Consumer Representation

A further innovation introduced by the Labour Government is the system of social and environmental guidance issued by ministers to regulators; here I shall concentrate on the social aspects of this. The review of utility regulation proposed a new approach under which government would issue such guidance in each sector; however it undertook that where new measures with significant financial implications were to be imposed, new primary legislation would be passed rather than using the guidance.[39]

The first example of the power to issue such guidance was contained in the Utilities Act 2000 and so applied to the energy regulator. Thus the Secretary of State was required to issue periodic guidance 'about the making by the Authority of a contribution towards the attainment of any social or environmental policies set out or referred to in the guidance' and the Authority was obliged to have regard to the guidance. Consultation was required before it was issued, and it was to be laid before Parliament under the negative resolution procedure.[40]

Draft guidance was issued for consultation in February 2000; after a considerable delay, a final draft was published in November 2002, though this was stated to be subject to review in the context of the Energy White Paper published soon afterwards.[41] The guidance comprises, firstly, an introductory statement of the wider context of the Government's social and environmental policy. Three social objectives are relevant to the regulator: tackling fuel poverty and social exclusion, improving the health of the population overall, and reducing the proportion of unfit housing stock. Moreover, the regulatory authority was invited to exercise its functions consistently with improving the health of the worst-off in particular. The rest of the guidance stated more detailed social and environmental objectives of the Government, including ensuring that the benefits of competition are fairly distributed between

[39] *A Fair Deal for Consumers: Modernising the Framework for Utility Regulation, op. cit.*, paras. 2.13–18, 5.4; *A Fair Deal for Consumers: The Response to Consultation, op. cit.*, paras. 10–14.

[40] Utilities Act 2000, s. 10 (inserting a new s. 4AB into the Gas Act 1986) and s. 14 (inserting a new s. 3B into the Electricity Act 1989).

[41] Department of Trade and Industry, *Social and Environmental Guidance to the Gas and Electricity Markets Authority* (2002).

different groups of consumers, and in particular that the poorest consumers and those suffering from fuel poverty should demonstrably share
in the benefits of competition. More specific guidance also dealt with
fuel poverty, payment options, debt and disconnection, energy efficiency,
the availability of gas, metering, and security of supply. The guidance is
thus an important means of communicating general government policy
in these areas to the regulators and, once more, making it clear that
the development of competitive markets is to be tempered by social
objectives.

Similar power to issue such guidance was also included in the Postal
Services Act.[42] In this case a final draft of the guidance was issued more
quickly, in March 2001.[43] The guidance stresses the statutory social
duties applying to Postcomm, notably that to ensure universal service,
and that the guidance is in addition to them, drawing together the
Government's social and environmental policies 'so that the Commission
can carry out its functions in a way that is alert to the wider policy picture
and, where possible, supportive of it'.[44] It is also emphasized that the
guidance is not a means of instructing Postcomm. The guidance also sets
out priorities for the Commission in applying it, the highest being universal service accessible and affordable for all and the next being accessibility of public post offices and the social functions that they perform,
particularly in rural and urban deprived areas. As in energy, Postcomm is
required to consider the effects of increasing competition on vulnerable
consumers. Greater detail is set out on the universal service requirement,
and it is emphasized that Postcomm 'must have regard to the social
objective of ensuring a universal postal service above other changes to
further the interests of users of postal services'.[45] Further guidance is also
provided on access to public post offices. The guidance is supplemented
by a direction requiring free postal services to be provided for the blind
and partially sighted in meeting their special needs.[46] This is only to
come into effect if voluntary arrangements prove inadequate.

Similar provisions for social and economic guidance are contained in
the Water Act 2003.[47] In this case the Welsh Assembly will also be able

---

[42] S. 43(2).

[43] Department of Trade and Industry, *Social and Environmental Guidance to the Postal Services
Commission Issued Under Section 43(2) of the Postal Services Act 2000* (2001).

[44] Ibid., Introduction, para. 2.   [45] Ibid., para. 9.2.

[46] Department of Trade and Industry, *Directions Under Section 41 of the Postal Services Act
2000* (nd).   [47] S. 40, inserting a new s. 2(A) into the Water Industry Act 1991.

to issue guidance. In the case of telecommunications, as we saw above, the regulatory system is now fundamentally different due to European Union liberalization, although the Secretary of State will have an important role in setting out universal service requirements by order; the requirements will then be applied by the new regulator. Once more, the system for rail is different. As a result of the Transport Act 2000 the Rail Regulator has come under a duty 'to have regard to any general guidance given to him by the Secretary of State about railway services or any other matters relating to railways'.[48] Such guidance has concerned general rather than specifically social matters; for example, working with other regulatory bodies.[49] Guidance to the Strategic Rail Authority, referred to above, has for example sought to link the Authority's strategies to the Government's own ten-year transport plan.[50]

Finally in this section, brief reference should be made to another important reform which had its origins in the Labour Government's utility review. This was to replace the somewhat untidy arrangements for consumer representation adopted when the original regulators were established with more independent consumer councils.[51] Measures were taken to implement this in the energy sector by the establishment of the Gas and Electricity Consumer Council (which operates as Energywatch) under the Utilities Act 2000.[52] Similarly, the Postal Services Act established the Consumer Council for Postal Services (PostWatch), and the Water Act 2003 will set up a Consumer Council for Water (WaterVoice).[53] These new bodies have had social concerns, and indeed their independence from the regulator may enable them to pursue these more vigorously; for example, we shall see below that Energywatch strongly opposed the regulator's abolition of price controls in the retail gas and electricity markets, and PostWatch has pressed for clearer definition of universal service by Postcomm.[54]

---

[48] S. 224(6) amending s. 4 of the Railways Act 1993.

[49] Department for Transport, *Statutory Guidance for the Rail Regulator* (2002).

[50] Department for Transport, *Directions and Guidance to the Strategic Rail Authority* (2002).

[51] For details of the original arrangements, see Prosser (1997) 49–50.

[52] S. 2 and Part III.

[53] Postal Services Act 2000, ss. 2 and 51–8; Water Act 2003, ss. 35 and 43–7.

[54] For conflict between regulators and consumer councils, see the House of Lords Select Committee on the Constitution, 'The Regulatory State: Ensuring its Accountability', HL 68, 2003–4, paras. 66–9.

Social Regulation in Practice

It has now been established clearly that the legal duties applying to the utility regulators include requirements of public service; initially in a somewhat incoherent manner but now with a clearer structure when reform has taken place after the 1998 utility review. Of course, the effect of legal duties can be highly uncertain, especially where there are a number of potentially contradictory duties to be weighed against each other, and in this section I shall examine the extent to which the regulators have engaged in social regulation in practice, hence implementing public service values as conceived in this book. The longest established of the utility regulators is that for telecommunications, and so this will be considered first.

Social Regulation of Telecommunications

In the case of telecommunications, social regulation has generally been conceived as part of the promotion and protection of universal service. Initially, the first Director General of Telecommunications was hesitant about implementing social goals; as he put it in his first annual report,

I do not think it would be appropriate for me to seek to impose a balance of prices in a way that is motivated primarily by a desire to achieve some particular redistribution of income ... nor do I think my powers would permit me to do this ... I do not believe ... that I could properly put forward a proposal for a rule that all people on low incomes should be given telephones free of rental: such a proposal would involve arbitrary judgements about matters of income redistribution and my making it would involve the usurping of the proper role of government.[55]

Nevertheless, in his price-control decisions a special tariff in the form of the light-user scheme was introduced by agreement with British Telecom; this was justified largely on the basis of the 'network externality', maximizing the value of the telephone network through encouraging as many people as possible to be linked to it. However, it can also be seen as in part based on social concerns.

Under the second Director General, Don Cruikshank, a more explicit approach was taken to social issues beginning with a review of universal service from 1994 onwards. Work on this area had already been undertaken by the European Commission (and later Community obligations

---

[55] Office of Telecommunications, *Annual Report* 1984, HC 457, 1984–5, 10–11.

were to become central in shaping universal service obligations).[56] Initially the review formed part of a more general consultation on interconnection and competition but concluded with a special consultation paper wholly concerned with universal service.[57] The policy objectives were geographical accessibility, affordability, and equal opportunities for customers with special needs, and the definition of universal service was to be 'affordable access to basic telecommunication services for all those reasonably requiring it regardless of where they live'.[58] This was the basis for proposals for a universal safety net including free itemized billing and selective call-barring; disconnection was to be replaced by the barring of outgoing calls and reasonable access to public call-box services was to be assured. Affordability meant that a more effective alternative to the existing light-user scheme be developed and a number of alternatives was put forward. In addition, special levels of universal service were to be set for schools and educational institutions, including high-speed network links, although, partly because of problems with compatibility with Community law, this in practice was followed up by other means.

It was clear that universal service concerns were developing beyond economic arguments based on the network externality into much more strongly social concerns, and the process culminated in the establishment of universal service requirements in 1997.[59] The level for universal service was established as a connection to the fixed network able to support voice telephony and low-speed data and fax transmission; the option of a more restricted service package at low cost; access to call boxes across the UK at affordable prices; free access to emergency services; and the option of an outgoing calls barred service as an alternative to disconnection. The universal services were to be provided at geographically averaged prices.

A further review took place during 1999–2001.[60] The objective was now explicitly social:

The policy objective behind universal service is to ensure that those telecommunications services which are used by the majority and which are essential to full social and economic inclusion are made available to everybody upon

---

[56] For the background, see Sauter (1998).

[57] Office of Telecommunications, *Universal Telecommunications Services* (1995).

[58] Ibid., para. 4.3.

[59] Office of Telecommunications, *Universal Telecommunications Services: Proposed Arrangements for Universal Service in the UK from 1997* (1997).

[60] Office of Telecommunications, *Universal Telecommunications Services* (1999); *Review of Universal Telecommunications Services* (2000); *Universal Service Obligation* (2001).

reasonable request in an appropriate fashion and at an affordable price. This principle is designed to ensure that people on low incomes, those in remote rural areas, those with disabilities and various other groups who might be described as more vulnerable do not miss out on the advantages telephony can bring.[61]

The context had changed somewhat in several respects; notably the rapid growth of mobile telephony which had dramatically reduced the numbers of those with no access to telephone services, and the growth of the Internet which had suggested to some that, to secure full social inclusion, a higher level of service with increased bandwidth should be included.

The conclusions of the review were as follows.[62] Firstly, despite the growth of mobile telephony, the universal service obligation should remain, and should consist of the provision of a basic connection to the fixed network, a more restricted scheme at low cost, and disconnection procedures which were proportionate, non-discriminatory, and published. The level of bandwidth required would be subject to further review, in conjunction with review by the European Commission; this concern had also been overtaken by other Government initiatives to facilitate the rapid roll-out of broadband.[63] Basic services should continue to be provided at geographically averaged prices as 'geographic averaging has delivered the benefits of competitive price levels nationally, rather than just in geographic areas where competition is strongest. It has also helped to ensure that telephony is affordable in areas where the high costs of provision would otherwise disadvantage certain groups of customers.'[64] British Telecom's existing prepaid scheme was to be reviewed to show that it fully met the needs of customers with low incomes and proposals would be sought to make the light-user scheme more effective. Disconnections of telephone services would be made subject to a good practice guide and regular meetings between consumer representatives and operators would be organized, linked to the publication of the disconnection statistics. Regulations had been passed requiring special services for the disabled.[65]

This process thus represents considerable progress on the part of the regulator in specifying and monitoring social goals in its regulation.

---

[61] *Universal Telecommunications Services* (1999), para. 1.2.

[62] See *Universal Service Obligation* (2001).

[63] See in particular the Office of the e-Envoy, *UK Online: Broadband Strategy* (2001) available at http://www.broadbanduk.org/reports/uk_online_broadband_strategy.pdf (consulted 14 July 2004).　[64] *Universal Service Obligation* (2001), para. 2.6.

[65] The Telecommunications (Services for Disabled Persons) Regulations 2000, SI 2000/2410. These have been revoked by the Communications Act 2003 in view of the new universal service arrangements to be described below.

It has certainly played a major role in the introduction of new social tariff and payment arrangements (such as the British Telecom's Pay&Call service introduced in 2003) and perhaps the most important effect has been in maintaining geographical averaging of charges. However disconnections in telecommunications are considerably higher than in other utility services, reaching a figure of over 1 million in 2002.[66]

The whole issue now has to be considered in the context of the new package of European regulation of electronic communications, including a new universal service directive, to be discussed in Chapter 8 below and implemented by the Communications Act 2003.[67] The content of the basic requirements is not significantly changed, but responsibility for setting them has passed to the Secretary of State with implementation by the regulator. Thus the Secretary of State has issued an order setting out the content of universal service requirements, covering the provision of telephone services, directories, public payphones, methods of billing (including requiring special tariff options and packages for those on low incomes or who have special needs), and special measures for the disabled.[68] Prices must be affordable for all users and uniform throughout the UK unless Ofcom has determined that there is a clear justification otherwise. It is then the responsibility of the regulator to designate universal service operators and to set the specific conditions necessary for each of them.[69] It should also be added that the UK has not established a universal service fund to pay for universal service, instead considering that in current conditions the requirement to provide universal service does not place an undue financial burden on universal service providers, though this could change in the future and is one of the reasons why Oftel recommended that the new Ofcom make a further review of universal service one of its priorities.[70] The first phase of this review identified difficulties in potential funding of universal service obligations from more profitable services as competition increases, and pointed to possible changes in their scope due to the growth of mobile telephony and the growing importance of broadband access.[71]

---

[66] Klein (2003) 8.   [67] Ss. 65–72.

[68] The Electronic Communications (Universal Service) Order 2003, SI 2003/1904.

[69] See Oftel, *Designation of BT and Kingston as Universal Service Providers, and the Specific Universal Service Conditions* (2003).   [70] Ibid., 2.8–11.

[71] Ofcom, *Strategic Review of Telecommunications: Phase 1 Consultation Document* (2004) paras. 5.94–5.100.

One particular aspect of universal service which merits further brief discussion is that of public call boxes. At the time of privatization, fears were expressed that the number of boxes would be drastically reduced, especially in rural and low-income areas. To avoid this, conditions were inserted into British Telecom's licence restricting the circumstances in which such public phones could be removed. The regulator also mounted a major campaign to ensure that the public phones actually worked. Public call boxes were included in the universal service consultations, but later merited reviews of their own. The most recent took the form of a consultation document issued in 2001 followed by a decision statement from the regulator in 2002; both were of course conducted against the background of the extremely rapid growth in mobile telephony which might appear to reduce the need for public call boxes.[72] The consultation document noted that there were more than 97,000 public call boxes, plus 58,500 operator-managed payphones on private land such as railway stations, almost double the number at privatization. This also compared favourably with comparable EU states, so the fear that privatization would lead to their removal had proved groundless.[73] Despite the growth of mobile telephony, the regulator concluded that adequate call-box coverage remained part of the basic universal service requirement, and that conditions restricting their removal should continue in revised form to be part of British Telecom's licence. The conditions require public consultation before removal of a call box and the consent of the local planning authority and parish council; provision is also made for the installation of new public call boxes on the ground of social need on request, for example by a local authority or community organization.[74] Once more, this system has been incorporated in the new system of protecting universal service under the new Community law regulatory package and the Communications Act.

It should finally be added that, apart from the explicit addressing of public service concerns in the universal service initiatives, they have also played some part in the more general work of the telecommunications regulator, including in price control.[75] Most recently, the 2002 British Telecom price control review has continued controls to ensure that the

---

[72] Oftel, *Public Payphones: A Consultation Document* (2001); *Public Payphones: A Statement Issued by the Director General of Telecommunications* (2002).

[73] *Public Payphones: A Consultation Document*, para. S.4.

[74] Oftel, *Public Payphones: Implementation of Universal Service Obligations* (2003).

[75] See Prosser (1997) 66–71.

prices for the lowest-spending 80% of customers will not rise, continues to require geographically averaged pricing, and maintains the light-user scheme and a ceiling on line rental.[76] This reflects the regulator's more general strategy that 'where competition cannot provide agreed services to all at affordable prices, regulation [will be used] to ensure that there is such provision in a way that minimises distorting effects'.[77]

In telecommunications, then, we have seen the development of the protection of universal service from a limited, economically based concept of network externality, to a much broader, more explicit and more dynamic socially based concept. This has been largely due to the influence of European Community law and as such illustrates an important theme of this book, which is that public services values have been more explicitly developed in Community law than in our own domestic law. Indeed, as a result of the Universal Service Directive the protection of specified universal service requirements is now legally prescribed; it is not simply a matter for regulatory discretion. That will be a major theme of my later chapters; first, however, we need to consider another area of utility regulation where the concept of universal service has not been developed so explicitly but where there have nevertheless been social principles adopted as part of the work of the regulator.

Social Regulation in Energy

In telecommunications the review of universal service has provided a method of approaching public service in the round, examining several aspects of it together. In energy, initially the approach was less clearly conceptualized, partly because at first gas and electricity were regulated separately. Now we do however see signs of a more coherent approach with the adoption of a social action plan by the unified regulatory authority and the regular examination of its implementation.

In both gas and electricity, the major social concern was the disconnection of supply. In gas, disconnection for failure to pay had been used widely before privatization; however, disconnections rose immediately at privatization from 35,626 in 1985 to 60,778 in 1987. Two years later, the Director General of Gas Supply announced a modification of British Gas's licence introducing new procedures aimed at

---

[76] Oftel, *Protecting Customers by Promoting Competition: Oftel's Conclusions* (2002).
[77] Oftel, *2000/1 Management Plan* (2000), para. 1.11.

limiting disconnections.[78] The new provisions effectively prevented disconnection unless the customer had first been offered a prepayment meter as an alternative; such a meter permits payment by prepaid token before consumption and can be set to recover debt. The effect was to reduce the number of disconnections dramatically, with a drop to under 20,000 by 1990 and to under 9,000 in 1996, although they were to rise again to almost 30,000 in 1997 and 1998; the 2003 figure was 15,973.[79]

Similarly, in electricity disconnections were running at the rate of 70,000 annually before privatization. Provisions in the Electricity Act 1989 and in the licences issued to electricity supply companies prevented disconnections where there was a serious dispute, and required a code of practice that largely precluded disconnection unless a prepayment meter had been offered.[80] As a result, disconnections dropped dramatically to below 20,000 in the year after privatization and by 1996 the figure had fallen to under 500, and to only 300 in 2000, though rising to 1361 in 2003.[81] Despite the more recent rise in gas disconnections (partly due to difficulties in installing prepayment meters in some circumstances), the general decline after privatization has been remarkable, especially in electricity, even if a couple of qualifications must be noted. First, developments in metering technology played an important part in the decline, and, second, the figures hide the extent of 'self-disconnection' through inability to pay with a prepayment meter, a matter addressed in the social action plan below.

The supply of gas and electricity was fully liberalized in 1998–9. As a result a large number of new suppliers entered the market. There were considerable fears about the effect of this development on social obligations. The first related to the threat of 'cream-skimming'. By definition, opening up the market signalled an end to universal tariffs (which had never fully applied to the energy supply markets anyway). The fear was that new entrants would offer service only to the most profitable customers, assumed to be the larger consumers, leaving the poor as an unprofitable rump retained by the former monopoly supplier. There was

---

[78] See Prosser (1997) 106–7.

[79] For general statistics on disconnections of supply by the public utilities, see 380 HC Debs col. 279W, 17 February 2002 and Ofgem, *Social Action Plan Indicators* (2004), Indicator 7.

[80] See Prosser (1997) 172–3; Electricity Act 1989, sch. 6, para. 1(6–10).

[81] See 380 HC Debs col. 279W, 17 February 2002, op.cit. and Ofgem, *Social Action Plan Indicators*, op. cit., Indicator 7.

also concern that social obligations applying to the monopoly supplier would not apply to new entrants.

A number of strategies were adopted to avoid these problems. In the case of gas, all competing operators had to be licensed, and the legislation forbade the granting of a licence framed in such a way as to exclude premises likely to be occupied by persons who are chronically sick, disabled, of pensionable age, or likely to default in the payment of charges.[82] This prevented a supplier from excluding poor inner-city areas from supply, for example. Licences required that all domestic customers in the licence area be supplied with gas without undue preference or undue discrimination in the processing of applications, thus retaining a limited form of universal service requirement.[83] Dominant suppliers were prohibited from undue preference and undue discrimination in charges, and price caps were temporarily retained for key tariffs, including those for prepayment meters. All social obligations in the licences, including the disconnection procedures and the special obligations towards elderly or disabled customers, applied to all suppliers, not just the former monopolist. Provision was also made for a levy on gas suppliers should any particular supplier be forced to bear an unfair share of the burden of uneconomic customers, though this provision has never been used.[84] Broadly similar provision was made for the introduction of the competitive retail electricity market, including the extension of social obligations to new entrants and the temporary retention of price controls.

For both gas and electricity, the Utilities Act 2000 introduced new powers permitting the Secretary of State to adjust charges for electricity and gas to help disadvantaged groups of customers, permitting cross-subsidy in their favour.[85] These were to be used, however, only as a last resort and it is unlikely that they will ever be employed given the development of the competitive markets. In addition to the legislative measures, the Government asked the (then) two energy regulators to draw up an action plan to ensure that disadvantaged customers benefited from the advantages of opening up the gas and electricity markets to competition. The plan confirmed that measures had already been taken to protect the interests of such consumers, but in its first version the plan did little more than to restate the existing arrangements to protect

---

[82] Gas Act 1995, s. 6(1), inserting a new s. 7A(8) into the Gas Act 1986.

[83] Department of Trade and Industry, *Gas Act 1995: Determination of the Standard Conditions of Gas Suppliers' Licenses* (1996), cond. 2(3).　　　　　　　　　　[84] Ibid., cond. 6.

[85] Ss. 69, 98.

vulnerable consumers in the liberalized markets as described above.[86] It was criticized by the Trade and Industry Select Committee on the grounds that '*[w]e are disappointed that it has taken a direct instruction from the Government for [the regulators] to prepare action plans to protect [choice and fairness for disadvantaged customers]. We are also disappointed that the Regulators' response should be so qualified.*'[87]

A second version of the social action plan, drafted after two rounds of consultation by the new, unified Ofgem, was considerably more far-reaching.[88] It contains four sections. The first is concerned with changes to be effected through licence modifications and new codes of practice. They include increasing access to cash payment facilities, improving service and information for prepayment meter customers, providing guidance on acceptable payment levels for the recovery of debt, provision of energy-efficiency advice, and improved provision of special services for the elderly, disabled, and chronically sick. The second part concerns broader structural changes, such as improved access to the competitive market for customers in debt and monitoring new tariff options including low-user tariffs. The third part sets out issues for further research that would be encouraged by Ofgem, for example on the extent of rationing and self-disconnection, and the final part establishes a timetable and indicators for monitoring progress. Ofgem publishes an annual report on progress in meeting the goals set out in the plan; for example, all the licence modifications were made quickly.

There has however been criticism of the effects of the liberalized markets in relation to vulnerable consumers and especially those on prepayment meters. Thus in relation to gas, after a detailed National Audit Office inquiry into the introduction of retail competition, the Public Accounts Committee of the House of Commons concluded that:

[w]e are concerned that low income customers who use prepayment meters to pay for their gas are not benefiting as much as other customers from the introduction of competition. We note OFGEM's concern that low income customers who use other methods to pay for their gas should not be asked to subsidise prepayment users. OFGEM should nevertheless look more closely at

---

[86] Office of Electricity Regulation and Office of Gas Supply, *The Social Dimension: Action Plan* (1998).

[87] Select Committee on Trade and Industry, *Developments in the Liberalisation of the Domestic Electricity Market*, HC 781, 1997–8, para. 38 (emphasis retained).

[88] Ofgem, *The Social Action Plan* (2000).

ways of promoting price competition in this part of the market, and ensuring that low income customers use prepayment meters only when they want to or benefit from doing so.[89]

After a related inquiry in electricity, the Committee reached similar conclusions.[90]

Nevertheless, the regulator has stressed the important role of liberalization itself in leading to lower prices and more choice for poorer consumers; since liberalization, retail prices in both gas and electricity had fallen by 14% in real terms. As Ofgem put it in its annual report for 2001–2, '[l]ower energy prices resulting from competition and effective regulation have lifted one million households out of fuel poverty since 1996 – by far the single biggest contribution to tackling this scourge. This year, Ofgem made a significant contribution to the Government's Fuel Poverty Strategy, which aims to remove all vulnerable households from fuel poverty by 2010.'[91] It has also noted that the switching rates for changing suppliers were as high in the case of some categories of vulnerable consumers as for the more affluent, and that switching by prepayment meter customers was increasing rapidly.[92] Moreover, as a result of liberalization, innovative tariffs had been introduced, for example permitting the elderly to pay a fixed monthly amount regardless of consumption.[93] As a result of this success of liberalization, the regulator decided to end all price controls in retail gas and electricity markets from 2002, including those on prepayment meter charges, although this was strongly opposed by Energywatch, the official consumer body, as premature.[94]

In energy, then, we have seen a substantial amount of activity concerned with social regulation, initially in relation to disconnections, and then to ensuring that the benefits of competition in retail markets became available to all consumers, including the most vulnerable. This has found expression in the social action plan, bringing together the key themes, although the main emphasis is on the benefits of a liberalized market in

[89] Committee of Public Accounts, *Office of Gas and Electricity Markets: Giving Customers a Choice – The Introduction of Competition into the Domestic Gas Market*, HC 171, 1999–2000, para. 3. The National Audit Office Report is HC 403, 1998–9.

[90] Committee of Public Accounts, *Office of Gas and Electricity Markets: Giving Domestic Customers a Choice of Electricity Supplier*, HC 446, 2001–2.   [91] HC 1020, 2001–2, 11.

[92] Ofgem, *Social Action Plan Annual Review 2002* (2002), 13–14.

[93] Ofgem, *Social Action Plan Annual Review 2003* (2003), 8–10.

[94] See also Klein (2003) 15–16.

reducing prices and in extending choice. It has yet to be seen how the abolition of retail price controls will affect the position of the most vulnerable.

It should be added that the work of the regulator forms only one part of the Government's broader Fuel Poverty Strategy, aiming to end fuel poverty by 2010.[95] This also includes action to tackle poverty and social exclusion, and energy efficiency programmes aimed at fuel-poor households. However, according to the National Consumer Council, it amounts to a 'cobbling together of existing strategies and reliance on market-driven solutions' which cannot achieve its aims. 'Responsibility for tackling this major social policy issue has been given to the regulator, Ofgem, whose primary driver is economic regulation, not the achievement of social objectives. The government retains various means of helping consumers with fuel bills but these are patchy and contradictory.'[96]

We shall see in Chapter 8 below that universal service in energy is another area in which Community law is beginning to play a role, although it is uncertain what the effect of this will be in the UK. Next I shall examine another part of the utility sector where, by contrast to energy, competition has remained extremely limited.

Social Regulation in Water and Sewerage Services

The issues of social regulation that arose in water and sewerage also centred around disconnection and the position of vulnerable groups. There were two differences from those in energy. The first is that there has been no question of a liberalized household market. However, the issue of cost-reflective pricing has arisen through the (limited) competition introduced for industrial users, raising similar concerns because of the adoption of lower large-user rates and the reduction of cross-subsidy. Secondly, the consequences of disconnection may be particularly severe in these sectors, not just for the disconnected consumers but for others who may be affected by resultant disease. Thus it is not surprising that disconnections of domestic supply became a major concern early on. Once more, there was a substantial rise in the number of disconnections after privatization: from between 10,000 and 15,000 per year to over

---

[95] Department for Environment, Food and Rural Affairs, and Department of Trade and Industry, *UK Fuel Poverty Strategy* (2001).   [96] Klein (2003) 27.

21,000 in 1991–2.[97] In 1992 the regulator issued guidelines to the water companies requiring improved procedures before disconnection took place.[98] These procedures resulted in a gradual but substantial drop in disconnections to under 6,000 in 1995–6, 3,148 in 1996–7, and only 1,129 in 1998–9. The introduction of prepayment meters as an alternative to disconnection is more difficult to implement for water, although a number of companies did employ budget payment units that allow use of a card for advance payment, followed by an emergency credit period of a week.[99] However, the High Court decided that the employment of these units was unlawful because they amounted to disconnection without the protections required by statute and licences.[100]

After the 1997 change of Government, the Water Industry Act 1999 was passed, which prohibits disconnection of water and sewerage services from residential consumers and also prohibits the use of budget payment units.[101] Thus all such disconnection ceased from June 1999, although the regulator has noticed an increase since in bad debt which has contributed to a need for interim tariff increases.[102] Indeed, by the end of 2002–3, over 4.7 million households in England and Wales (20% of all households) were in debt to water companies.[103]

The same legislation also required the Director General of Water Services to approve companies' individual charges in an annual charging scheme, and this must be in accordance with regulations issued by the Secretary of State.[104] Regulations were issued which enable those who receive social security benefits and either have three or more children or medical conditions requiring high water use to pay an average charge rather than that based on their metered consumption.[105] As a result each company has produced vulnerable group tariffs. However, the scheme has had a low take-up, the figures being only between 0.03% and 0.2% of

---

[97] See Ernst (1994) 149.

[98] Office of Water Services, *Guidelines on Debt and Disconnection* (1992).

[99] See Herbert and Kempson (1995) 69–73.

[100] *R v. Director General of Water Services, ex parte Lancashire County Council* [1999] Env. LR 114, noted at (1998) 9 Utilities Law Review 123–8.

[101] Ss. 1–2, inserting new ss. 61A and 63A and sch. 4A into the Water Industry Act 1991.

[102] Director General of Water Services, *Annual Report 2002–3*, HC 679, 2002–3, 15.

[103] Klein (2003) 8.   [104] Ss. 3–5.

[105] The Water Industry (Charges) (Vulnerable Groups) Regulations, SI 1999/3441, as amended by the Water Industry (Charges) (Vulnerable Groups) Regulations, SI 2000/519 and the Water Industry (Charges) (Vulnerable Groups) Regulations, SI 2003/552, the latter adding further benefits to extend access to the scheme.

metered customers; only £86,000 of the £7.5 million earmarked for the scheme in its first year of operation was spent.[106] It is now subject to review to make it more effective by the Department of the Environment.[107] The scheme has been criticized by the consumer council on the grounds that financial help could be better channelled through the social security system to avoid administrative duplication and the need to provide personal information to both a government department and a water company.[108] These special tariffs are thus the result of government intervention; the water regulator has made it clear, after consultation, that he will not approve charges schemes which propose the introduction of other new optional low-user tariffs with no standing charge.[109]

Social Regulation in Postal Services

The major difference in postal services is that universal service is given clear statutory priority in the Postal Services Act, as we have seen above. The issue has arisen most immediately in the context of opening up postal services to competition, where Postcomm has the direct ability to increase competition by issuing licences to rival companies to the Royal Mail, as well as the power to initiate modification of the area reserved to the Royal Mail by the Secretary of State.[110] After extensive consultation, Postcomm announced a phased programme for liberalization, culminating in the full lifting of restrictions on market entry in 2007.[111] It had earlier been subject to criticism by the Public Accounts Committee concerning the relationship between liberalization and universal service. The National Audit Office had suggested that liberalization could result in a breakdown in universal service.[112] The Committee concluded that Postcomm 'need to be cautious about the potential consequences of their proposals on the universal service'.[113] In response, Postcomm undertook that it would continue to monitor whether universal service

---

[106] Klein (2003) 36.

[107] Department for Environment, Food and Rural Affairs, *Water Industry (Charges) (Vulnerable Groups) Regulations 1999: A Consultation Paper: Reductions for Vulnerable Groups* (2003).

[108] WaterVoice, *Annual Report 2001–2*, (2002), 9.

[109] Office of Water Services, *Approval of Companies' Charges Schemes 2002–3: Tariff Policy Issues*, RD 14/01, 2001.   [110] Postal Services Act 2000, ss. 6–8.

[111] Postcomm, *Promoting Effective Competition in UK Postal Services* (2002).

[112] *Opening the Post: Postcomm and Postal Services – The Risks and Opportunities*, HC 521, 2001–2, paras. 2.21–2.39.

[113] *Postcomm: Opening the Post*, HC 632, 2001–2, para. 4; see also paras. 21 and 35.

was threatened by liberalization and, if it was, it would take appropriate action.[114] It has also undertaken a consultation on what should comprise the universal service, proposing only minor changes in its scope.[115] Further relevant activity includes a consultation on the extent to which the Royal Mail's special privileges (such as exemption from value added tax) are necessary for universal service and the extent to which they distort competition.[116]

Postcomm also has responsibility for another task different from that of other utility regulators; that of providing the Secretary of State with advice and information on the number, location, and accessibility of public post offices.[117] A detailed report by the Cabinet Office Performance and Innovation Unit recommended that the Government should require the Post Office to maintain the rural network and that a subsidy should be granted for that purpose under the Act.[118] As a result, the government required the Post Office to prevent avoidable rural closures until 2006, and Postcomm was given a key role in monitoring the network by reporting annually on whether the range of services provided remains relevant to the needs of customers and meets the needs of rural and deprived urban communities. It also advises the government on the best way to channel financial assistance and on future policy. Postcomm has commissioned a research study into what customers want from their post offices, and has issued three annual reports on the network.[119] The first stressed the need to concentrate on the accessibility of post offices to those who need them rather than simply on the number of closures; the second stressed the importance of branches for vulnerable groups; it included a summary of confidential (because of the commercial sensitivity of information included) advice to government on financial support, and covered the introduction of universal banking services. The third report covered changes to the network including the effect of the new banking services; advice was also issued to government on the future role of the rural network.

---

[114] *Treasury Minute on the Thirty-first to the Thirty-fifth Reports from the Committee of Public Accounts* 2001–2, Cm 5549 (2002), 1.

[115] Postcomm, *The Universal Postal Service in the UK: What Services Should Be Provided: A Consultation Document* (2003); *Decision Document: The UK's Universal Postal Service* (2004).

[116] Postcomm, *A Review of Royal Mail's Special Privileges: A Consultation Document* (2004).

[117] Postal Services Act 2000, s. 42.

[118] *Counter Revolution: Modernising the Post Office* (2000); Postal Services Act 2000, s. 103.

[119] *Post Offices, Customers and Communities* (2001); *Access to Post Office Services: Time to Act* (2002); *Banking on the Future* (2003).

Social Regulation and Transport

The main type of transport in which universal service has been directly protected has been that of rail. In the UK the future running of the rail network is subject to considerable uncertainty with the chaos resulting from the serious problems associated with privatization and the financial collapse of Railtrack. Even before privatization, government had made separate payments to protect socially necessary but economically unviable services, and as we shall see this has continued as part of the franchising requirements for rail operators.[120] In addition, special procedures for consent for the withdrawal of all passenger services over a route had existed under nationalization, and the closure hearings had become prolonged and controversial.[121] After privatization the procedures were retained in amended form. Service withdrawals had to be advertised, with the opportunity of lodging objections with the rail regulator. Objections were then sent to the relevant regional Rail Users' Consultative Committee, part of the consumer representation machinery, which would investigate whether the closure would cause hardship, reporting to the regulator who would take the closure decision, with appeal to the Secretary of State.[122] Shortly after the new procedures came into effect, important clarification was given by the Court of Session which held that it was unlawful to run 'ghost trains', services of minimal public use introduced merely to circumvent the closure procedures.[123]

The new procedures have remained untested, as there have been no major withdrawals of passenger services which qualify for their protection since privatization. Some changes were made to the procedures in the Transport Act 2000. This had been foreshadowed in the Government's proposals for tidying up regulatory responsibilities which were untidily divided between the Rail Regulator and the Office of the Franchising Director (the predecessor of the Strategic Rail Authority). Responsibility for the closure decision passed to the Secretary of State from the Rail Regulator; it was thought not appropriate for the Authority as the latter funded rail services and so had a potential conflict of interest.[124] The role of the Consultative Committees remained, although

---

[120] See the Transport Act 1968, ss. 38–40.   [121] See Prosser (1986) 65–8.
[122] Railways Act 1993, ss. 37–44, 55.
[123] *Highland Regional Council v. British Railways Board* 1996 SLT 274 (1st Div.).
[124] Department of the Environment, Transport and the Regions, *A New Deal for the Railways* (1998) para. 38, implemented by the Transport Act 2000, ss. 234–9.

they became sponsored by the Strategic Rail Authority and were renamed Rail Passengers Committees. It is too early to see yet how the new system will work, although the minister is also subject to a potential conflict of interests as part of a government which provides public funding for uneconomic services.

Apart from the question of total withdrawals of service from a line, there was considerable concern at the time of privatization about the reduction of uneconomic services, for example those in the late evening. As part of the franchising of the operators of rail services, the franchise agreements contained minimum service levels which had to be met (the Passenger Service Requirement), based on the British Rail levels immediately before privatization. In some cases, however, there were substantial reductions and these were successfully challenged by judicial review, although the response of the minister was simply to amend his instructions and guidance to the franchising director to permit such reductions.[125] At the end of 2002, faced with serious problems in renewing franchises, in the performance of operators, and in the level of financial support needed, the Strategic Rail Authority adopted a new strategy involving shorter franchises (five to eight years) with more clearly and closely specified service levels and quality standards. As it put it:

This differs from the model from the first round of franchising, which sought to create a set of business opportunities, subject to regulation, with obligations not to let services fall below specified base levels. However, the opportunity for further unilateral franchisee expansion of services has largely been exhausted. Further, some of the protected services are of dubious economic value, particularly now that network capacity is constrained.[126]

Once more the future is uncertain, though there is clearly an important move to a closer specification and monitoring of franchise terms.

It should already be apparent that competition has had only a limited role to play in the operation of the privatized rail network. As the first Rail Regulator put it, 'unrestricted freedom to compete could lead to operators concentrating on the most profitable routes and ignoring others. This could make it more expensive for the taxpayer to support services with significant social and environmental benefits. Unrestricted

---

[125] *R v. Director of Passenger Rail Franchising, ex parte Save Our Railways and Others*, The Times, 18 December 1995 (CA), and see 268 HC Debs Cols. 1236–7, 18 December 1995.

[126] Strategic Rail Authority, *Franchising Policy Statement* (2002), 9.

competition can also undermine investment plans.'[127] Together with the heavily subsidized nature of the rail businesses, public service has played a much greater role vis-à-vis competition than in the other utilities studied here.

Only a little need be said about other types of transport. For buses no specialist regulator was established, although when the sector was liberalized by the Transport Act 1985 local authorities were permitted to subsidize socially necessary services through a process of competitive tendering.[128] More recently, the Transport Act 2000 has permitted the establishment of 'quality partnerships' and 'quality contracts' between bus operators and local authorities. As we saw in the preceding chapter, a block exemption has been issued to protect certain ticket schemes, between operators from challenge under the Chapter I prohibition in the Competition Act 1998, and the Transport Act introduces a special form of public interest test for assessing the compatibility of quality partnerships, ticketing schemes, and tendering for subsidized services with the Competition Act.[129] In the field of civil aviation, regulation is now predominantly at a European level, and the liberalizing regulation permits the recognition of public service obligations on thin routes which are important for the economic development of particular regions. The process involves competitive tendering followed by exclusive access by only one carrier for up to three years.[130] This provision has been employed by a number of Member States, including the UK for routes in the Scottish Highlands and Islands.

Conclusion

What has been apparent in this chapter has been the gradual development of social regulation based on public service concerns, notably in relation to protecting universal service and the interests of vulnerable consumers in newly competitive markets. Initially this was a very untidy process, but since the 1998 Utility Review there has been a move to

---

[127] Office of the Rail Regulator, *Annual Report of the Rail Regulator*, 1998–9, (1999), para. 4.2. See also Prosser (1997) 197–8.   [128] S. 89.

[129] The Competition Act 1998 (Public Transport Ticketing Schemes Block Exemption) Order 2001, SI 2001/319, and the Transport Act 2000 sch. 10.

[130] Reg. 2408/92 of 23 July 1992 on access for Community air carriers to intra-Community air routes [1992] OJ L240/8 Art. 4.

greater clarity with revised statutory duties and the issuing of government guidance on social matters. Despite this welcome degree of clarification, however, criticisms of the adequacy of the work of the utility regulators in implementing social goals have continued, culminating in a wide-ranging report from the National Consumer Council in 2003.[131] Amongst its many detailed criticisms, two themes are of particular importance for this book. The first is that protections are uncoordinated and inconsistent. Thus:

It is inconsistent to have the need for universal service formally recognised and defined only in one of the utility services – telecommunications. Legislation indicates a need for universal access to water and energy, but it is not clearly defined... Inconsistent policy approaches to universal access are especially apparent when we examine continuity of supply. Disconnections are banned in water, and discouraged in energy but still possible. In telecommunications, consumers can be disconnected, despite the need to call helplines or families in an emergency... Government also needs to clarify the roles and responsibilities of the various players, including the State, in ensuring affordable access to these essential services.[132]

Secondly, '[t]he general promotion of cost-reflective pricing, combined with selective (although not necessarily equitable) use of cross subsidies and a complicated system of taxpayer support, has led to inefficiencies and inequities'.[133] Thus:

[a]lthough water and sewerage charges are averaged within each region in England and Wales, there are large variations between the regions. For instance, average household bills for sewerage in South West Water's area in 2002/3 were over twice those of the lowest charging company, Thames Water... Water consumers living in the South-West and Wales will pay £72.80 more, on average, than those living in London, yet they have an average income of £27,350.50 less than Londoners. Government assistance for people on low incomes does not take into account these regional price differences.[134]

Both these criticisms are of relevance when we come to consider the Continental tradition of public service. Thus, unlike the UK approach, it has tended to start from general principles rather than relying on a gradual, pragmatic development of practice. It has also established a strong insistence on geographically averaged charges for public services. A further difference from the UK is that, in the latter, the courts have played only a minimal role; instead it has been government and the

---

[131] Klein (2003).   [132] Ibid., 52.   [133] Ibid., 56.
[134] Ibid., 31 (reference omitted).

regulators themselves who have developed empirically the public service initiatives, mainly through licence modifications. In the following chapter we shall see the opposite in our examination of the public service traditions in France and Italy. In France in particular, we shall find a concept which is based around the articulation of principle at a high level, but which leaves some doubts as to its practical application. We shall also see the courts, and national constitutions, play an important role in the development of such principle.

5

The Continental Tradition of Public Service

Introduction

In the previous chapter we saw that there has been a considerable amount of activity by the UK utility regulators to protect public service, especially when markets have been opened up to competition. However, this activity has been highly pragmatic and lacks any general principles about the meaning of public service, the limits to competitive markets, and the extent to which competition law is applicable to its delivery. By contrast, in Continental Europe there is a considerable body of doctrine devoted precisely to developing the distinctive missions of public service, especially in the French law of *service public* and the Italian law of *servizio pubblico*. Moreover, this body of doctrine is accepted as having a form of constitutional status (although, in common with other constitutional values, its precise content may remain controversial).

This chapter will provide an outline of the principles of these bodies of law, with two objectives. The first is to permit us to see public service in the round as a coherent set of principle and doctrine, thereby enabling us to pass beyond British pragmatism and instead to develop a stronger theoretical basis for determining the limits to competition law. The second is to provide essential background for understanding the fierce debate within European Community law and politics on the degree to which competition law is applicable to services of general interest, for much of the controversy is drawn from Continental public service traditions which are perceived as potentially in conflict with market liberalization; these debates will be discussed in the following three chapters.

The countries discussed will be France and (in less detail) Italy. The former, in effect, chose itself for inclusion, both as the home of the most developed concept of public service in Europe and the nation in which *le service public* performs the strongest role in defining a national self-identity. Largely for this reason, it has also been the most vigorous proponent of public service-based limits to liberalization and to the ordinary application of competition law in this area. Italy has similar doctrine, but has moved further in privatizing public services and in particular public utilities. It has done more to integrate public service doctrine with developments such as independent regulatory authorities and charters of service standards derived from those of the UK. This experience may provide the basis for the possible integration of the British and Continental traditions.

Before embarking on the main task of this chapter, however, two warnings must be given. Firstly, particularly in France, the definition of public service is notoriously difficult and elusive; as one expert has put it, 'it is easier to put back the mercury lost from an old barometer, than to capture the concept of *service public* in a definition'.[1] Secondly, and not entirely without connection to this last point, it should always be remembered that law may perform different functions in different cultures and this has to be borne in mind in making comparisons between different legal concepts and principles.[2] Thus law may have particularly important symbolic value and may not always be expected to be transformed into concrete protections on the ground; as we shall see, the symbolic value of *service public* as a mission of the French state has been extremely high, and in Italy, despite the presence of such a tradition enshrined in law, the concrete protections for consumers may be very weak. Whatever difficulties this poses for transplanting legal provisions from one culture to another, in the context of this book the different approaches should be useful through pointing a contrast to the British situation where concrete regulatory protections are unaccompanied by an appeal to wider principle, and once more in illuminating the European debates which, as we shall see in Chapter 7, have been as much at the symbolic as the practical level.

---

[1] M. Waline, quoted in Melleray (2003a) 117. All translations are my own unless otherwise stated.   [2] See e.g. Nelken (1997); Nelken and Feest (2001).

France

Public Service and the Constitution

In France, of course, we are dealing with a radically different constitutional regime from that of the UK, although one which is less than unique in world terms. There is thus a written constitution and the Parliament is not sovereign because the constitution lays down restrictions on the legally permissible scope of its laws.[3] The method of checking the constitutionality of laws is less familiar; rather than using a supreme court, the Conseil Constitutionnel may examine a proposed *loi* after it has passed both houses of the French parliament but before it has been finally promulgated. Reference may be made *inter alia* by sixty members of either house of the parliament. Although the original function of the Conseil was to preserve governmental autonomy vis-à-vis parliament, it has transformed itself into a protector of basic constitutional rights against the legislature.

It is not unknown for constitutions to contain references to economic values, although this has become less marked with the development of more liberal economic regimes globally.[4] France retains one of the most striking examples of a constitutional provision providing some degree of economic direction. This is in the form of one of the 'political, economic and social principles . . . especially necessary in our times' in the Preamble to the 1946 Constitution, incorporated into the current Constitution of the Fifth Republic by the latter's own Preamble. It provides that '[a]ll property and all enterprises of which the operation has, or acquires, the character of a national public service or of a monopoly [*monopole de fait*] are to become public property'. Although there was for some years doubt as to the legal force of these principles, the Conseil Constitutionnel has in fact been prepared to apply them, as we shall see shortly. Thus at first sight it would appear that the concept of public service acts as an institutional boundary restricting the private ownership of such services. The truth is, however, considerably more complicated.

Continental writers have in fact distinguished between two different concepts of public service to which this provision refers.[5] On the one

---

[3] For background see Bell (1995) and Graham and Prosser (1991) ch. 2.

[4] For a useful survey of such provisions see Daintith and Sah (1993).

[5] See in particular Thirion (2002) esp. at 639–41, 646–7.

hand there is 'constitutional public service' where the Constitution requires that the relevant services are in public hands, subject of course to constitutional amendment. These are narrowly defined, corresponding to those closely connected to the traditional attributes of state sovereignty, such as defence, justice, foreign affairs, or policing. A much wider range of public services, more closely related to the subject matter of this book, fall under a looser, 'existentialist' concept of public service. Rather than embodying an essentialist definition, this concept of public service refers to those activities defined as such by law, either legislation or case law interpreting it.[6] This is of particular importance as it permits the privatization of public service activities subject to legal controls to ensure that the goals of public service remain protected even in private hands.

The first relevant decision of the Conseil in which the meaning of the concept was elucidated was that concerning the empowering legislation for the privatization programme; it should be noted that this did not include the public utilities.[7] The Conseil established that, outside the central core of services referred to above, the legislature was free to determine whether an enterprise fell within the concept of public service or not, and it would only intervene in the case of manifest error; none of the enterprises to be privatized fell within it. Similarly, in determining the constitutionality of the sale of the main television channel, the Conseil found that the Constitution did not require this to be in public ownership as a public service.[8]

The most important decision in this respect is however that concerning the partial privatization of France Télécom.[9] As part of its moves to liberalize telecommunications, the French Government had decided to reduce its holding in the enterprise to 56%. The Conseil confirmed that France Télécom was a public service designated as such by the legislature and that the state could not reduce its holding in it to less than a majority. However, it also stated that in the future such a reduction could take place through a further law. The conditions on which such a further law could be approved remained unclear, but it was suggested that the

---

[6] Ibid., 639–40.

[7] Déc. 86-207 DC, 25 and 26 June 1986, *Loi autorisant le Gouvernement à prendre diverses mesures d'ordre économique et social*, AJDA 1986, 575.

[8] Déc. 86-217 DC, 18 September 1986, *Loi relative à la liberté de communication*, AJDA 1987, 102.

[9] Déc. 96-380 DC, 23 July 1996, *Loi relative à l'entreprise nationale France Télécom*, AJDA 1996, 696; see Thirion (2002) 640, and Chevallier (1996a) at 937–41.

legislator is not completely free to decide as it wishes in the matter, but rather that if it wishes to do so it must effectively deprive the enterprise of its character as a national public service first.[10] This could take the form of ensuring that public service is protected through other means, and notably through the conferral of public service functions on local authorities or private enterprises, so long as they are subject to supervision and regulation by public authorities.[11] This flexibility was reinforced by the stress in the Conseil's decision on the fact that the partial privatization had done nothing to remove France Télécom's public service mission. Thus the enterprise was required, by the *cahier des charges* under which it operated, to serve the whole of the national territory and to protect the equality of users and the neutrality and confidentiality of its services. It remained the responsibility of the public authorities to ensure strictly that France Télécom continued to comply with the constitutional requirements of public service.

At the time of writing the French Government retains a 55% stake in France Télécom, and further sales are on hold due to the financial state of the enterprise. However legislation was passed at the end of 2003 to prepare for further sales which would take the state holding to below 50%.[12] The law proceeds by, firstly, amending the code of posts and telecommunications so that, whilst continuing to state that the obligations of public service are to be assured in accordance with the principles of equality, continuity, and adaptability, France Télécom is no longer to be the sole provider of universal service. The latter is defined as a set of obligations in accordance with Community law (see Chapter 8 below), and it will be for the minister to designate those enterprises responsible for its delivery after seeking bids for the designations, financing being by way of a universal service fund. Thus the responsibility for ensuring the delivery of public service now lies with the Government, not with France Télécom. The *loi* then adds the latter to the list of enterprises covered by the *loi* of 1993 permitting privatization, and it is made subject to ordinary company law.

Unfortunately (from the viewpoint of this book) the *loi* was not referred to the Conseil Constitutionnel by the Socialist Group in the

¹⁰ Schrameck (1996).   ¹¹ See Espluglas (1998) 42–3.

¹² Loi no. 2003-1365 du 31 décembre 2003 relative aux obligations de service public des télecommunications et à France Télécom, JO 1 janvier 2004, 1. For background see Melleray (2003b) and Rapp (2004).

National Assembly, as the Group had achieved its major objective of retaining the status of civil servant for the enterprise's employees. A further piece of legislation in July 2004 implemented the European Community regulatory package on electronic communications, for which see Chapter 8 below.[13]

The French Government also announced that it intended to change the legal status of Eléctricité de France and of Gaz de France to ordinary companies during 2004, which would require further legislation.[14] A law to change their status was passed by the French Parliament in July 2004, but the state holding will not be reduced below 50% and geographically averaged pricing for household customers will be retained; indeed, geographical uniformity of electricity tariffs and harmonization of gas charges are stated as key objectives for the enterprises.[15] Thus this fresh legislation does not raise the issue of the constitutionality of privatization in the same way as the *loi* on France Télécom, and the Conseil Constitutionnel held that there was in fact no privatization as the state would retain a majority holding.

Thus the provision in the Preamble does permit considerable flexibility in relation to the ownership of enterprises providing public services, so long as the provision of the services themselves is protected. It also appears to require public ownership of monopolies; this has however had limited effect so far as it does not prevent privatization where a competitive market is created prior to the sale, as in the case of the European utility liberalization to be considered in detail in Chapter 8 below and exemplified by the opening of universal service provision in telecommunications to competition by the recent French legislation.[16]

However, the question of ownership is much less important than two other features of the French constitutional arrangements. The first is that there is a clear recognition at the level of constitutional principle of the distinctive nature of public service. The second is that this continues to require that constraints are imposed on enterprises providing public service to meet certain constitutional goals, for example to serve the whole of the national territory and to treat consumers equally. These constraints are derived from the concept of *service public* in French

[13] Loi no. 2004-669 du 9 juillet 2004 relative aux communications électroniques et aux services de communication audiovisuelle, JO 10 juillet 2004, 12483.

[14] 'France Confirms Plan to Alter Utilities' Status', *Financial Times*, 17 December 2003.

[15] Loi no. 2004-803 relative au service public de l'électricité et du gaz et aux entreprises éléctriques et gazières, Art. 1, JO 27 août 2004, 14256.   [16] Thirion (2002) 645.

administrative law, and it is to this that we shall now turn as it provides both the historical basis for the constitutional provisions and offers more detailed guidance on what a regime of public service actually requires.

Public Service in Administrative Law

Public service has provided a central, perhaps *the* central, concept in French administrative law. It has perhaps been most celebrated in forming a criterion for the assertion of jurisdiction by the administrative courts, though that is outside the scope of this book.[17] In addition, however, it has provided a major source of substantive principle both in terms of providing restrictions on the freedom of public bodies and providing them with a major source of legitimacy; in this respect it must not be forgotten that, as John Bell has put it, 'French administrative law is first and foremost about the proper functioning of the administration in its principal activity of serving the public *(le service public)* and only secondarily about the control of the administration.'[18] French literature on the subject is voluminous, as is that which attempts to update it for a more competitive environment and for compatibility with European liberalization; in both these respects considerable controversy currently exists.[19]

Service Public: *Origins and General Principles*

The concept of public service originally appeared in the celebrated decision of the Tribunal des Conflits (responsible for allocating jurisdiction between the administrative and the ordinary courts) in the case of *Blanco* in 1873.[20] However, its theoretical development is closely linked to the work of the social theorist Duguit, discussed in Chapter 2 above.[21] As Loughlin has put it, '[I]n seeking a legitimatory principle he embraced a functional approach. Duguit took the view that the state was simply an apparatus for performing certain functions. Consequently, the concept of sovereignty was replaced with that of "public service";

---

[17] See Brown and Bell (1998) 129–35. The requirements of *service public* have also been applied by the private law courts; see Melleray (2003a).   [18] Bell (1999) 190.

[19] For accounts in English see Brown and Bell (1998); Bell (1999); and Malaret Garcia (1998). In French see in particular, for an introduction, Fournier (2001); for more detail Conseil d'Etat (1995) and the essays in Kovar and Simon (1998).   [20] TC 8 February 1873.

[21] For a useful account of his work in English see Loughlin (1992) 110–12.

the state exists merely to perform certain tasks which are necessary for the preservation and promotion of social solidarity.'[22] It will be apparent from this that it is closely linked to the approach outlined in Chapter 2 in which protecting social solidarity and cohesion is one of the reasons for limiting the application of the normal rules of competition law.[23]

Around this theoretical basis, the administrative law courts and academic writers built up a set of rules of considerable sophistication. The meaning of the concept can be defined as follows: 'in French public law, public service is an activity in the general interest, provided by a public or private actor and subject to a special legal regime requiring equality of treatment, adaptation to changing needs and security of supply, etc.'[24] It is also important to note that, reflecting the concern for social solidarity and social cohesion, the concept of *service public* is essentially non-economic and distributive in nature: 'it is the essence of *service public*, as a means of consolidation of the social contract and of social solidarity, that it contributes to some types of redistribution and of transfers between social groups'.[25]

The central core of *service public* can be found in the so-called 'laws of Roland', which have been described as the 'natural laws' of public service.[26] The three core principles are the continuity of public service, equality of users of public service, and the adaptability of public service, although, as we shall see, more recently a number of others, notably the quality of public service, have been added. I shall now examine these principles one by one before discussing their adaptation to recent conditions.

The principle of continuity has been defined as follows: 'if the public authorities have decided to create a public service to satisfy the general interest, the service must function in a continuous manner, without interruption, properly to satisfy its users'.[27] A number of obvious implications apply in the context of the public utilities discussed in the previous chapter; the obligation to restore power supplies cut off by storms as soon as possible, the obligation to ensure security of supply, and the obligation that, should an operator go out of business, there is no interruption in the supply of the service for users. It also has implications

---

[22] Ibid., 111 (footnote omitted).   [23] See also Malaret Garcia (1998) 64–5.
[24] Debène and Raymundie (1996) 186. As elsewhere in this section, my translation is inevitably a loose one given the difficulty of conveying the flavour of the concept in English.
[25] Conseil d'Etat (1995) 53.   [26] Malaret Garcia (1998) 67–8.
[27] Oberdoff (1998) 94.

for the right to strike, although these have never been fully grasped in France; in Italy, by contrast, limits are set on this latter right to ensure the provision of a minimum service.[28] A further implication, of importance when we consider European Community policy later, is that continuity may be inconsistent with frequent competitive tendering for the provision of the service.

The principle of equality imposes more far-reaching requirements for public services. Firstly it requires equality of access to public services for all citizens; this is based both on social concerns to prevent discrimination on the basis of social status, and on territorial concerns to prevent inequality between regions.[29] Indeed, the reform of the French Constitution in 2003 to permit decentralization explicitly provides for the principle of equality between different territories.[30] Secondly, it requires equality of treatment of users by public services. Not only does this prevent overt discrimination but it also forms the basis for the French principle of *péréquation*, the charging of equal prices to all users irrespective of cost of supply. As we saw in Chapter 2 above, this is precisely the principle most threatened by the introduction of cost-based pricing to enable more effective competition and to enhance allocative efficiency.

There is a considerable body of administrative case law setting out the implications of, and the limits to, this principle. The basic rule is that legitimate reasons must be found in the different situations of different consumers to justify variations in pricing, or a difference must be justified by an overriding public interest. For example, the Conseil d'Etat (the highest administrative court) in 1993 gave an advisory opinion to the minister permitting higher tariffs for the TGV Nord than for other rail services, based on its higher standards of speed and comfort and to permit a higher return from the service by reflecting particular characteristics of its clientele, so long as precautions were taken to ensure that the tariff differentials were indispensable to attain these objectives and that the provision of services as a whole, including those at a lower tariff, did not compromise basic principles of public service.[31] More recently, however, decisions by local authorities to adopt discounted tickets for ski-lifts

---

[28] See Sciarra (1998).   [29] Fournier (2001) 4.

[30] Loi constitutionnelle no. 2003-276 du 28 Mars 2003 relative à l'organisation décentralisée de la République, Art. 7, JO 29 mars 2003, 5568.

[31] Assemblée Générale (Section des travaux publics) no. 353 605—24 juin 1993. For a similar, more recent decision relating to urban transport see Conseil d'Etat, 13 mars 2002, *Union fédérale des consommateurs* [2003] AJDA 772.

based on place of residence, and free travel for certain types of unem-
ployed persons, have been struck down by the administrative courts as in
breach of the principle of equality.[32] The case law is backed up by tariff
requirements set in some detail by ministers and included in the *cahiers
des charges* under which public enterprises operate; as we shall see below,
this ministerial price-setting role has survived the creation of independent regulatory authorities with other responsibilities.

A linked principle is that of the neutrality of the public service. This
prohibits discrimination between users, for example on the basis of
political or religious belief, and has had more importance in the field of
education than of public utilities or other public services supplying
commodities. However, once more it illustrates the importance of citizenship as the basis for the special treatment of users of public services.

The final principle traditionally included in the basic concept of public
service is that of the adaptability of public service. This in turn can be
broken down into two separate principles; adaptability itself and what the
French term the 'mutability' of public service.[33] The former refers to the
right of the users of public services to receive services whose quality
reflects the development of new forms of technology and responds to
their changing needs. The second, by contrast, refers to the power of the
state to modify the functioning of public services as it thinks fit to meet
new needs. Thus the operators, even if private, of public services have no
right to refuse to adapt to new social needs (even, if necessary, ending the
provision of a service no longer required); however, the public authorities
may have to compensate them for any additional costs incurred.

It will immediately be apparent that these 'laws' of public service are at
an extremely high level of generality, although they may have important
practical implications. As Fournier has put it, 'we see that the principles
of the functioning of public service have often more the character of
objectives to be pursued than of rules to be respected in practice. Their
existence is however no less essential. They are evidence of the sort of
special requirements which the state imposes in relation to tasks carried
out in its name.'[34] There is also a further striking characteristic of these
principles, especially for the British reader. They appear outdated
through assuming that the state has a much more fundamental and far-
reaching role in the economy than is now the case in Western economies;

---

[32] *Commune de Saint-Sorlin-d'Arves* [2000] AJDA 849; *M. Daniel Brindel* [2002] AJDA 1409.
[33] For a developed discussion of the distinction see Markus (2001).   [34] Fournier (2001) 5.

in particular they appear to have ignored the processes of privatization and the creation of independent regulation which have characterized the 1980s and 1990s. Moreover, they raise serious questions of compatibility with European Community law, as we shall see later in Chapter 8. For all these reasons, there have been important attempts to update the principles of public service for modern conditions, and I shall now describe some of them.

Restatement as 'Le Service Public à la Française' *and the* Market Economy

One means of updating the principles of public service has been to formulate further principles to supplement them. As mentioned above, one is the principle of quality of service; this has been derived partly from similar requirements in the Community law relating to liberalized telecommunications, and is linked to the development of service standards, also a central requirement of European liberalization.[35] Other further principles applicable to the public service include accessibility, simplicity, rapidity, transparency, mediation, participation, and responsibility, all of which are included in a 1995 circular on the reform of the state and of public services.[36] In particular, and echoing concerns in Anglo-Saxon utility regulation, participation of consumers in the administration, or at least the regulation, of public services and transparency of administration are seen as part of the requirements of the public service regime.[37]

However, the most sustained and ambitious restatement of the principles of *service public* for a competitive European economy took the form of the report commissioned by the prime minister in 1995 and published in 1996 by a team lead by Renaud Denoix de Saint Marc, the vice-president of the Conseil d'Etat, and I shall examine this is some detail.[38] It began by restating the traditional doctrines of *service public*, but then made the crucial point that this doctrine does not require any particular from of organization for the delivery of public services: 'recent debate has suffered from the confusion of two levels of analysis; it has confused the doctrine of public service itself, on the one hand, with the forms of organization of public services, especially the public utilities, on the other. Many amongst the French have sincerely believed that in

---

[35] See Voisset (1999).
[36] Circular of 26 July 1995, JO 28 juillet 1995, 11217; see Chevallier (1996b) 197.
[37] For more details see Conseil d'Etat (1995) 69–100.   [38] Saint Marc (1996).

reforming the latter we attack the former.'[39] This meant that *service public* was distinguishable from the extent of the public sector, and in particular that the traditional French organizational model of a publicly owned monopoly with the status of civil servant for its employees was merely a historically specific form, not an inherent requirement of doctrine. Indeed, it had always been true that private enterprises had delivered local public services, notably water, and this had not always involved the grant of a monopoly, or at least not an indefinite monopoly.[40] Thus public service does not require the use of public enterprises nor any special status for employees, except for the very narrow constitutional requirement discussed earlier in this chapter.

As a result of this separation between doctrine and institutional form, and in particular the lack of an intrinsic requirement of a monopoly provider, according to the Report the French doctrine was not incompatible with the requirements of European Community law.[41] Rather than concentrating on institutional form, public service was a means of satisfying the needs of users of public services and of ensuring social cohesion, in particular through limiting differences in the delivery of public services in different parts of the nation.[42] Public intervention was thus needed to meet four types of goals; the first was to prevent social exclusion, not just on a geographical basis but also on the basis of economic situation or disability. This did not require uniform treatment for *all* users, for example a subsidized telephone line to all households, unless it was impossible to identify those in disadvantaged groups. The second goal was to maintain what is now termed geographical universal service (see below and also Chapter 8) so that services were provided throughout all areas, for example uneconomic rural postal services and urban transport services. The third goal was to co-ordinate services for policy goals such as the security of long-term energy resources, and the fourth was to maintain a form of symbolic social cohesion, for example through uniform postal charges signifying membership of a common community.[43] The report concluded that a rejuvenated and clarified notion of public service was required and that this would be compatible with Community law, but on the other hand the organizational model for the delivery of public services in France (particularly public utilities) must be improved, both for the satisfaction of the needs of users and to develop competitiveness.

---

[39] Ibid., 17; see also 13, 21.   [40] See Richer (1997).   [41] Saint Marc (1996) 59–64.
[42] Ibid., 49–50.   [43] Ibid., 53–5.

The restatement of the requirements of *service public* expressed most clearly in the 1996 report has been influential for a number of reasons; it has suggested that there is no basic incompatibility between the doctrine and the measures of European Community liberalization to be discussed in the following chapters, and it has paved the way for the privatization, at least partially, of public utilities, whilst suggesting that the values intrinsic in the public service principles must be preserved. In fact, in recent years the French Government has acknowledged this last point through incorporating into statute specific reference to these values.[44] Thus both the laws of 1990 and of 1996 on telecommunications made such a reference, the latter requiring that the service be provided in a manner respecting equality, continuity, and adaptability; this reference is even retained despite the 2003 law permitting further privatization of France Télécom.[45] Similar provisions were also included in later laws on electricity, gas, and postal services, and on the body owning the rail infrastructure.[46] This might appear a largely symbolic attempt to reassert the importance of the specifically French doctrine in sectors facing European liberalization; nevertheless, the important point to make is that the principles of *service public* are felt still to be of such fundamental importance as to require legislative reassertion.

Similarly, there has been considerable debate in France about the relationship between *service public* and the concept of universal service, developed in the United States and now increasingly used in European Community liberalization.[47] The universal service concept will be analysed in detail in Chapter 8 below, but the point should be made here that there has been reluctance in France to accept the two as synonymous; universal service is seen as concerned with only the provision of a minimal and residual service where the market cannot do so. Thus it presupposes an essentially competitive regime, but one subject to market failure.[48] As we have seen, *service public* goes far beyond this, being derived from constitutional and citizenship values. Once more, despite the restatement of *service public* for liberalized conditions it retains a flavour and importance of its own.

---

[44] See Moderne (1998) 13–16.

[45] Lois 90-568 du 2 juillet 1990 and 96-659 du 26 juillet 1996, introducing a new art. 35 into the code of posts and telecommunications.

[46] Lois 2000-108 du 10 février 2000, 2003-8 du 3 janvier 2003, 96-659 du 26 juillet 1996, 97-135 du 13 février 1997.   [47] See Debène and Raymundie (1996).

[48] See Hancher (1996) 136–8.

Liberalization and Reform

Reflecting the discussion above concerning the restatement of public service principles, they now form part of a broader system of regulation of public utilities within a context of overall liberalization and application of general competition law, even in France. This has had several implications. The first is the development alongside these principles of a body of public competition law applied both by the general competition authority, the Conseil de la Concurrence, and the administrative courts.[49] Thus there is complete acceptance that public bodies, even those delivering public services, are subject to competition law; indeed, the commercial code, which now incorporates the provisions of competition law, states that: 'The rules defined in this part shall apply to all production, distribution and service activities, including those which are carried out by public persons, in particular in the context of public service concessions.'[50] There is an exemption for practices which result from the application of a *loi* or a regulation implementing it, but this is interpreted narrowly and would not include action not necessary for that application.[51] Examples of cases where the competition law rules in principle apply include purchase of electricity for onward sale from independent producers by Eléctricité de France and anti-competitive conduct by the state postal service.[52]

Competition law thus clearly applies to the activities of public service bodies themselves; there has been more controversy, however, about the extent to which it can be applied to the acts of public authorities setting the conditions under which markets are to operate, for example through the granting of concessions. However, even here the administrative courts, strongly influenced by developments in Community law, have been prepared to apply competition law principles. Thus as early as 1996 the Conseil d'Etat annulled a decree because of its incompatibility with the European competition rules, and in the following year it decided that a contract delegating the carrying out of funeral services to a private company could not lawfully put the enterprise in a dominant position in breach of domestic competition law.[53]

The development of competition law doctrine as it is applied to public service bodies has led to difficult questions of jurisdiction between the

---

[49] Bell (1999) 195–7; Bazex (1998); Nicinski (2004).   [50] Code de Commerce, Art. 410-1.
[51] Bazex (1998) 794.   [52] Bell (1999) 196–7.
[53] *Féderation française des sociétés d'assurances et autres* AJDA 1997, 204, and *Société Million et Marais* AJDA 1998, 247; for detailed analysis see Bazex (1998).

public and civil law systems, but it is of interest to us for two other reasons. The first is that it illustrates the general tension which is the theme of this book; rather than competition law and public service being quite distinct spheres, as had been envisaged by the older work on *service public*, they now interact strongly. Rather than having an institutional distinction between the scope of each body of doctrine, both may be applied to the same institution. The second point is that the doctrine in this area is to a very large degree derived from European Community law, and this will be analysed in detail in the next three chapters. Overall, the existence of a strong set of principles of *service public* has not freed the French from the need to grapple with the difficult questions of competition law and its limits, especially in the context of Community law. As two French writers have put it, rather than separating the areas of public service and competition, 'to-day it is more appropriate to think of competitive activities impregnated with the public service obligations. Public service no longer seems to be a derogation from competition rules, but a factor in shaping the direction of competitive activity.'[54]

If this integration of public service and competition law forms part of a form of convergence with jurisdictions such as the UK, a further form of convergence can be found in the development of independent regulatory authorities for the French utilities.[55] Again partly under the influence of European Community law, these have been established in a number of sectors; a further influence has been linked to the discussion above about the restatement of the principles of *service public*, seen as requiring the effective protection of consumers through the use of independent agencies. We have seen in the previous chapter that, in the UK at least, it is of the essence of the regulatory authorities that they both apply rules and principles designed to protect the operation of competitive markets, and have a role in protecting public service values.

The first example of such a body was in telecommunications with the creation of the Autorité de Régulation des Télécommunications in 1996.[56] A similar body was created for electricity regulation, which later acquired responsibilities for gas also, and is now termed the Commission de Régulation de l'Énergie.[57] Indeed, the influential Haut Conseil du Secteur

---

[54] Nicinski and Pintat (2003) 229.   [55] For a general survey see Braconnier (2001).

[56] Loi no. 96-659 du 26 juillet 1996, JO 27 juillet 1996, 11384; see Maisl (1995); Chevallier (1997) and the website at http://www.art-telecom.fr/ (consulted 14 July 2004).

[57] For electricity see loi no. 2000-108 du 10 février 2000, JO 11 février 2000, 2143, and décret no. 2000-381 du 2 mai 2000, JO 4 mai 2000, 668. For gas see loi no. 2003-8 du 3 janvier 2003,

Public even proposed a new regulatory authority for the water sector, previously highly fragmented in local authority hands, though this has not been implemented. In a slightly different context, once more partly as a result of requirements of Community law, in the French railways a separate enterprise in charge of the infrastructure was created as Réseau Ferré de France. Although no independent regulatory body was established, and the degree of opening up the rail network to competition was placed in the hands of the public rail operator and the minister, the law setting up the new enterprise itself pays respect to the principles of public service.[58]

Even though this move to independent agencies seems similar to developments in the UK, it must be added that there are some important limits to their powers. Thus the setting of prices remains to a large extent in governmental hands, either directly where the enterprise is managed by the state, or when it is delegated through the setting of *cahiers des charges*. The telecommunications authority sets tariffs for universal service, and other tariffs where competition has not yet been established, in conjunction with the government, and the approval of both is required. Similarly, it will be the minister who, under the December 2003 law, designates the providers of universal service, although the authority assesses its cost. The legislation implementing the European Community package does permit a *décret* to set out conditions under which the authority may set out a framework for universal service tariffs and object to a tariff; the provision survived a challenge before the Conseil Constitutionnel alleging that this amounted to an unconstitutional delegation of legislative power.[59]

The energy commission merely gives its opinion on tariffs for household customers and proposes tariffs for the use of the public electricity and gas systems and the annual charges attributable to public service, leaving the ultimate decision for government; the minister also has the power to impose sanctions for breach of competition rules or of those imposing public service requirements.[60]

JO 4 janvier 2003, 265. The Commission's website is at http://www.cre.fr/ (consulted 14 July 2004).

[58] Loi no. 97-135 du 13 février 1997, JO 15 février 1997, 2592, Art. 1; see Broussolle (1997).

[59] Loi no. 2004-669 du 9 juillet 2004 relative aux communications électroniques et aux services de communication audiovisuelle, JO 10 juillet 2004, 12483, arts. 13, 15; Conseil Constitutionnel, Déc. 2004-497, 1 juillet 2004, *Loi relative aux communications électroniques et aux services de communication audiovisuelle*.

[60] Braconnier (2001) 49; Nicinski and Pintat (2003) 228.

This division of responsibilities makes it clear that *service public* is still regarded as essentially the responsibility of government, even if this no longer implies that public services are directly provided by the public sector. As a writer on the new regulatory bodies has put it, '[t]hey do not in fact contribute, or at best do so only at the margin, to the control of quality of service, and in particular to compliance with the requirements of *service public*...This mission remains the prerogative of government.'[61] There is also of course the potential for conflict between Government and regulator, where the government's social goals come into conflict with the latter's economic objectives, one example being where the competition authority supported a report from the telecommunications regulator finding anti-competitive a low price for Internet in schools; the low price had been set by France Télécom at the request of the Government.[62]

The final point to be made in relation to this process of maintaining public service in a liberalized environment concerns something rather different; the use of public service charters. In 1992 the French Government issued a Charter of Public Services restating the principles of public service and adding eighty-nine detailed requirements; this was supplemented in 1995 by a circular adding a list of other principles, as already mentioned above.[63] It has more recently been supplemented by other charters, for example on municipal public services. Once more we see convergence with the UK where the *Citizen's Charter* and *Service First* have been the basis for important developments in setting and implementing quality standards for public service. Detailed discussion is outside the scope of this work, but once again it is evident that the principles of *service public* are becoming concretized and expressed through means more similar to those of the UK than was previously the case.

France: Conclusions

In this discussion of France it is apparent that the starting point for determining principles which might limit the use of competition law for public services is diametrically opposed to that of the UK. In the latter this has been left either to politics through public ownership, or has developed pragmatically and incrementally through the work of the

---

[61] Braconnier (2001) 49.   [62] Curien and Henry (1999) 118.
[63] See generally Chevallier (1996b).

regulators. In France it has developed from first principles, determined by the administrative courts and by academic writers; indeed it is at the level of principle that *service public* is at its strongest. Recent years have seen attempts to restate the principles in a form suitable for a liberalized environment where services are delivered by private bodies within the framework of European Community law. This has led to innovation in the meaning and scope of the doctrine and in the institutional means for its delivery. However, it has been felt necessary to restate the requirement that *service public* be respected when new regulatory regimes are created and, although France has now adopted (under the influence of Community law) independent regulatory agencies in telecommunications and energy, the implementation of *service public* remains ultimately the responsibility of government. There are also potential problems of compatibility with European Community law, and the strength of the French attachment to public service means that debates around this are likely to be particularly heated. This is made all the more true by the evident political dimension to the protection of public service, which can serve as a slogan for the left and as a justification for industrial action amongst public sector workers.

The relationship with European law will be discussed in later chapters. For the moment, however, we shall consider another European country. France has not yet fully privatized any of its public utilities; even in telecommunications government retains a majority stake in the major enterprise, though the ground has been prepared for a larger sale. Moreover, liberalization has often taken the form of a reluctant and minimalist response to European requirements. Italy will be an instructive comparison as it also has a public service tradition whilst having gone further in the process of privatization and, in some fields, liberalization. What tensions result from this, and what solutions can be reached?

Italy

Public Service and the Constitution

The Italian constitutional requirements in this context at first sight appear considerably more flexible than the French. Thus Article 43 of the Constitution merely states that a law *may* reserve to the state, to public enterprises or to co-operatives, enterprises supplying essential public services, or energy sources, or those in monopoly situations. It is thus permissive rather than obligatory.[64] Article 41 also protects the freedom of private enterprise; however, this is to be subject to limitations and to appropriate planning and control, defined by law, to meet social aims. As a result of these provisions, where an enterprise has been given exclusive rights by law, this has been treated as requiring that it is subject to a 'reservation to the state' through public ownership, or is at least subject to state control through its operation under concession by a public or in some cases private enterprise.[65] The effect is that where an enterprise delivering a public service is to be privatized, it must lose its exclusive rights or it must continue to be subject to close public supervision by means of a concession.

Amendments were made to the Constitution in 2001 as part of a move towards a greater decentralization of Italy. A new Article 117 lists the legislative powers of the central state and of the regions; matters allocated exclusively to the central state include 'supervision of competition' and also 'determination of the basic levels of services concerning civil and social rights that must be guaranteed throughout the entire nation'.[66] Apart from the allocation of authority to the state, this appears to give both competition and the achievement of national levels of public service a form of normative constitutional force. As the Italian competition authority put it in a paper prepared for the prime minister and Parliament:

the guarantee of the universality of public utility services remains unavoidable, even in a context of partial or complete liberalization, because the right 'to a basic service' is now to be considered a general principle of constitutional status. The regulation of basic guaranteed services, that has brought with it a considerable improvement in the quality of public utility services, must thus be permanent. However, it must not become the reason for introducing unjustified restrictions on competition, limiting access to the market or advantaging the dominant enterprise through financing above the costs needed for the provision of universal service.[67]

These constitutional provisions have not prevented Italy from developing a privatization programme over a number of years.[68] Moreover, as we shall see in the following chapters, the retention of exclusive rights by enterprises has been called seriously into question through the

[64] See Thirion (2002) 643–5 and Cassese (2004) 83–94.

[65] Thirion (2002) 644–5. For controversy on the different meanings of public service involved, see Parisio (1998) 712–14.   [66] Art. 117(2)(e), (m). See Clarich (2003) 110–16.

[67] Autoritá Garante della Concorrenza e del Mercato, *Riforma della Regolazione e Promozione della Concorrenza; Segnalazione del 14 Gennaio 2002 (AS226)* (2002).

[68] For early details see Cassese (1994), and for fuller information, including the legal norms employed, Marchetti (1995).

development of European Community law. Partly as a result of Community law, important utility markets have been liberalized, and, unlike in France where liberalization has usually seemed to represent a reluctant and minimalist response to European initiatives, this has been undertaken with relative alacrity and in some cases has gone beyond European Union requirements. Thus in 1999 32% of ENEL, the major electricity utility, was sold with a further sale in 2003 reducing the state holding to just below 61%. It has been required to divest itself of important activities, including generating capacity, transmission, and urban distribution networks. In gas, the holding company ENI and its subsidiary Snam have been partially privatized, with the state retaining only 35% of the former, and this has been accompanied by extensive liberalization in both energy sectors.[69] Finally, the whole of Telecom Italia has been sold (except for a small residual state holding associated with a 'golden share') and telecommunications were fully liberalized from 1998.

As we shall see in a moment, this privatization and liberalization has been accompanied by the development of new regulatory institutions. However, as in France there is also an acceptance that general competition law is applicable to public services. Thus the Italian competition law specifies that its prohibitions of anti-competitive agreements and abuse of a dominant position 'apply both to private and public undertakings and to those in which the state is the majority shareholder'.[70] There is a limited exception for services of general economic interest, reflecting that in Community law to be discussed in the following chapters.[71] Nevertheless, in Italy as in France, rather than competition law and public service being in separate institutional spheres, they are increasingly intertwined.

The Italian Concept of Servizio Pubblico *and the New Regulatory Regimes*[72]

The Italian concept of public service has much in common with that of France; however, it is even more difficult to define and lacks some of the

---

[69] See notably the 'Decreto Bersani', Decreto Legge n. 79 del 16 marzo 1999, *Gazzetta Ufficiale* n. 292, 14.12.1999.

[70] Legge 10 ottobre 1990, n. 287, Norme per la tutela della concorrenza e del mercato, *Gazzetta Ufficiale*, no. 240, 13.10.1990, Art. 8 (1), as amended by Legge 5 marzo 2001, n. 57 (art. 11), Disposizioni in materia di apertura e regolazione dei mercati, *Gazzetta Ufficiale*, n. 66, 20.3.2001.   [71] Art. 8(2).

[72] There has been something of an outpouring of new works on public service in Italy recently; see notably Rangone (1999), Scotti (2003), and de Falco (2003).

principled character of the latter. Thus 'the definition of "public service" seems to be amongst the most vexing in the Italian legal system as legislation, especially in the administrative law field, has never provided a clear identification of this concept'.[73] In addition, it has played a more marginal role in Italian administrative law and lacks coherence or general principle.[74] However, there have been extensive debates on whether the concept is 'subjective' or 'objective', the former implying that public service is defined only by the application of a suitable regime by the legislator, the latter that there is a deeper underlying concept of public services derived from constitutional norms, but one which can be delivered by private operators subject to regulation.[75] Moreover, the French 'laws of Roland' discussed earlier in this chapter have had an influence, and indeed reflect other constitutional norms, for example the principle of equality in Art. 3 para. 2 of the Constitution. What is now striking, however, is that, as we shall see in a moment, they have been built into new initiatives for the improvement of public services and new regulatory regimes.

A further Italian characteristic has been extensive debates, as in France, on the compatibility of the Italian regime with European Community law, concerning both the reservation of exclusive rights and the relationship between public service and universal service.[76] The debates have been usefully summarized as follows:

French legal theory, treating the concept of *service public* as the reflection and foundation ... of state sovereignty (the state as guarantor of services of general interest and of social and economic and social cohesion), treats universal service as an attack on the traditional concept of public service and, moreover, as inadequate to guarantee the citizen access to the use of essential services according to the well-known principles of equality, continuity and adaptation ... In Italy the situation is different. Part of the doctrine points out that the concept of universal service is contained within the traditional concept of public service, representing its core ... In other words, universal service may be the seed of public service or could have been present within it in a latent form until it emerges at the time when it is decided to liberalize markets and the public authorities assume the responsibility of guaranteeing to all users the accessibility of defined essential services in a competitive market.[77]

---

[73] Parisio (1998) 686.   [74] Rangone (1999) 239, 299.
[75] Ibid., 292–311; Scotti (2003) ch. I, ch. II s. II.
[76] See Ragnone (1999) 265–88; de Falco (2003); Napolitano (2000).
[77] Bonadio (2003) 3; see also Cassese (1999).

What is most interesting, however, is the attempt to combine the Continental traditions of public service with more concrete institutional guarantees of their effective delivery.[78]

The first stage in doing so was the Directive of 1994 on the delivery of public services.[79] It applies to all parts of the administration which deliver public services; where services are delivered under concession by private bodies, the administration is to secure that the principles set out in the Directive are observed by them. The Directive sets out fundamental principles of public service very much on the French model; they are stated as six principles. The first is that of equality, including that of users in different geographical areas. The second is impartiality and the third, continuity. In addition to these traditional French principles, however, the remaining ones are choice for consumers, consumer participation (including the right to information and to be consulted on quality of service), and efficiency and effectiveness. These reflect a more Anglo-Saxon concern with a consumer-oriented approach to the delivery of services, and this is developed further as the legislation then follows the British model in requiring the implementation of these principles through the setting of service standards (*gli standard*) which include both general and individual standards, breach of the latter giving rise to a right to compensation. Grievance procedures are also required to be established. The standards and procedures are published in the form of a *Carta del servizio pubblico* for each industry and implementation is supervised by a special committee. Further reinforcement of the obligation to develop charters has been provided by more recent legislation, and in 1999 a further law provided for the participation of users and their associations in the drawing up of service standards.[80]

This procedure represents an important innovation through attempting to combine the general principles of French administrative law with concrete institutional means for their delivery; the similarity of the latter to the British *Citizen's Charter* is striking.[81] There has been considerable progress in developing the more detailed charters; for example, in the

---

[78] See generally de Lucia (2002) ch. 3.

[79] Direttiva del Presidente del Consiglio dei Ministri, 27 gennaio 1994, *Gazzetta Ufficiale* n. 43, 22.2.1994.

[80] de Lucia (2002) 208–9; Decreto Legislativo, 30 luglio 1999, no. 286, art. 11.

[81] For the background see Cassese (1995) and for more recent assessments of the process see Vesperini (1998), Battini (1998), and Marconi (1998).

case of electricity supply, by the end of 1997, 99% of electricity consumers were covered by such charters. It should be mentioned, however, that the standards are often relatively unsophisticated; for example, that on disconnection of electricity supplies merely provides for notice to be given and the restoration of supply to take place if evidence is produced that the debt has been paid in full. This is far behind the British provisions limiting disconnections discussed in the preceding chapter.[82]

A further phase occurred with the preparations for the privatization of utility enterprises and the liberalization of the telecommunications and energy markets. As Giuliano Amato, former prime minister and President of the Competition Authority put it:

[t]he process [towards the creation of independent regulators] is similar to what it has been in the United Kingdom, and the reasons why we should prefer independent rather than politico-administrative regulation are fundamentally the same, with rejection in Italy of politico-administrative regulation which is associated with the poor condition of public services, and even with corruption.[83]

A law of 1995 set out the general principles to be adopted in the creation of independent regulatory authorities for energy and communications (including telecommunications and broadcasting) and defined in detail those for the energy sector; detailed arrangements for communications were introduced later.[84] Again, there is a strong influence from the British experience. The new authorities, the Autorità per l'Energia Elettrica e il Gas and the Autorità per le Garanzie nelle Communicazioni are placed at arm's-length from government. In the case of energy, appointments are made by the President of the Republic on the recommendation of the government and after hearings by the appropriate parliamentary committee. Indeed, the latter must give an absolute majority for a nomination to go ahead. For communications, each house of the Parliament elects four members whilst the president of the authority is appointed by the President of the Republic on a proposal from the government. Both examples indeed go considerably further than the British arrangements in securing parliamentary scrutiny.

---

[82] ENEL, *Carta del servizio elettrico*, (1996) punto 3.3.3, available at http://www.aduc.it/dyn/sosonline/leggienorme/legg_mostra.php?id = 49163 (consulted 14 July 2004). Anecdotal evidence from Italy suggests that even the minimal Italian standard is often breached.

[83] Quoted in Curien and Henry (1999) 128.

[84] Legge n. 481, 14 novembre 1995, *Gazzetta Ufficiale* no. 270, 18.11.1995; legge n. 249, 31 luglio 1997, *Gazzetta Ufficiale*, no. 177, 31.7.1997. On regulatory bodies in Italy, see Giani (2002).

The authorities take the form of commissions of three members with seven years' security of tenure.[85] Their functions include the formulation of advice to government and parliament, including on the amendment of concessions and authorizations, and protecting both the principles of competition and efficiency and of public service, here characterized as delivering services on terms of equality, which meet all reasonable needs of users including the old and disabled, and to respect the environment, security of installations, and safety of employees.[86] They also supervise the implementation of service standards and determine complaints. As regards tariffs, the authorities were given the power to set basic tariffs in the remaining regulated sectors themselves through price caps on the British model. In the field of universal service, the telecommunications regulator has negotiated a 50% reduction in Telecom Italia's tariffs for low income families and set contributions to the universal service fund. In energy, the regulator has established and monitors service standards and the application of a Citizens' Service Charter. Thus the regulators possess considerably greater powers than their French equivalents to implement public service goals (alongside the role of government in issuing concessions and authorizations), and are in this sense closer to their UK counterparts. However, a reminder of continuing government involvement occurred in 2002 when Prime Minister Berlusconi, by decree, froze electricity and gas prices for three months, overruling the energy authority in pursuance of his general economic policy.[87]

Italy: Conclusions

In Italy we have a role for the principles of public service which falls in between the case of the UK described in the previous chapter and that of France. On the one hand there is a strong tradition of the distinctiveness of public service, even at a constitutional level, and the inherent duties of the state to ensure its proper delivery, either through ownership or through effective supervision of private operators. This has also found expression in some general principles similar to those so important in France. However, the development of privatization and liberalization of

---

[85] Detailed information on the Authorities can be found on their websites (in English) at http://www.autorita.energia.it/inglese/about/eng_index.htm (consulted 14 July 2004) and http://www.agcom.it/eng/eng_intro.htm (consulted 14 July 2004).

[86] Art. 2(12) of legge n. 481, 14 novembre 1995.

[87] Decreto-Legge, 4 settembre 2002, n. 193, *Gazetta Ufficiale* no. 207, 4.9.2002.

utility markets on a larger scale than in France, and the requirements of European Community law, have necessitated some rethinking and the wider application of competition law. Moreover, the often very low standard of customer service in Italian public services has also given impetus to the development of measures to improve standards, with a greater trust being placed in independent regulation rather than potentially corrupt government.[88]

The effect has been the adoption of a number of measures much closer to those favoured in Britain than those associated with the Continental tradition, whilst retaining reference to the general principles derived from France. This has taken the form of charters and service standards reminiscent of the *Citizen's Charter* and *Service First* initiatives in the UK, and the development of regulatory authorities with power to supervise the delivery of such standards and to set tariffs, rather than these matters being solely for government. The implication is that it may be possible to combine a more principled approach to public service with the more pragmatic and specific means for its protection described in the previous chapter.

All the developments in this chapter, however, must be seen in the context of European Community law and the often heated debates around the relationship between competition law and public service as part of European liberalization. This will be the subject of the next three chapters of this book.

---

[88] See Cassese (1995).

6

Public Service and European Community Law

Introduction

It is now time to move from discussion of public service and competition law in national jurisdictions to describe their treatment in European Community law. This is of considerable interest as here the potential conflict between the two themes has been highly controversial and has produced a very large amount of legal material, without, it must be said, coming to clear solutions on many of the most important questions. However, a pattern is now starting to emerge. The earlier approach, closely linked to the development of the single internal market, was to see services of general interest (as public services are termed in this context) as an unwelcome impediment to the task of market creation. Thus provisions permitting special treatment for such services were interpreted narrowly and restrictively. More recently, and particularly since the Treaty of Amsterdam, there has been a fuller recognition of the independent value of public services as exemplifying a Community commitment to citizenship, partly as a result of their partial constitutionalization in the new Article 16 of the Treaty. The objective is no longer only to limit their scope but to improve their delivery through applying principles of good governance, including (but not limited to) the use of competitive markets.

This chapter will make no attempt to provide general coverage of the treatment of public services by Community law as that would require discussion at far greater length than is possible in one chapter. Fortunately, excellent general treatises already exist and will be drawn on extensively here.[1] Instead of such comprehensive treatment, I shall provide a discussion of the way in which Community law has attempted to handle tensions between public service and competition objectives in key areas, notably in the application of general Community competition law and in the scrutiny of state aids. A warning must be added at this point; even within such a limited treatment the law is often very complex and sometimes almost unfathomable. Advance notice of this should be very apparent from the fact that the law on two key issues has been characterized as of 'obscure clarity' and of 'clear obscurity'; neither of these epithets suggest that understanding will be easy.[2] The next, briefer, chapter will discuss attempts by the European Commission to develop general principles in this area as part of a continuing process of reform, and Chapter 8 will examine the developing role of public service obligations in those areas in which utility services have been liberalized. The central theme will be the same in all three chapters: the progress from market building to citizenship.

Much of the difficulty can be traced to two central elements in the background to the Community law in this area. The first is that which has become apparent earlier in this book; different Member States have radically different approaches to public service and different degrees of attachment to public service values. This has led not only to very different systems of national law on which Community law may draw, but also to different perceptions of the legitimacy of the application of Community competition law to public services. Thus, on the one hand, support from the Commission for the model of liberalized public utilities operating in a competitive market place, with a residual role for universal service only in the case of market failure, led to sustained criticism from Continental Member States that the Commission is 'a liberalization machine, ultra-liberal and dogmatic'.[3] On the other hand,

---

[1] Buendia Sierra (1999); Quigley and Collins (2003). The subject is also covered in the major texts on EC Competition Law; see e.g. Jones and Sufrin (2004) ch. 8. A further source is the European Commission's annual *Report on EU Competition Policy*, which now contains an informative section on recent developments relating to services of general economic interest. A good recent summary is also Szyszczak (2001).

[2] Colliard (1964); Tesauro AG in Case C-202/88 *French Republic v. Commission of the European Communities (Telecommunications Terminal Equipment)* [1991] ECR I-1243, para. 11, both quoted in Buendia Sierra (1999) 77 and 129.

[3] See speech of Karel van Miert, 'L'Europe, Vecteur de la Libéralisation', Paris, 21 October 1996; available at http://europa.eu.int/comm/competition/speeches/text/sp1996_053_fr.html (consulted 14 July 2004).

attempts to protect the special treatment of public services have been condemned by Anglo-Saxon sources as maintaining the privileges of inefficient monopoly providers; for example, a British edited version of the Amsterdam Treaty entitled the section dealing with services of general economic interest and public service broadcasting 'Vested Interests'.[4]

The effect of these different approaches will be dealt with more fully in the following two chapters, but here it is necessary to point out a second source of tension. On the one hand, the fundamental principles of the Community are essentially pro-competitive, especially through the construction of a single internal market.[5] Moreover, amongst the fundamental principles in the Treaty, Article 4 (inserted by the Treaty on European Union in 1993) provides that the activities of the Member States and of the Community shall include 'the adoption of an economic policy which is ... conducted in accordance with the principle of an open market economy with free competition'. This emphasis has led to an increasingly firm application of the basic competition law rules contained in Articles 81 and 82 of the Treaty, and indeed their application to state monopolies and the liberalization of public utilities have been some of the last areas in which serious limits to a single market have been tackled. This in turn leads to a form of presumption that the values associated with competition law and liberalized markets are the most appropriate ones unless a very strong reason exists otherwise. On the other hand, however, the fundamental principles contained in the Treaty also refer to other, more collective goals associated with social solidarity. To give merely a few examples, from the Treaty's fundamental principles Article 2 setting out the task of the Community includes 'a high level of employment and of social protection' and 'economic and social cohesion and solidarity among Member States'. Article 3(1)(k) sets out as an activity of the Community 'the strengthening of economic and social cohesion'. In more specific provisions, Article 152 states that '[a] high level of human health protection shall be ensured in the definition and implementation of all Community policies and activities', and Article 158 that:

[i]n order to promote its overall harmonious development, the Community shall develop and pursue its actions leading to the strengthening of its economic and social cohesion.

---

[4] Duff (1997) 84–5.   [5] On the internal market see Armstrong and Bulmer (1998).

In particular, the Community shall aim at reducing the disparities between the levels of development of the various regions and the backwardness of the least favoured regions or islands, including rural areas.[6]

As we saw in Chapter 2, in recent years attempts have been made to strengthen the protection of non-market values in this context through the introduction of a new Article 16 amongst the fundamental principles of the Treaty; this requires Member States to ensure that services of general economic interest (a concept to be analysed below) operate on the basis of principles and conditions which enable them to fulfil their missions. Moreover the Charter of Fundamental Rights adopted in 2000 includes a Chapter on solidarity (Chapter IV) and, within it, rights to social security, to health care, and to access to services of general economic interest.[7]

Thus, in view of these radically diverse principles underlying Community law, it is hardly surprising that difficulty has been found in reconciling liberalized markets and competition on the one hand with the promotion and protection of public service goals on the other. With this background, it is now time to examine the application of Community competition law and its exceptions in more detail. The first relevant Treaty article can be disposed of quickly.

State Monopolies and Article 31

A provision of Community law which at first sight appears to have considerable importance for public service is Article 31, especially given the historical adoption of a state monopoly as the main means of delivering public services. As amended by the Treaty of Amsterdam, it provides *inter alia* that 'Member States shall adjust any state monopolies of a commercial character so as to ensure that no discrimination regarding the conditions under which goods are procured and marketed exists between nationals of Member States'. It is also provided that the provisions apply to monopolies delegated by the State to others.[8] The provision has both been difficult to interpret and of limited scope, applying most clearly to statutory national monopolies for tax-raising

---

[6] For the social dimensions of Community policy see Burrows and Mair (1996).

[7] Arts. 34–6.

[8] See generally Buendia Sierra (1999) ch. 3. In the text of the new Constitutional Treaty produced by the European Convention it remains effectively unchanged as Article III-44.

purposes such as tobacco and alcohol monopolies, although in principle it can be applied to public service activities which are commercial rather than merely regulatory in nature, and this may include exclusive rights of production.[9] It applies to goods rather than services but this may include energy and water, thus potentially covering some public utilities.[10]

Fortunately, we need not examine the complexities of this provision in greater depth as its content is now effectively identical to that of other provisions which have been used more frequently, notably Article 86, to be considered in detail in a moment.[11] Crucially, should Article 31 be employed, the qualified exception to the competition rules for services of general economic interest under Article 86(2) also applies to it, and this will also be discussed in detail later.[12]

The General Rules of Competition Law and Article 86

Introduction

Of much greater importance are the general rules of Community competition law set out in Articles 81 and 82, which should be familiar to most readers. Article 81 prohibits agreements between undertakings and concerted practices which have as their object or effect the prevention, restriction, or distortion of competition within the common market. Exemptions may be granted in certain circumstances under Article 81(3), application of which has now been decentralized to national courts and competition authorities.[13] Article 82 prohibits abuse of a dominant position by one or more undertakings.[14]

In the context of this work, it is essential to add to these provisions Article 86(1) and (2) of the Treaty.[15] They provide as follows:

(1) In the case of public undertakings and undertakings to which Member States grant special or exclusive rights, Member States shall neither enact nor

---

[9] Buendia Sierra (1999) 80–81, 84, but cf. 123–5.   [10] Ibid., 87–8.

[11] Ibid., 101, 117, 259–60.

[12] Ibid., 126–7, and see e.g. Case C-159/94 *Commission v. France* [1997] ECR I-5815, para. 49.

[13] For details of the extensive law on Article 81, see Jones and Sufrin (2001) chs. 2–3 and Whish (2001) chs. 3–4.

[14] Similarly, see Jones and Sufrin (2004) chs. 3–6; Whish (2001) ch. 5.

[15] The Constitutional Treaty also retains this Article essentially unchanged as new Article III-55.

maintain in force any measure contrary to the rules contained in the Treaty, in particular to those rules provided for in Article 12 and Articles 81 to 89.

(2) Undertakings entrusted with the operation of services of general economic interest or having the character of a revenue producing monopoly shall be subject to the rules contained in this Treaty, in particular to the rules on competition, insofar as the application of such rules does not obstruct the performance, in law or in fact, of the particular tasks assigned to them. The development of trade must not be affected to such an extent as would be contrary to the interests of the Community.

Article 86 thus operates as a 'reference rule' applying other Treaty provisions, in particular Articles 81 and 82, both to action taken by Member States and that taken by public undertakings or those given exclusive or special rights.[16]

In practice, the application of Article 81 in conjunction with Article 86 has been the less important.[17] Nevertheless, it is not difficult to think of situations in which these Articles may have a potential role in relation to public services; a notable one would be that referred to in Chapters 2 and 3 of the co-ordination of bus services through agreements between undertakings to adopt integrated timetables and fare structures; as we have seen, this has been partially facilitated through the adoption of a block exemption under the UK Competition Act. Article 81 requires that any agreement must affect trade between Member States; this might appear improbable in relation to bus operations but as we shall see later the requirement has been interpreted extremely generously and may include them, and would certainly include co-operation between enterprises which effectively closed markets to outside competition from other Member States.

Much more important in practice has been the application of Article 86 in conjunction with Article 82 prohibiting abuse of a dominant position, and this raises obvious questions about the delivery of public services. In particular, to what extent is cross-subsidy permitted to provide a uniform universal service? This has special importance where an undertaking undertakes both public service activities and competitive activities in the marketplace; to what extent is cross-subsidy permissible between the two?[18] In addition, restrictions on entry may exist to preserve the position of the undertaking offering the public service and funding it by internal cross-subsidy which would no longer be possible if new entrants

---

[16] Buendia Sierra (1999) 140–1, 260–1.   [17] Ibid., 189–90, 261–7.

[18] For the general treatment of cross-subsidy in Community Law see Abbamonte (1998).

could 'cream-skim' the most profitable business. Thus one of the leading cases on Article 86 concerned the extent to which it was permissible for the Belgian postal service to benefit from exclusive rights to collect, transport, and deliver mail, including special courier services, to protect its basic universal service.[19] In a more recent case, the Court of Justice had to consider the legality of restrictions, justified by the need to protect emergency ambulance services, on opportunities for commercial operators to provide general ambulance services.[20]

It must be added as well that Article 86 may also be applied in conjunction with other Treaty articles which are addressed to Member States; in addition to application to the states themselves the articles can be applied to actions taken on their behalf through their undertakings.[21] Many of these articles are of course subject to limitation or exceptions themselves, and these may be relevant to public services; examples would include Articles 28 and 29 concerning quantitative restrictions on imports and exports, subject to exceptions under Article 30 including restrictions based on public morality, public policy, public security, and the protection of the health and life of humans, animals, and plants. Others would be the freedom to provide services under Article 49 and freedom of establishment under Article 43. Nevertheless, in is in relation to the competition rules that the major controversy has arisen, and these will be the main subject of this section.

The Scope of Article 86 and the Concept of an Undertaking

How, then, will Article 86 be applied in practice and what is its scope? One potentially important restriction on the scope of both Articles 86(1) and (2) is through their application only to undertakings. Both public and private undertakings granted exclusive rights are covered, but to qualify as an undertaking the entity involved must carry our economic activities.[22] Entities carrying out non-economic activities will not be covered by the competition rules. The case law on this is complicated (and I have already addressed the matter in Chapter 3 in discussion of the *BetterCare* decision).

---

[19] Case C-320/91 *Procureur du Roi v. Paul Corbeau* [1993] ECR I-2533.
[20] Case C-475/99 *Ambulanz Glöckner v. Landkreis Südwestpfalz*, [2001] ECR I-8089.
[21] See Buendia Sierra (1999) ch. 6 which analyses this question in considerable detail.
[22] Buendia Sierra (1999) 43–62, 275–6 gives a detailed analysis of this question; see also Szyszczak (2001) 39–46.

On the one hand, the concept of economic activities will exclude 'matters which are intrinsically prerogatives of the State, services such as national education and compulsory basic social security schemes, and a number of activities conducted by organisations performing largely social functions, which are not meant to engage in industrial or commercial activity'.[23] Thus in *Humbel* the Court held that courses provided under a national education system were not 'services provided for remuneration' as the state is 'not seeking to engage in gainful activity but is fulfilling its duties towards its own population in the social, cultural and educational fields'.[24] The concept may also exclude what may be termed non-economic regulatory activities; for example, the control and supervision of air space on safety grounds in *Eurocontrol* and anti-pollution surveillance services in *Calì*.[25] It is clear however that other activities which form part of economic regulation, such as the granting of exclusive rights to a particular enterprise, will be subject to competition law, as we shall see. Further complex questions have arisen in relation to social security schemes. Here organization on the basis of 'social solidarity' with contributions proportional to income and equal benefits has been held to preclude classification as an economic activity.[26] The Court of Justice has held that the management of a compulsory scheme providing insurance against accidents at work and occupational diseases did not constitute an economic activity as it was based on the principle of solidarity.[27]

On the other hand, no problems will arise in relation to service provision on the part of public utilities funded at least in part by charging consumers as these are clearly economic activities; '[a]ctivities such as postal services or the distribution of electricity have always been considered to be economic activities in Community law, even when their tariffs are largely based on the principle of solidarity'.[28] Similarly, where there is a direct participation in markets by a public authority this is covered by Article 86. Thus the body managing Paris airports was held to be an undertaking engaging in economic activities insofar as it provided services to others, such as airlines, and was remunerated by commercial fees. This was distinct, and severable, from its role in the exercise of

---

[23] Commission of the European Communities, *Green Paper on Services of General Interest*, COM(2003)270 final, para. 45.

[24] Case 263/86 *Belgium v. Humbel* [1988] ECR 5365.

[25] Case C-364/92 *Eurocontrol* [1994] ECR I-43; Case C-343/95 *Calì* [1997] ECR I-1588.

[26] Cases C-159/91 and C-160/91 *Christian Poucet v. Assurances Générales de France* [1993] ECR I-637.   [27] Case C-218/00 *INAIL* (2002) ECR I-691.

[28] Buendia Sierra (1999) 58.

public authority through, for example, supervision of air traffic control, which had earlier been held to fall outside the scope of competition law.[29] In the German ambulance case mentioned above, the Court also concluded that, as ambulance facilities had not always been provided by public authorities, their provision even by such authorities was clearly an economic activity for the purposes of Article 86(1).[30]

It is clear from these later cases that the concept of an undertaking and of economic activity will be widely interpreted and, as *BetterCare* suggested, participation in markets even in ways shaped by public interest requirements will fall within these concepts. Social solidarity may be the reason for public intervention in the marketplace, but that is quite distinct from the replacement of the marketplace as in the case of compulsory social security and insurance schemes. This approach was summarized in the 2003 Commission Green Paper as: 'any activity consisting in offering goods and services on a given market is an economic activity... Thus, economic and non-economic services can co-exist within the same sector and sometimes even be provided by the same organization.'[31]

However, some possible doubt might be cast on this approach (and that in *BetterCare*) by the decision in *FENIN*, where it was held by the Court of First Instance that purchasing decisions by Spanish health organizations were not covered by the competition rules as the supplies were not purchased for an economic activity but for use in the context of a principle of solidarity by providing free services on the basis of universal cover.[32] It has however been convincingly argued that this case can be distinguished from *BetterCare* because, in the latter, the purchasing body was also actively engaged in the direct provision of services in the market, and because in *FENIN* it was assumed that no services were provided directly for remuneration by the purchasing authority, whilst in *BetterCare* they clearly were.[33] Thus the approach in the Green Paper, under which the key test is whether the activity involved participation in markets which can be made the subject of the competition rules, could still

---

[29] Case C-82/01 *Aéroports de Paris* [2002] ECR I-9297; Case C-364/92, *SAT v. Eurocontrol* [1994] ECR I-43.   [30] *Ambulanz Glöckner* (above n. 20), para. 20.

[31] Commission of the European Communities, *Green Paper on Services of General Interest*, COM(2003)270 final, para. 44. This approach draws on the Court of Justice in Cases C-180–184/98 *Pavel Pavlov and Others v. Stichting Pensioenfonds Medische Specialisten* [2000] ECR I-6451.

[32] Case T-319/99, *FENIN v. Commission of the European Communities* [2003] ECR II-357.

[33] Rodger (2003) 6–9.

be the correct one. However, in a further decision, the Court of Justice, not following the opinion of its Advocate-General, held that Germany's state-run sickness funds did not constitute undertakings. Although they competed with each other and with private undertakings, they performed an exclusively social function, founded on the principle of national solidarity and which was entirely non-profit-making.[34] The emphasis was thus on the underlying purpose of the activity, not participation in the market.

It has also been argued convincingly that much of the confusion has been due to a failure to separate two distinct issues; whether an activity is economic and so falls within the scope of Community competence, and whether there are nevertheless good reasons, such as the role of social solidarity, for modifying the application of the competition rules.[35] This whole area cries out for clarification, perhaps through a framework directive, a matter to be discussed in the following chapter.[36]

On a related issue, the limitation of Articles 81 and 82 to restrictions on competition which affect trade between Member States seems to be interpreted in such a way as to give the Treaty provisions a wide effect. To take one example, that of the German ambulance case once more, the Court of Justice considered that the provision of ambulance services in one German *Land* was capable of affecting such trade as restrictions on competition could partition the common market and thereby restrict freedom to provide services, and entry restrictions could prevent an undertaking from another Member State from establishing itself, though the question was ultimately to be left to the national court. Given the degree of participation in health and utility services by undertakings from other Member States, it is difficult to see how this condition could not be met.[37]

Exclusive and Special Rights

The next question to be briefly addressed is that of the meaning of exclusive or special rights under Article 86(1), which, it will be recalled, applies in the case of a public undertaking or of any undertaking granted

---

[34] Joined Cases C-264/01, C-306/01, C-354/01 and C-355/01 *AOK Bundesverband* OJ [2004] C94/2, para. 51.   [35] Szyszczak (2001) 42–5.
[36] See Santamato and Pesaresi (2004) 20–1. For the Office of Fair Trading's interpretation, see *The Competition Act and Public Bodies*, Policy Note 1/2004.
[37] *Ambulanz Glöckner* (above n. 20), para. 49.

such rights. It is directed towards actions by Member States, whilst Article 86(2) is directed at undertakings themselves, although the latter may also apply to state measures granting exclusive rights to such undertakings. An exclusive right broadly corresponds to a monopoly but does not include the organization of a market by the state through regulation; the legal form of the award of the right is irrelevant.[38] Special rights arise when there is a limitation of the number of undertakings which can benefit from rights granted by the state, or where special advantages are conferred by the state on an enterprise or a number of enterprises.[39] An important distinction is between such special rights and 'regulated access activities'. In the latter case access to, for example, a profession, is limited on objective grounds, such as training and qualification requirements. An example which the Court of Justice has treated as falling within this latter category and so not amounting to special rights is relevant to our earlier discussion, that of pharmacies, where numbers had been limited by the state and a minimum distance required between outlets.[40] As we saw in Chapter 3 above, this policy of public authorities of maintaining a widespread geographical distribution of pharmacies has proved controversial in the UK and has required some restrictions on the scope of competition.

Finally, in relation to the application of Article 86 in conjunction with Article 82, there has been considerable judicial and academic controversy over whether the simple grant of exclusive rights is sufficient to create a breach of the articles, or whether actual abuse is necessary as well.[41] In the *Corbeau* case referred to above, the Court implied that the mere grant of exclusive rights was adequate to establish abuse, thus rendering all exclusive rights not capable of objective justification in breach of Article 86. The Court has however retreated from this in later decisions.[42] As a result, Buendia Sierra concludes that an exclusive right will breach Article 86 in combination with Article 82 where an undertaking enjoys a dominant position, and where it carries out, or is capable of carrying out, abusive behaviour as an inevitable result of the grant, or where similar

---

[38] Buendia Sierra (1999) 5–6, 17–18, 23, 25–6, and see the Commission Directive (EC) 94/46 in relation to telecommunications liberalization [1994] OJ L268/15, where the definition was set out in detail; Recitals 6 and 11, and Arts. 1(1)(b) and 2(1)(a)(ii). For the more recent developments in telecommunications liberalization see Chapter 8 below.   [39] Buendia Sierra (1999) 64–9.

[40] Ibid., 69–70 and 214; see Case C-387/93 *Criminal proceedings against Giorgio Domingo Banchero* [1995] ECR I-4667.   [41] Buendia Sierra (1999) 151–89; see also Hancher (1999).

[42] See notably Case C-323/93 *Le Crespelle* [1994] ECR I-5077.

effects to abuse are produced as a result of the grant.[43] This is also reflected in later cases; for example, in the German ambulance case the Court noted that the mere creation of a dominant position through the grant of special or exclusive rights was not incompatible with Article 86. However, there would be incompatibility if the undertaking, by exercising those rights, is led to abuse its dominant position or where the rights are liable to create a situation in which the undertaking is led to commit abuses.[44]

In this section I have considered in outline the, somewhat technical and frequently complex, rules concerning the application of Community law, especially Community competition law, to the grant of exclusive or special rights to undertakings and to the related conduct of such undertakings themselves. The most important exception is that concerning non-economic activities and those carried out by bodies other than undertakings, but this is not likely to apply to entities which participate in markets rather than replace them. There is however another exception to the application of competition law and this is contained in Article 86(2); it is of the utmost importance for this study.

Services of General Economic Interest and the Article 86(2) Exception

Introduction

It is clear from the discussion above that the general application of competition law and other provisions of Community law designed to maintain a single, open, market is well established even where Member States have sought to protect public service goals through giving exclusive or special rights to enterprises, although an important, though not clearly defined, potential exception to this is where the intervention is not carried out through an undertaking exercising economic activities. The major controversy has however concerned a further exception set out in Article 86(2). It will be recalled that this states that the Treaty rules are applicable to '[u]ndertakings entrusted with the operation of services of general economic interest . . . insofar as the application of such rules does

---

[43] Buendia Sierra (1999) 186–7, summarizing his detailed earlier discussion.

[44] *Ambulanz Glöckner* (above n. 20), para. 39. See also Case C-67/96 *Albany* [1999] ECR I-5751; Cases C-147-148/97 *Deutsche Post* [2000] ECR I-825.

not obstruct the performance, in law or in fact, of the particular tasks assigned to them. The development of trade must not be affected to such an extent as would be contrary to the interests of the Community.'

This is clearly of enormous importance in establishing the possibility of special treatment for public services and for the achievement of public service goals. The exception is potentially of very wide scope; thus it applies not just to undertakings themselves but also to state measures referring to such undertakings, including the grant or maintenance of exclusive rights.[45] It does of course also apply both to public and private undertakings, although the *activity* involved must be economic for the reasons discussed above; otherwise there would be no need to apply this exception. Despite the wording of the Article, however, the *interest* involved need not be economic in nature, and indeed will normally be social.[46] Indeed, the term 'economic' is often omitted and reference made simply to 'services of general interest'. As has been pointed out, the concept of 'services of general economic interest' corresponds roughly to the concept of public service used by the Continental Member States and discussed in my previous chapter.[47]

It is only fairly recently that a strong interest has developed in the interpretation of Article 86(2), but there is already a substantial case law on it. As we shall see below it has importance outside the main provisions of competition law in Articles 81 and 82 as it is also now a key test in determining the legitimacy of state aid to undertakings. The first question which arises is the degree to which a Member State is free to define a service of general interest. As I shall describe in the following chapter, this has been a subject of considerable political controversy, but the current position is that the choice of services of general interest is essentially a matter for the Member States themselves; as the Commission has put it (note the reference to 'public service mission' here):

Member States' freedom to define means that Member States are primarily responsible for defining what they regard as services of general economic interest on the basis of the specific features of the activities. This definition can only be subject to control for manifest error ... However, in every case, for the exception provided for by Article 86(2) to apply, the public service mission needs to be clearly defined and must be explicitly entrusted through an act of public authority.[48]

---

[45] Buendia Sierra (1999) 273.   [46] Ibid., 277–8.   [47] Ibid., 279–80.

[48] European Commission, *Communication from the Commission – Services of General Interest in Europe* COM/2000/0580 final (2000).

Moreover, the Court of First Instance has also stated, in a challenge concerning the activities of the French postal undertaking and the maintenance of a network in rural communities, that 'the Commission is not entitled to rule on the basis of public service tasks assigned to the public operator, such as the level of costs linked to that service, or the expediency of the political choices made in this regard by the national authorities, or La Poste's economic efficiency in the sector reserved to it . . .'.[49]

It is clear from the above that the discretion of Member States is not absolute, and, as we shall see, the rest of the wording of Article 86(2) does permit a considerable degree of scrutiny by the Court. Nevertheless, the onus is firmly on the Member State to choose, and, very importantly, to define, the nature of the service of general interest in question.

The Proportionality Test

In the application of Article 86(2), the basic principle applied by the Court to assess the Member State's definition of a service of general interest is that of proportionality, and it is in this connection that we see the most interesting shifts in direction by the Court.[50] This is of course evident from the wording of the Article itself; application of the competition rules (and other Treaty rules) will only take place insofar as it does not obstruct the general interest tasks assigned to an undertaking. The final requirement that '[t]he development of trade must not be affected to such an extent as would be contrary to the interests of the Community' is also now treated as part of the proportionality test, meaning incidentally that it is probable that Article 86(2) as a whole has direct effect.[51]

The exception to the competition rules must be necessary for the undertaking to perform its task. The meaning of this necessity has given rise to much of the controversy, especially in relation to measures designed to protect universal service for all citizens, notably in the public utilities. The key questions are whether some other means of achieving

---

[49] Case T-106/95 *Fédération française des sociétés d'assurances (FFSA) et al. v. Commission (La Poste)* [1997] ECR II-229, para. 108; see also para. 192; Buendia Sierra (1999) 282–3. The last point about economic efficiency needs to be qualified should state aid be provided; the relevant decisions will be discussed near the end of this chapter.

[50] For a detailed examination of proportionality in this context see Buendia Sierra (1999) 300–41.   [51] Ibid., 341–52.

the same goals might be available which are less restrictive of competition, and what the effect of failure to apply the exception would be. Is it necessary that it would be completely impossible to perform the general interest task, or is it sufficient that failure to apply the exception would simply render the task more difficult? To understand the approach adopted it will be most convenient to examine some of the key cases.

Early decisions took a highly restrictive approach to applying the Article 86(2) exception, applying a strict interpretation of the proportionality principle.[52] For example, in the 1974 case of *Sacchi*, it was held that the exception could only be employed if the competition rules were incompatible with the performance of the undertaking's assigned tasks.[53] In the 1991 case of *RTT* the Court held, in effect, that the exception would only apply where this was indispensable to achieve the objective of general interest.[54] This approach was in turn applied strictly by the Commission, which determined that:

It is not sufficient in this regard that compliance with the provisions of the Treaty makes the performance of the particular task more complicated. A possible limitation of the application of the rules on competition can be envisaged only in the event that the undertaking concerned has no other technically and economically feasible means of performing its particular task.[55]

In one context this approach was applied as late as 1997, when the Court of First Instance decided in *Air Inter* that:

The application of [the Treaty Articles] could ... be excluded only in as much as they 'obstructed' the performance of the tasks entrusted to the applicant. Since that condition must be interpreted strictly, it was not sufficient for such performance to be simply hindered or made more difficult.[56]

Thus, on this view, 'only those restrictions which are *indispensable* in order to achieve an objective of general interest will be allowed. Accordingly, faced with a particular measure the question which must be asked is whether or not other less restrictive measures exist by which this end could be achieved. If such measures exist Article 86(2) cannot be relied on.'[57] It should be noted, however, that these decisions relate to areas in which building a single market was a particularly pressing task for the

---

[52] Ibid., 303–4. [53] Case 155/73 *Sacchi* [1974] ECR 409, para. 15.
[54] Case C-18/88 *RTT* [1991] ECR I-5941, para 22.
[55] Commission Decision (EEC) 82/371 *Navewa-Anseau* [1982] OJ L167/48, para. 66.
[56] Case T-260/94 *Air Inter* [1997] ECR II-997, para. 138.
[57] Buendia Sierra (1999) 304 (emphasis retained).

Community; telecommunications in the case of *RTT* and the Commission decision referred to, and the liberalization of civil aviation in the case of *Air Inter*. Moreover, these were contexts in which it was well established at least by the beginning of the 1990s that competitive markets were feasible as a means of allocation, and public service considerations were not as strong nor as symbolically important as in, for example, posts and energy. It is thus hardly surprising that the logic of completing a single, competitive, market was dominant in the approaches of the courts and of the Commission.

The case which represented the most important early application of a different approach to Article 86(2) was in the context of protecting rights to universal service; it was the celebrated *Corbeau* decision.[58] Corbeau had set up a local postal service in breach of the exclusive rights given to the Belgian Régie des Postes, and was faced with criminal proceedings. The Régie's monopoly was justified on the basis that it was necessary to ensure the provision of a basic postal service at a uniform rate throughout Belgian territory; in order to achieve this goal and to finance the basic service, the monopoly applied to all postal services, basic and special. It was thus a classic example of the grant of an exclusive right to prevent 'cream-skimming' by competitors who were free to accept only the most profitable business. The Advocate-General accepted that this justified the monopoly for the basic service. However, he considered that special services such as those offered by Corbeau were a distinct market and application of the monopoly to them represented an unjustified extension of a dominant position. The Court of Justice took a somewhat different approach, deciding that it was necessary to ask whether a restriction on competition was necessary to permit the holder of the exclusive right to perform its task of general interest in economically acceptable conditions.[59] Thus it was not necessary that the task of general interest be completely impossible to perform without the benefit of the restriction. On this basis, the Court accepted the legitimacy of the 'cream-skimming' argument; the obligation of the undertaking to break even 'presupposes that it will be possible to offset less profitable sectors against the profitable ones and hence justifies a restriction of competition from individual undertakings where the economically profitable sectors are concerned'.[60] Competitors could 'concentrate on the economically

---

[58] Case C-320/91 *Procureur du Roi v. Paul Corbeau* [1993] ECR I-2533; see also Hancher (1994). [59] *Corbeau* (above n. 58), para. 16.
[60] Ibid., para. 17.

profitable operations and . . . offer more advantageous tariffs than those
adopted by the holders of the exclusive rights since, unlike the latter, they
are not bound for economic reasons to offset losses in the unprofitable
sectors against profits in the more profitable sectors'.[61] The exclusion of
competition for special services would be permissible if competition in
them would compromise the economic equilibrium of the service of
general economic interest.[62]

The decision in this case was seen as a considerable step forward by
proponents of public service. Not only was the 'cream-skimming' argument accepted, but it seemed that the restriction on competition was not
only justified where otherwise the provision of the basic service at uniform tariffs would be impossible, but also where it would not be possible
to achieve conditions of economic equilibrium as a result.[63] Indeed, the
Court did not ask whether there might be other means of providing
a universal service more compatible with open competition, such as
a central universal service fund to support unprofitable services for which
competing operators might bid. A similar response was given to the later
decision in the *Almelo* case.[64] Here exclusive purchasing and sales contracts had been entered into between electricity companies; these had the
effect of precluding imports from other Member States. The Court noted
that the regional distribution company in question had been given the
task of ensuring that 'throughout the territory in respect of which the
concession is granted, all consumers, whether local distributors or end-
users, receive uninterrupted supplies of electricity in sufficient quantities
to meet demand at any given time, at uniform tariff rates and on terms
which may not vary save in accordance with objective criteria applicable
to all customers'.[65] The Advocate-General had stated that 'the competition rules may be disapplied not only where they make it impossible for
the undertaking in question to perform its public service task but also
where they jeopardize its financial stability'.[66] He had however also
required that it be proved that no other less restrictive way of achieving
the public service objectives was available. The Court did not ask this
last question, instead stating that restrictions on competition 'must be
allowed in order to enable the undertaking entrusted with such a task of

---

[61] Ibid., para. 18.   [62] Ibid., para. 19.

[63] See para. 17 of the judgment; the term 'economic equilibrium' is not defined.

[64] Case C-393/92 *Almelo* [1994] ECR I-1477.   [65] Ibid., para. 48.

[66] At para. 146 of his opinion; see Buendia Sierra (1999) 332.

general interest to perform it. In that regard, it is necessary to take into consideration the economic conditions in which the undertaking operates, in particular the costs which it has to bear and the legislation, particularly concerning the environment, to which it is subject.'[67]

Confirmation of this more generous approach came in further cases in late 1997 in a number of cases concerning gas and electricity monopolies, where it was stated explicitly that the survival of the undertaking itself need not be threatened to justify restrictions on competition, and that it does not have to be shown that there is no other conceivable means of fulfilling the general interest goals if the Member State can provide arguments justifying the maintenance of the exclusive rights.[68] By this time, however, an important constitutional change was beginning to make its present felt.

The Treaty of Amsterdam and the New Article 16

On 2 October 1997 (three weeks before judgment in the electricity and gas monopolies cases) the Treaty of Amsterdam was signed, though the relevant provisions were not to come into effect until 1 May 1999. The background to these provisions will be discussed in detail in the following chapter. The most important is the new Article 16 of the EC Treaty, which states:

Without prejudice to Articles 73, 86 and 87,[69] and given the place occupied by services of general economic interest in the shared values of the Union as well as their role in promoting social and territorial cohesion, the Community and the Member States, each within their respective powers and within the scope of application of this Treaty, shall take care that such services operate on the basis of principles and conditions which enable them to fulfil their missions.[70]

The Final Act of the Amsterdam Treaty also contained a declaration that the new Article 'shall be implemented with full respect for the jurisprudence of the Court of Justice, inter alia as regards the principles of

---

[67] *Almelo* (above n. 64), para. 49.

[68] Case C-157/94 *Commission v. Netherlands* [1997] ECR I-5699, paras. 43, 58; see also C-158/94 *Commission v. Italy* [1997] ECR I-5789 and C-159/94 *Commission v. France* [1997] ECR I-5815.

[69] Art. 86 has been discussed above; Arts. 73 and 87 concern state aids and will be analysed below.

[70] In the Constitutional Treaty there are only minor changes to this provision; thus, apart from drafting changes, the 'principles and conditions' are 'in particular economic and financial' and are to be defined in new European laws; new Art. III-6, and see the following chapter.

equality, quality and continuity of such services'; this is of course an explicit reference to the French concept of *service public*. Finally, the Treaty also included a special protocol on public broadcasting; this is of considerable importance and will be discussed in detail in Chapter 9 below.

The new Article 16 is placed in the section of the Treaty dealing with fundamental principles; thus it 'cannot be dismissed as an insignificant side-show'.[71] However, opinion is divided on its effect. On the one hand, it may be perceived as essentially symbolic; thus Buendia Sierra has argued that it has not modified Article 86(2) nor the case law on the latter; it does not introduce a new legal test and is explicitly made subject to the main existing articles.[72] Similarly, Szyszczak has suggested that its importance lies in its support for the provision of public services through competitive markets rather than outside them.[73]

On the other hand, it has been argued that the potential effect of Article 16 is of fundamental importance in imposing a positive duty (rather than merely giving a possible derogation) for Member States to ensure that the European concept of service of general interest is respected and facilitated by them. As a result,

Article 16 represents a critical step in the concretising of non-market (or post-market) concerns in both the psyche and legal hierarchy of legal development. The express references to shared Union values and to the particular objectives of social and territorial cohesion upgrade general interest services into positive horizontal policy-shaping considerations for both member States and the Community institutions . . . The leaving intact of the Article 86 principles ensures that the *acquis* is not diluted, whilst the development of the new, obligatory, element of Article 16 provides a steering mechanism for the future. In these terms the new provision is a microcosm of a recurring issue in the Union's current process of development: the balancing or prioritising of market-based considerations and those more aligned to cohesion and social solidarity.[74]

In turn, this provides a recognition of the values of services of general interest as part of a 'minimum overlapping Union consensus' on which European citizenship can be developed.[75]

This is an ambitious interpretation, the evaluation of which must await a definitive interpretation by the Court of Justice of the new Article.

---

[71] Jones and Sufrin (2004) 590.
[72] Buendia Sierra (1999) 329–34; see also Hancher (1999) 730–1.
[73] Szyszczak (2001) 63–4.   [74] Ross (2000) 34 (footnote omitted).
[75] Ibid., 34–8 (the quotation is from 37).

However, especially in conjunction with the new right of access to services of general interest in the Community Charter of Fundamental Rights,[76] it would seem difficult to argue that the new Article can do anything but reinforce a growing recognition that the values associated with public service do have an important role as limits on the scope of competition law values. As we shall in Chapter 9, the Protocol on Public Broadcasting, also introduced by the Amsterdam Treaty, does seem to have made a difference to the attitude of the Commission in approving non-market based activities by broadcasters. Although no cases have yet been brought on the basis of Article 16, there does seem to be growing liberalism in judicial decisions which may indirectly reflect this new approach. In particular, rather than concentrating only on the negative role of services of general interests as restrictions on free competition in the internal market, there is a growing recognition of their positive value.

This could already be seen in the gas and electricity monopoly cases, and is also apparent in the case of *Albany*, decided in September 1999, where the Court of Justice stated (reiterating *Corbeau*) that '[i]t is sufficient that, in the absence of the rights at issue, it would not be possible for the undertaking to perform the particular tasks entrusted to it, defined by reference to the obligations and constraints to which it is subject ... or that maintenance of those rights is necessary to enable the holder of them to perform tasks of general economic interest which have been assigned to it under economically acceptable conditions'.[77] In *Deutsche Post* a similarly broad approach was taken, leading one commentator to suggest that, in connection with Article 86(2), 'this provision, originally an exemption and therefore to be interpreted narrowly, seems to be becoming a rule that allows for the activities falling within the individual Member States' competences to be taken account of more broadly'.[78]

Perhaps most vividly, in the German ambulance case discussed above, the Court took a generous approach to cross-subsidy, referring once more to the ability to provide the service of general interest in 'economically acceptable conditions' as the test for whether a restriction on competition was necessary, and holding that the markets for emergency and non-emergency patient transport were so closely linked that losses in one could threaten the economic viability of the other and so 'jeopardize

---

[76] Art. 36.   [77] Case C-67/96 *Albany* [1999] ECR I-5751, para 107.
[78] Cases C-147-148/97 *Deutsche Post* [2000] ECR I-825, [2000] 4 CMLR 838; Bartosch (2001) 196.

the quality and reliability of that service'.[79] It would only be if the service benefiting from the restriction of competition was manifestly unable to satisfy demand for services that the restriction would not be acceptable. Thus here the reference was not only to the maintaining of an economically acceptable outcome but to the maintenance of quality and reliability of service.

We do then see a clear shift of emphasis in these more recent cases. As has been pointed out in relation to the electricity monopoly cases, '[I]nstead of using the economic viability of the undertaking as the very essence of whether tasks were obstructed by complying with the Treaty, the revised view appears to concentrate on the justifications for protecting the service. Put another way, the crucial methodological switch is from economic measurement to value judgement in the application of the derogation.'[80] The burden of showing that it can benefit from Article 86(2) rests with the Member State, but this will be easier to satisfy than had been supposed earlier, and arguments which are essentially distributive in nature are clearly acceptable in doing so. The most important decisions in suggesting a more liberal approach are however in the field of state aids, and we shall now consider that before reaching some overall conclusions to this chapter.

Public Services and State Aids

Introduction

An area of Community law of equal importance for many public services is that of state aids. The concern here, as with the grant of exclusive rights, is of course to ensure that financial support is limited to what is necessary to enable them to perform their tasks; it is particularly acute where undertakings are also active in other, competitive, markets, where aid could give them an unfair advantage; '[t]he compensation that certain undertakings rightly receive for providing [services of general interest] must not constitute advantages that enable them to compete unfairly in the most profitable liberalised sectors'.[81] Here two questions arise; which payments constitute state aid as against mere compensation for the

---

[79] *Ambulanz Glöckner* (above n. 20), paras. 58–62.   [80] Ross (2000) 24.

[81] European Commission, *Report from the Commission on the State of Play in the Work on the Guidelines for State Aid and Services of General Economic Interest* (2002).

carrying out of uncommercial activities at government request, and, if it is state aid, can it be justified as compatible with the common market, in particular under Article 86(2)?

The basic law on state aids is contained in Articles 87 and 88 of the Treaty.[82] Article 87(1) provides that:

[s]ave as otherwise provided in this Treaty, any aid granted by a Member State or through state resources in any form whatsoever which distorts or threatens to distort competition by favouring certain undertakings or the production of certain goods shall, insofar as it affects trade between Member States, be incompatible with the common market.

The Treaty then goes on in Article 87(2) to list categories of aid which are compatible with the common market, and in Article 87(3) those categories which may be considered by the Commission to be compatible on the exercise of discretionary judgment. Article 88 provides for supervision of state aids by the Commission, including, crucially, imposing a duty on Member States to notify the latter of any plans to grant or alter aid.[83] It should be noted that, in the case of public enterprises, the system is reinforced by a Directive requiring transparency in their financial relations with government, and this has been amended to require that separate accounts are kept for services of general economic interest and for commercial activities.[84]

Compensation for Public Service and State Aids

There is a substantial body of law on state aids, both in general and in specific sectors, which will not be rehearsed here.[85] Rather I shall concentrate on the key issues relevant to public service. The first is the degree to which compensation for public service activities constitutes state aid. This is of crucial importance, for if such compensation does not constitute state aid at all, not only will it be compatible with the common market but it will not require notification to the Commission.[86] One point is quite

---

[82] They are unchanged in the new Constitutional Treaty as Arts. III-56-7.

[83] Art. 88(3).

[84] Council Directive 80/723/EEC on the transparency of financial relations between Member States and public undertakings, [1980] OJ L195/35, as amended by Directive 85/413/EEC [1984] OJ L229/20, Directive 93/84/EC [1993] OJ L254/16 and, most importantly in this context, Directive 2000/52/EC [2000] OJ L193/75.

[85] For a detailed account see Quigley and Collins (2003).

[86] Ibid., 267-8. The general issue of the status of compensation for services of general economic interest is discussed ibid., 45-8.

clear; if the undertaking in question is overcompensated by the provision of compensation which is more generous than the cost of providing the service of general economic interest, that will constitute state aid.[87]

The uncertainty arises where the payment does accurately reflect the extra costs imposed as a result of the public service requirement; here rather than state aid, it can be seen as merely a payment similar to a contractual system of compensation from the state. Thus in the case of *La Poste*, discussed earlier in this chapter, the state aids issue was appealed to the Court of Justice, which held that both the Commission and the Court of First Instance had been correct in examining the compatibility of aid with the common market under Article 86(2) instead of treating it as compensation, not aid.[88] Similarly, in a case concerning state financing for Portuguese public service broadcasting, the Court of First Instance annulled a Commission decision which had not treated as state aid payments intended merely to offset the additional costs of public service, considering that 'the fact that a financial advantage is granted to an undertaking by the public authorities in order to offset the cost of public service obligations which that undertaking is claimed to have assumed has no bearing on the classification of that measure as aid within the meaning of Article 92(1) of the Treaty'.[89] Clearly, much will depend on the adequacy of the accounting arrangements adopted; if they are not capable of identifying accurately the costs for which compensation is paid it will not be possible to exclude it from the category of state aid.

There has been more major controversy about recent case law, in particular the decision in *Ferring v. ACOSS*, which concerned a tax exemption for wholesale distributors of pharmaceutical products in France.[90] This was justified on the ground that they were required to carry sufficient stocks to supply the needs of the local population. The Court of Justice held that:

provided that the tax on direct sales imposed on pharmaceutical laboratories corresponds to the additional costs actually incurred by wholesale distributors in discharging their public service obligations, not assessing wholesale distributors to the tax may be regarded as compensation for the services they provide and hence not State aid within the meaning of Article 92 [now Article 87] of the

---

[87] Ibid., 45 and see Case T-14/96 *BAI v. Commission* [1999] ECR II-139. For a recent example of overcompensation see European Commission, *Thirty-Second Report on EU Competition Policy* (2003), points 590–93.　　　　[88] Case C-174/97 *FFSA v. Commission* [1998] ECR I-1303.

[89] Case T-46/97 *SIC v. Commission* [2000] ECR II-2125, para. 84.

[90] Case C-53/00 [2001] ECR I-9067.

Treaty. Moreover, provided there is the necessary equivalence between the exemption and the additional costs incurred, wholesale distributors will not be enjoying any real advantage for the purposes of Article 92(1) of the Treaty because the only effect of the tax will be to put distributors and laboratories on an equal competitive footing.[91]

This decision proved highly controversial. It was heavily criticized by Advocates-General in later cases. Thus in *Altmark*,[92] Advocate-General Léger invited the Court to review *Ferring* as that decision had deprived the Commission of its ability properly to apply Article 86(2) (as this could only be done where a payment was classified as state aid) and to reconcile on the basis of that Article the needs of the service of general economic interest and the requirements of an undistorted market. In *GEMO*,[93] Advocate-General Jacobs suggested that a distinction be made between cases where, on the one hand, the link between the state financing and clearly defined general interest obligations was direct and manifest, and, on the other, where there was no such clear link. An example of the former would be where public service contracts had been awarded after public procurement procedures. In the first category, financial support should be treated as compensation rather than state aid; in the latter as state aid but subject to possible exemption under Article 86(2).[94]

The plenary formation of the European Court of Justice delivered its judgment in *Altmark* on 24 July 2003. It did not overrule *Ferring*, but clarified it in terms drawing on the approach of Advocate-General Jacobs.[95] Thus:

where a State measure must be regarded as compensation for the services provided by the recipient undertakings in order to discharge public service obligations, so that those undertakings do not enjoy a real financial advantage and the measure thus does not have the effect of putting them in a more favourable competitive position than the undertakings competing with them, such a measure is not caught by Article [87(1)] of the Treaty.[96]

However, this was subject to four conditions. First, the public service obligations must be clearly defined. Second, 'the parameters on the basis of which the compensation is calculated must be established in advance in

---

[91] *Ferring*, (above n. 90), para. 27.

[92] Case C-280/00 *Altmark Trans GmbH* [2003] ECR I-7747.

[93] Case C-126/01 *GEMO SA* [2004] 1 CMLR 9.

[94] See also Advocate-General Stix-Hakl in Cases C-34/01 and C-38/01 *Ensirisorse SpA* [2004] 1 CMLR 10.

[95] C-280/00 *Altmark Trans GmbH* [2003] I-7747. See Bartosch (2003); Santamato and Pesaresi (2004).   [96] Para. 87.

an objective and transparent manner'. If the basis for payment is not set in advance but where it becomes apparent after the event that the operation of services meeting the public service obligations is not economically viable, that will constitute state aid. Third, compensation must not exceed the costs of meeting the public service obligations, allowing for a reasonable profit. Fourth, where the undertaking to discharge the obligations is not chosen through a public procurement procedure based on the lowest cost, 'the level of compensation needed must be determined on the basis of an analysis of costs which a typical undertaking, well run and adequately provided with means...so as to be able to meet the necessary public service requirements, would have incurred in discharging those obligations, taking into account the relevant receipts and a reasonable profit for discharging the obligations'.[97] The decision interpreted widely the requirement that intra-Community trade be affected, applying it to local transport in view of the potential role of undertakings based in other Member States in supplying it.

The effect of this decision will be to permit detailed scrutiny of state aid decisions in relation to public services where the strict conditions set out are not complied with; indeed, in a further decision the Court has held that there was state aid where payments were not linked to a clearly defined public service remit and no objective parameters for their calculation were prepared in advance.[98] In particular, in the absence of award by a public procurement procedure (which, as we shall see in Chapter 9 below, may not be appropriate for some types of public service) examination of the efficiency of the enterprise providing the service is likely to be necessary. Even this is by no means certain, however, in view of a decision of the Court three weeks before *Altmark* to the effect that such an efficiency examination was not appropriate where there is only one possible supplier of a service, and hence no benchmark against which to judge efficiency.[99] However, putting these uncertainties to one side, it should be underlined that, even if compensation does constitute state aid, there may be grounds for approving it as compatible with the common market, and this will be the next subject for discussion.

---

[97] Paras. 88–93.

[98] Cases C-34/01 and C-38/01 *Enirisorse SpA* [2004] 1 CMLR 10, paras. 32–40. See also Case C-126/01 *GEMO SA* [2004] 1 CMLR 9 where the same result was reached through less transparent reasoning.

[99] Cases C-83/01, C-93/01 and C-94/01 *Chronopost and Others* [2003] ECR I-6993, and see Bartosch (2003).

State Aid which is Compatible with the Common Market

It will be recalled that Article 87 contains several types of exceptions from the general incompatibility with the common market of state aids. The first is where the Commission is required to find categories of aids compatible, the second where it has a discretion whether to do so, and the third is where the Council may decide that certain categories of aid are compatible or may decide that particular aid is justified in exceptional circumstances.[100] Of the *de jure* exceptions, the most relevant here is the first; 'aid having a social character, granted to individual consumers, provided that such aid is granted without discrimination related to the origin of the products concerned'. A hypothetical example used by the Commission was that of aid to assist elderly people with electricity bills; if the aid were for all forms of heating within the market it would not constitute state aid as it would have no distorting effect.[101] The important point is of course that the aid must be granted to individuals rather than directly to an undertaking.

In the case of the discretionary exceptions, these include a number of examples which may be relevant to public service. The first is 'aid to promote the economic development of areas where the standard of living is abnormally low or where there is serious underemployment'.[102] This may include sectoral aid or aid to specific industries so long as the regional criterion is met.[103] Aid to facilitate the development of certain economic activities or certain economic areas may also be held compatible with the common market, and this may be used for broader schemes of regional aid than the former exception.[104] A rather different exception also permits the use of aid to promote the execution of an important project of common European interest or to remedy a serious disturbance in the economy of a Member State.[105] In addition to these exceptions, aid may be found to be compatible with the common market on the basis of other Community objectives, for example Articles 6 and 174 on environmental policy. In this latter area the Commission has issued specific guidelines on state aids, most recently in 2001.[106] Similarly, as Article 152

---

[100] Arts. 87(2–3), 88(2); see Quigley and Collins (2003) ch. 2.

[101] European Commission, *Twenty-Fourth Report on Competition Policy* (1994) point 354.

[102] Art. 87(3)(a).   [103] Quigley and Collins (2003) 84.   [104] Art. 87(3)(c).

[105] Art. 87(3)(b).

[106] European Commission, *Guidelines on State Aid for Environmental Protection*, OJ 2001 C37/3, and see Quigley and Collins (2003) 183–9.

requires a high level of health protection to be ensured in the definition and implementation of all Community policies and activities, this may also be a basis for finding aid compatible with the common market.[107]

Most importantly in the context of this book, however, Article 86(2), perhaps in conjunction with Article 16, may also provide the basis for treating state aid as compatible with the common market. The key principles have been discussed above, and in the past, it has been used, for example, in the electricity sector to permit state aid in the funding of an electricity cable from the Finnish mainland to isolated islands, and support for the construction of a natural gas network and the distribution of natural gas in Denmark.[108] By contrast, more recently the Commission has decided that tax exemptions and loans on advantageous terms for companies established by municipal authorities could not be justified as no general interest obligation could be deduced from the legislation empowering the setting up of such companies, which did not clearly define a public service mission.[109]

State Aid in Special Sectors

This discussion of state aid must conclude with a brief examination of some special sectors where more specific state aid regimes exist, for example through the provision of special guidelines by the Commission; in a number of these areas public service concerns are particularly likely to arise, and in some cases they are sectors where extensive liberalization is taking place.[110] One of these is that of public service broadcasting, where guidelines were published in the form of a Communication in late 2001;[111] this will be considered in detail in Chapter 9 below. Another important example is that of transport, which has figured in many of the most important judicial decisions in this area, including *Altmark*, and on which more will be said in Chapter 8 below. Articles 70–80 of the Treaty provide a special regime for rail, road, and inland water transport in

---

[107] Quigley and Collins (2003) 190.

[108] European Commission, *Twenty-Eighth Report on Competition Policy* (1998), 247–8; Quigley and Collins (2003) 120.

[109] European Commission, *Thirty-Second Report on Competition Policy* (2003), points 602–5.

[110] See generally Quigley and Collins (2003) ch. 5.

[111] European Commission, *Communication from the Commission on the Application of State Aid Rules to Public Service Broadcasting*, 2001/C320/4 [2001] OJ C320/5.

addition to Article 87, and Article 73 states explicitly that '[a]ids shall be compatible with this Treaty if they meet the needs of coordination of transport or if they represent reimbursement for the discharge of certain obligations inherent in the concept of a public service'. There is also a considerable amount of secondary legislation; thus as long ago as 1969 a Council Regulation was passed to regulate compensation for fulfilling public service obligations in this area, and a new replacement for it is currently proposed, though it has been delayed due to opposition to the proposed extent of competitive tendering for awarding public service contracts.[112] The Regulation, *inter alia*, sets out common procedures for the award of public service contracts to undertakings and for the calculation of compensation. A further Council Regulation sets out the conditions for the award of aid for the co-ordination of transport, including that covering infrastructure costs, and for the meeting of public service obligations by transport undertakings, and a third on the normalization of accounts for rail undertakings provides for compensation for additional financial burdens which they carry in comparison with other transport undertakings.[113] Finally, the Directive on the development of the Community's railways includes some provision for financial aid for new investment.[114] Different provision is made in the case of air transport, where there is a set of general guidelines in relation to state aids in the aviation sector, and in addition, under the regulations liberalizing air transport markets, public service obligations may be imposed on certain routes vital for the economic development of a region; compensation may be provided only after a public tendering process.[115]

Finally some mention should be made of the energy sector.[116] Here, in line with broader Community objectives, state aid has been approved to

---

[112] Regulation (EEC) No. 1191/69 of the Council of 26 June 1969 on action by Member States concerning the obligations inherent in the concept of a public service in transport by rail, road and inland waterway, [1969] OJ L156/1, as amended by Council Regulation (EEC) No. 1893/91, [1991] OJ L169/1, and see the *Altmark* decision, above. The new proposal is COM(2002)107 final.

[113] Council Regulations (EEC) 1107/70 on the granting of aids for transport by rail, road and inland waterway, [1970] OJ L130/1; (EEC) 1192/69 on common rules for the normalization of accounts of railway undertakings, [1969] OJ L156/8.

[114] Council Directive 91/440/EEC on the development of the Community's railways, [1991] OJ L237/25.

[115] European Commission, *Application of Articles 92 and 93 of the EC Treaty and Article 61 of the EEA agreement to State aids in the aviation sector*, OJ 1994 C350/07; Council Regulation (EEC) 2408/92 on access for Community air carriers to intra-Community air routes, [1992] OJ L240/8, Art. 4(1–2).   [116] See Quigley and Collins (2003) 206–9.

secure diversification of supply and for the production of energy from renewable sources, for example the British non-fossil fuel obligation.[117] As part of the liberalization process, which will be discussed more fully in Chapter 8 below, provision has also been made for state aid for 'stranded costs' in the form of long-term commitments undermined by the introduction of competition.[118]

The Choice of the Holder of Exclusive Rights and the Recipient of State Aids

To conclude this chapter reference should be made to a further issue which has caused considerable controversy, involving both exclusive rights and state aids; as a result of the decision in *Altmark* it is likely to assume a much higher profile in the future. It has already been hinted at in relation to transport, although much of the general discussion falls outside the scope of this book.[119] Let us assume that a Member State has decided that a public service can best be delivered through the mechanism of exclusive or special rights, perhaps with the provision of state aid. Can the Member State deliver the service itself, and, should it decide to delegate delivery to a public or private undertaking, does it have a full discretion in exercising its choice or must it adopt a process of competitive tendering? This is of considerable importance in a number of areas where it might be considered that such a tendering process is inappropriate; for example, by reason of transaction costs, because the disruption incurred in periodic tendering may disrupt the continuity of public service delivery, or because a particular undertaking has built up a body of special expertise over time which should be respected through assurances of continuity. As we shall see in Chapter 9, this is a specially important issue in relation to public service broadcasting, notably in funding the BBC. A further problem may be that competitive tendering results in a 'race to the bottom', reducing quality in order to cut costs.[120]

In this context Article 43 of the Treaty becomes important; it provides a right of establishment for an undertaking in any Member State. This

---

[117] European Commission, *Twenty-Eighth Report on Competition Policy* (1998), 256–7.

[118] European Commission, *Communication Relating to the Methodology for Analysing State Aid Linked to Stranded Costs*, 26 July 2001; Quigley and Collins (2003) 208–9. For the broader context of energy liberalization see Chapter 8 below.

[119] See generally Buendia Sierra (1999) 363–74; Cox (2003).   [120] See Cox (2003) 18–26.

implies that any grant of exclusive or special rights should be undertaken through an open and non-discriminatory process. The law is further developed through the public procurement directives covering the acquisition of public works, goods, and services; these make special provision for 'public works concessions' where an undertaking is given the task of carrying out a public service activity and is remunerated by a right to exploit the works in question, assuming the risk in doing so.[121] The requirements for the award of such concessions are limited to advertising rather than a full process of tendering. No similar requirements exist in relation to procurement of services or of supplies, nor are such requirements included in the new Directive of 2004 which revises the requirements.[122] However, in an interpretative communication in 2000 the Commission maintained strongly that as a result of the general requirements of Community law all candidates for such concessions should be treated equally and that objective criteria, specified in advance, should be used in assessing applications.[123] This clearly suggests that competitive tendering should be the normal means of allocation of such concessions. Further procedural rules are proposed in the Commission's Green Paper on Public–Private Partnerships.[124]

This position is reinforced by some aspects of the law relating to state aids. As we have seen, secondary legislation may require the adoption of tendering in certain specific situations, for example the award of support for undertaking public service obligations in civil aviation, and in the award of other transport concessions; in that sector the matter is currently highly controversial and has delayed the passing of a new Regulation. As a result of the *Altmark* decision, discussed above, a requirement of competitive tendering may become more clearly a matter of general principle in Community law. It will be recalled that the court permitted the exclusion of public service compensation from the category of state aid only where the obligations were clearly defined, and the basis for the compensation determined, in advance. Where the undertaking

---

[121] Council Directive (EEC) 93/37 concerning the co-ordination of procedures for the award of public works contracts, [1993] OJ L199/54, Art. 3.

[122] Directive 2004/18/EC on the procedures for the award of public works contracts, public supply contracts and public service contracts, [2004] OJ L134/114.

[123] European Commission, *Commission Interpretative Communication on Concessions Under Community Law*, 12 April 2000.

[124] Commission of the European Communities, *Green Paper on Public–Private Partnerships and Community Law on Public Contracts and Concessions*, COM(2004)327 final.

was chosen by means other than a public procurement procedure which would allow the selection of the tenderer who would provide services at least cost, then compensation would be determined on the basis of an efficient undertaking rather than by the costs actually incurred.[125] This could raise serious difficulties in calculating the costs of such a notional efficient undertaking and, as acknowledged in *Chronopost*, may well prove impossible where there is only one possible supplier of a service. Thus the decision in *Altmark* is most likely to result in the further adoption of competitive tendering for reasons of certainty and simplicity;[126] however, as we shall see in Chapter 10, it is not necessarily the case that competitive tendering will have these effects.

Conclusion

We have seen in this chapter that the European Community law relating to the interaction of competition law and public service goals is much more fully developed than our domestic law, even if it remains unclear on some key issues. It is also at a crucial stage in its development. The case law on Article 86(2) in particular has adopted an increasingly generous attitude to the permissibility of cross-subsidy and other means of meeting clear public service goals, and this growing liberality is reinforced through the developing effect of Article 16 of the Treaty, which appears to constitutionalize certain public service values. Considerable relief has been expressed by proponents of public service at the *Altmark* decision which has accepted the legitimacy of public service compensation outside the definition of notifiable state aid. It also reinforces the necessity for a clear and explicit definition of public service obligations, which will itself create the need for their fuller protection through law rather than only by political means. The most controversial implication may be increased adoption of competitive tendering procedures in the allocation of such compensation, a subject to which I shall return in Chapter 10.

My concentration on the formal legal position and decisions of the Court of Justice only tells half the story, however. It is important to see it within a political context, where controversy has been heated in recent years. Moreover the Commission itself has played a major role in attempting to determine the legitimate scope of services of general

---

[125] *Altmark* (above), paras. 89–93.   [126] See Bartosch (2003) 17.

interest. This political and administrative context will be the subject of the next chapter, where we shall see a similar shift from regarding such services as impediments to the single market towards treating them as citizenship rights, followed in Chapter 8 by an analysis of the specific measures taken to protect public service in those areas where utility markets have been successfully liberalized.

7

Services of General Interest, the Commission, and Reform

Introduction

Although the subject matter of this chapter will be similar to that of the preceding one, the emphasis and approach will be different. Chapter 6 concentrated on the legal position and on past developments in the Community law treatment of public services. This chapter will discuss the political background to the developing Community approach to them, and will be forward-looking through examining the continuing reform process and the debates around a possible framework directive on services of general interest. This will lead the way into the discussion in Chapter 8 of experience in the sectors where liberalization has taken place and a more clearly articulated approach to the treatment of public service has been adopted. This chapter will also discuss the effect of the new Constitutional Treaty adopted in 2004. The theme will be similar to that of the preceding chapter; the move from conceiving services of general interest as a restriction on the single market towards seeing them as a positive expression of citizenship rights.

The Background: Conflicting Values and Models

It will be evident from the previous chapter that, behind the recent developments in Community law, is a fundamental conflict of values which results in different models for the treatment of public services.[1] On the one hand there is the competition-based model, in which public

---

[1] See also Scott (2000).

service provision is best undertaken through market-based mechanisms and in which the normal provisions of Community competition law are applied; this was the approach particularly associated with the UK. On the other, there is the public service-based model based on Continental traditions in which quite distinct principles are applied, and the values of public service are perceived as threatened by the application of competition law.[2]

This conflict became particularly acute after the Treaty of European Union (the Maastricht Treaty), signed in 1992. It added to the basic principles in Part I of the Community Treaty the new Article 4, which states *inter alia* that the activities of the Member States and of the Community shall include 'the adoption of an economic policy which is...conducted in accordance with the principle of an open market economy with free competition'. Thus '[t]his provision elevated a policy directed at effective competition to the level of a constitutional imperative, loosing competition policy for the first time from its traditional role as a handmaiden of integration concerns'.[3] Did this mean that the competition-based model had ultimately triumphed?

The response of the advocates of the public service model was to campaign vociferously for Treaty amendment to recognize more clearly the distinctive role of public service and for a Charter of Public Services setting out basic principles including the right of access of European citizens to public services and the standards which services should meet.[4] Key actors in this were the French and Belgian Governments, the Centre Européen des Entreprises à Participation Publique (CEEP), an international grouping of public undertakings,[5] and the Initiative pour des Services d'Utilité Publique en Europe (ISUPE), a similar but larger and looser coalition. The French Government had proposed a new charter for public services in 1993, and later some interest was expressed by the Commission. In 1994 Jacques Delors, its then President, requested CEEP to draft a public service charter to give legitimacy to public services and to define more clearly the role of exclusive rights and obligations. In 1995 CEEP produced proposals to replace Article 90(2) (now Article 86(2)) with a new Article 94, which would clarify the objectives and obligations

---

[2] See in particular Kovar (1996) esp. 215–16, 219.

[3] Flynn (1999) 186 (footnote omitted).

[4] See generally Buendia Sierra (1999) 330–2; Egenhofer (1995) 155–60; Pelkmans (1997) 111–16.   [5] See http://www.ceep.org/ (consulted 15 July 2004).

of services of general interest as well as setting out the situations where exclusive rights would be permitted; these would be made more explicit in the new Charter.[6] The proposals were criticized, however; for example, '[t]he fundamental aim of these proposals was to establish an almost complete presumption of the legality of those monopolies granted for carrying out tasks of public service, so that the control of proportionality would be practically without any effect'.[7] This would clearly have gone much too far for the Commission and for supporters of the competition-oriented approach.

Indeed, the division of national opinion was also reflected in greater support for change within the various European institutions. The Parliament became a strong defender of the public service model.[8] In 1994, it passed a resolution to express its concern that the concepts of public service and of general interest were undefined, whilst guidelines on liberalizing markets were more clear-cut. Thus competition policy should be brought into harmony with the recognition of the public interest and citizens' rights to accessible public services, through the Commission taking the initiative in a public service charter identifying the common principles with which public services should comply to meet the requirements of true European citizenship and equal treatment.[9] The Heads of State and Government at the Cannes summit in 1995 also resolved that:

The European Council reiterates its concern that the introduction of greater competition into many sectors in order to complete the internal market should be compatible with the general economic tasks facing Europe, in particular balanced town and country planning, equal treatment for citizens – including equal rights and equal opportunities for men and women – the quality and performance of services to consumers and the safeguarding of long-term strategic interests.[10]

In the Commission itself, as has been mentioned above, the President had sought a draft charter from CEEP; later the Competition

---

[6] *Centre Européen des Entreprises à Participation Publique* (1995).

[7] Buendia Sierra (1999) 330–1.

[8] It has been suggested that this was 'for obvious electoral reasons'; Pelkmans (1997) 113.

[9] Resolution of the European Parliament, 6 May 94, Debates of the European Parliament No. 3-448/272, based on the report by Mr R. Speciale, on behalf of the Committee on Economic and Monetary Affairs and Industrial Policy, A3-0254/94/A.

[10] Cannes European Council, 26–7 June 1995, Conclusions of the Presidency – SN 211/95, point A.I.1.7.

Commissioner, Karel van Miert, suggested in a speech that more explicit recognition of the objectives of public service be added to the Treaty; he also found it necessary to defend the Commission against charges that it had been a 'liberalization machine, ultra-liberal and dogmatic'.[11] The most important development at this stage was however the Commission's 1996 Communication on services of general interest in Europe, and this will now be discussed in detail.

The 1996 Communication on Services of General Interest in Europe[12]

The next President of the Commission, Jacques Santer, formed a task force on services of general interest and produced this document, summarized by one observer as 'a horizontal, non-technical document, providing a general but politically useful contextual perspective, [which] identified a set of overall objectives, sketched the place of the various sectoral approaches and made a modest proposal for the treaty's revision'.[13]

The first point worth noting is that the title of the Communication refers to 'services of general interest', not services of 'general *economic* interest'. The definition of terms within it suggests that the former covers market and non-market services, whilst the latter refers only to market services, and this is the distinction which has usually been adopted; the former term is also useful in indicating that, although the activity must be economic to be covered by Article 86, the interest will in fact be social.[14] The change of emphasis indicated by the title does reflect a broadening of interest on the part of the Commission, although it will be recalled from the previous chapter that non-economic activities will be outside the scope of Community competence and so competition and freedom of movement rules will not be applied to them (although the scope of non-economic activities has narrowed in recent years).[15]

The Communication did not present new policy, but rather

in terms of explaining the rationale, the emphasis on the guaranteed public services and their quality, the connection to the internal market (hence, free

---

[11] *L'Europe, Vecteur de la Libéralisation*, 21 October 96, available at http://europa.eu.int/comm/competition/speeches/text/sp1996_053_fr.html (consulted 25 July 2004).
[12] COM(96)443 of 9 September 1996.   [13] Pelkmans (1997) 114.
[14] Buendia Sierra (1999) 278.   [15] See Szyszczak (2001) 39–42.

movement and some regulation, rather than competition per se), and the juxta-position of sectoral approaches, the communication does what is long overdue: justify liberalization in policy terms and show, without legal jargon and too much Eurospeak, that this presents no threat to universal service, affordability, solid-arity, or equal treatment.[16]

It actually commenced by acknowledging the importance of '[s]olidarity and equal treatment within an open and dynamic market economy' as fundamental Community objectives, and states that general interest services, often regarded as social rights that make an important con-tribution to economic and social coherence, are 'at the heart of the European model of society'.[17] It noted that services of general interest play an important role as 'social cement', have a symbolic value and form part of the cultural identity of everyday life. They require certain basic operating principles: continuity, equal access, universality, and open-ness.[18] On the other hand, '[m]arket forces produce a better allocation of resources and greater effectiveness in the supply of services, the principal beneficiary being the consumer, who gets better quality at a lower price'.[19] Market forces nevertheless have their limits, and, according to the Communication the Community's approach was based on respect for diversity in the organization of services of general interest, under-pinned by the principles of neutrality on public or private ownership[20] and freedom of Member States to define general interest services and, within the limits of Community law, to grant them exclusive rights and to fund them. In turn this was an application of the principle of subsidiarity, but exceptions to the single market rules must be subject to the test of proportionality. This principle

is designed to ensure the best match between the duty to provide general interest services and the way in which the services are actually provided ... The principle is formulated to allow for a flexible and context-sensitive balance that takes account of the Member States' different circumstances and objectives as well as the technical and budgetary constraints that may vary from one sector to another. It also makes for the best possible interaction between market efficiency and general interest requirements ... [21]

Having stated these general considerations, the second part of the Communication proceeded to summarize progress in sectoral liberal-ization and in the development of universal service obligations; these will

---

[16] Pelkmans (1997) 115.   [17] 1996 Communication (above n. 12), para. 1.
[18] Ibid., paras. 6–8.   [19] Ibid., para. 15.
[20] See Article 295 of the Treaty.   [21] 1996 Communication (above n. 12), para. 21.

be discussed in detail in the following chapter. It then set out the Commission's objectives for the future. These were summarized as, firstly, introducing evaluation tools to assess the operation, performance, and competence of services of general interest on a sector-by-sector basis.[22] Greater openness was to be adopted, for example through publishing a communication on the application of what is now Article 86 and through more consultation; there could be greater coordination of national general economic interest bodies in matters such as public financing arrangements and control systems, and further development of the universal service concept.[23] Further Community measures would be taken in relation to matters such as trans-European networks where commitments had already been made by Heads of Government, and the Community could offer further support to national and regional government in the provision of other general interest services such as health, welfare, education, water, and housing.[24]

On the issue of Treaty Amendment, the Commission firmly rejected change to Article 90 (now Article 86), which 'has proved its worth in fully guaranteeing the beneficial interaction between liberalization and general interest. It is best left untouched.'[25] However, 'the role of services of general interest in the development of the concept of European citizenship should be commensurate with the place they occupy among the shared values on which the European societies are founded'.[26] Thus a new subparagraph should be added to the list of activities of the Community in the Principles section of the Treaty to cover 'a contribution to the promotion of services of general interest'.[27] This would not create any new legal base for Community action but would 'establish that general interest services are something which the Community should take into account when drawing up its policies and planning its activities'.[28]

In the 1996 Communication there was thus a welcome recognition of the value of services of general interest, but they were placed firmly within a single market context; despite the autonomy given to Member States in the organization of these services, their legitimate role was limited to cases of market failure.[29] The proposals for future promotion and improvement of such services were relatively modest. Against this background, the importance of the Amsterdam Treaty amendments of the following year comes as something of a surprise.

---

[22] 1996 communication (above n. 12), para. 61.   [23] Para. 64.   [24] Paras. 66–9.
[25] Para. 71.   [26] Para. 72.   [27] Para. 73.   [28] Para. 74.   [29] See para. 15.

The Amsterdam Treaty

The debate on the appropriate Community model for services of general interest continued in the Intergovernmental Conference culminating in the Amsterdam Treaty signed in October 1997. Once more, a number of different proposals for reform were made; thus the French and German Governments proposed revising the Treaty to recognize and guarantee a universal right of access to services of general interest;[30] CEEP reiterated its proposals for the replacement of what has become Article 86(2)[31] with a new Article to establish a balance between competition and public service, together with a European charter of services of general economic interest. The Parliament also called for amendment of several Treaty articles, including what is now Article 86, and resolved once more that 'fundamental principles of public service, i.e. accessibility, universality, equality, continuity, quality, transparency, and participation in the context of the single market and respecting the principle of subsidiarity, should be incorporated in the Treaty'.[32] There was thus considerable support for some degree of reform, and indeed, when it is recalled that the Commission itself also favoured limited Treaty amendment, 'there do not seem to have been any public defenders of a retention of pre-existing broad application of the competition rules'.[33]

The outcome in the Treaty of Amsterdam was different from anything which had been proposed earlier, reflecting considerable political division within the Conference between the Member States favouring major Treaty amendment and those, including the UK, which would only support very limited change as they believed that the current Treaty provisions ensured an adequate balance between competition policy and the needs of public services. What was eventually agreed was a French-inspired amendment adding a new Article 16 to the Treaty, placed within Part I of the Treaty covering fundamental principles of the Community. Although it has been discussed in the previous chapter, it is worth repeating the provisions here:

Without prejudice to Articles 77, 90 and 92, and given the place occupied by services of general economic interest in the shared values of the Union as well as

---

[30] For criticism of such a right see Buendia Sierra (1999) 332.   [31] Then Article 90(2).
[32] Resolution of the European Parliament on the Intergovernmental Conference [1996] OJ C96/77, point 11.3; Flynn (1999) 197.   [33] Flynn (1999) 197.

their role in promoting social and territorial cohesion, the Community and the Member States, each within their respective powers and within the scope of application of this Treaty, shall take care that such services operate on the basis of principles and conditions which enable them to fulfil their missions.

A Declaration stated that these provisions should be implemented 'with full respect for the jurisprudence of the Court of Justice, inter alia as regards the principles of equality of treatment, quality and continuity of such services'.[34] Finally, there was also an important Protocol on public broadcasting, which will be discussed in detail in Chapter 9 below. The Amsterdam changes took effect from 1 May 1999.

As I discussed in the previous chapter, Article 16 is a highly opaque provision whose interpretation has given rise to much difficulty, although so far there has been no help from the Court of Justice in the form of an authoritative decision on it. In an important and sophisticated account of the possible meanings of the Article, Ross has suggested three possible meanings.[35] The first is that it makes no legal difference to the pre-existing position and is merely a 'political gloss'.[36] This view is shared by Buendia Sierra, who maintains that if anything it could result in a less flexible interpretation of Article 86(2) because it may seem weaker than the latter's requirement of not impeding the fulfilment of tasks of general economic interest.[37] Ross rejects this interpretation of the Article on the ground that it cannot represent the intention of the Member States involved, and this seems correct. The second possible meaning is that it enlarges the national competence of Member States in relation to services of general economic interest. This would seem more probable, particularly given the forceful claims made by the countries which campaigned most vociferously for change that their own powers to provide public services were being threatened by liberalization. However, Ross also considers this interpretation to be inadequate as, rather than simply ceding decision-making to Member States, Article 16 is a 'clarification of the values embedded in the Community regime of control'.[38] He favours a third interpretation; that Article 16 is not merely a derogation from the Treaty rules, but places an obligation on both Member States and the Community to take care that services of general interest operate on the basis of principles and conditions which enable them to fulfil their

---

[34] Treaty of Amsterdam, Art. 2(8) and Declaration on Art. 7d of the Treaty Establishing the European Community.   [35] Ross (2000) 28–38.
[36] Ibid., 28.   [37] Buendia Sierra (1999) 333.   [38] Ross (2000) 30.

missions: 'Article 16 seems to envisage a duty to facilitate the achievement of general service missions.'[39] However, this remains subject to the *acquis* of the established competition law jurisprudence. Indeed, the values represented by services of general interest can provide the basis for developing a concept of European citizenship.[40] A radical interpretation of the Article has also been suggested by Flynn: '[I]t is clear that, post-Maastricht, the idea that the process of European integration can proceed as though it were no more than a functionalist and technocratic matter has lost its dominant character.'[41]

The radical interpretation of Article 16 has been criticized on the ground that it does not in fact represent such a fundamental change of direction; both before and after Amsterdam, the emphasis has been on 'the delivery of public services *through* competitive markets' and services of general interest 'are being manipulated to further the process of market integration and liberalization'.[42] A definitive answer to these questions must await further decisions by the Commission and the Court of Justice, but there has certainly been a growing interest since Amsterdam in clarification by means other than Treaty amendment of the approach to be taken to services of general interest. These developments do suggest a growing recognition of the positive value of services of general interest as expressions of citizenship rights.

The 2000 Communication on Services of General Interest in Europe[43]

The Lisbon Summit in March 2000 requested an updating of the 1996 Communication and this was quickly published. The objectives of the new Communication included to 'further develop the European framework relating to the good functioning of services of general interest', in line with Article 16, and this theme was particularly strong in the new Communication, suggesting that the first effect of Article 16 was to inspire a stronger positive programme from the Commission to ensure that services of general interest operate transparently and effectively to meet the needs of citizens.[44] Thus '[I]n order to fulfil their mission, it is necessary for the relevant public authorities to act in full transparency, by

---

[39] Ibid., 32.   [40] Ibid., 37.   [41] Flynn (1999) 198.
[42] Szyszczak (2001) 64 (emphasis retained).   [43] COM/2000/0580 final.   [44] Para. 6.

stipulating with some precision the needs of users for which services of general interest are being established, who is in charge of setting up and enforcing the relevant obligations and how these obligations are going to be fulfilled.'[45] Moreover, '[f]or consumers, a guarantee of universal access, high quality and affordability constitute the basis of their needs'.[46] Principles to help define users' requirements included:

- clear definition of basic obligations to ensure good quality service provision, high levels of public health and physical safety of services;
- full transparency e.g. on tariffs, terms and conditions of contracts, choice and financing of providers;
- choice of service and where appropriate, choice of supplier and effective competition between suppliers;
- existence, where justified, of regulatory bodies independent of operators and redress in the form of complaint handling and dispute settlement mechanisms.

They might also include representation and active participation of users in the definition of services and choice of forms of payment.[47]

What we see here is thus a positive programme to improve the operation of public services, based on measures already taken in the liberalized sectors. There is still a reference to the work of CEEP and the European Trades Union Confederation in proposing a public service charter, but this is merely referred to as 'an important contribution to the current debate' rather than as a forthcoming development.[48] The Communication accepted that '[t]he existence of a network of services of general interest is an essential element of social cohesion; conversely, the disappearance of such services is a telling sign of the desertification of a rural area or the degradation of a town. The Community is committed to maintaining the function of these services intact, while improving their efficiency.'[49] This was used to justify a 'pro-active stance on general interest services, which incorporates and goes beyond the approach based on the single market'.[50] In an interesting reference, the Commission stated that '[t]he special place of services of general economic interest in the shared values of the Union, recognized by Article 16 of the Treaty, calls for a parallel recognition of the link between access to services of general interest and European citizenship'.[51] It was also made clear that the Community is committed to maintaining services of general interest in WTO negotiations.[52]

---

[45] 2000 Communication (above n. 43), para. 9.   [46] Para. 10.   [47] Para. 11.
[48] Para. 12.   [49] Para. 54.   [50] Para. 57.   [51] Para. 64.   [52] Para. 67.

We do see here a shift in emphasis, and one which gives support for the more radical reading of Article 16. The link between services of general interest and European citizenship is accepted, at least as a matter of general principle, and, rather than seeing the former as obstacles to the completion of a competitive single market, it portrays them positively as an important contribution to the values of European life. However, this contribution may be marred by inefficient operation and ineffective delivery of services; hence the need to develop effective tools for the evaluation of the operation of services of general interest.

Developments Since the 2000 Communication: Towards a Framework Directive?

Since 2000 there has been considerable activity in relation to each of these themes. As regards citizenship, the most important development has of course been the new Article 36 of the Charter of Fundamental Rights, adopted at the end of that year. This is entitled *Access to Services of General Economic Interest* and provides that:

The Union recognizes and respects access to services of general economic interest as provided for in national laws and practices, in accordance with the Treaty establishing the European Community, in order to promote the social and territorial cohesion of the Union.

This raises difficulties in a number of respects. Apart from the vagueness of the terms 'recognizes and respects', the Community lacks the competence and resources necessary to guarantee social rights of this kind, as Buendia Sierra has pointed out.[53] Thus the effect of the Article can only be to reinforce Article 16 by imposing a negative obligation not to hinder the actions of Member States promoting such access. A further limitation is that the Charter is not directly incorporated into the Treaty, but was instead promulgated in a declaratory form through the institutions of the Union, thus denying it full legal effect.[54] The new Constitutional Treaty based on the work of the Constitutional Convention will retain Article 36 unchanged as Article II-36.

[53] Buendia Sierra (1999) 332.
[54] Solemn Proclamation of the European Parliament, the Commission and the Council of 7 December 2000, OJ 2000 No. C364/1, and see Shaw (2001) 199.

In relation to a further major theme of the 2000 Communication, that of the evaluation of the effectiveness of services of general interest, a new Communication was published in 2002 setting out the proposed methodology, which was to include both evaluation of each sector and horizontal evaluation of the effectiveness of services of general economic interest as a whole.[55] A baseline had been provided by a report already published.[56] Further progress was reported in the Commission's report to the Laeken European Council in 2001.[57] The Commission proposed various measures to develop legal certainty and transparency in this area. A Community framework for state aid granted to undertakings entrusted with the provision of services of general economic interest would be developed, and certain aids in this area might be exempted from the requirement of prior notification.[58] It had been suggested that a list be drawn up of services of general interest that are of a non-economic nature; however, although a list of examples could be drawn up, the Commission considered that a definitive a priori list would not be possible as an abstract definition would be very difficult and the range of services is constantly evolving.[59] The Commission would also add a specific section to its annual report on competition policy covering services of general interest.

On the now controversial question of the selection of the provider of a service of general economic interest, the Commission reiterated that the procedures in the public procurement directives should be followed if they were applicable and, even if not, the choice of supplier should be made transparent through advertising and the impartiality of procurement procedures; this would apply to service concessions and other forms of public–private partnership. Further detail was provided on the evaluation of performance, including sectoral and horizontal reporting; the latter would include an economic and social assessment of public service obligations. Most innovatively, however, the Report contains a section on 'Developing the Principles of Article 16'. It had been suggested that

---

[55] *A Methodological Note for the Horizontal Evaluation of Services of General Economic Interest*, COM(2002)331 final.

[56] *Market Performance of Network Industries Providing Services of General Interest: A First Horizontal Assessment*, SEC(2001)1998, annexed to the *Report on the Functioning of Product and Capital Markets*, COM(2001)736 final.

[57] *Report to the Laeken European Council: Services of General Interest*, COM(2001)598.

[58] Paras. 28–9. See also the Commissions 'Non-Paper' *Services of General Economic Interest and State Aid*, November 2002. The preparation of such a framework was delayed by the legal uncertainty discussed in the previous chapter.   [59] Para. 30.

the principles on services of general economic interest underlying Article 16, which had previously been implemented through sectoral policies, could be consolidated and specified in a single framework directive. This would 'highlight the importance the European Union attaches to services of general interest and could help to clarify some of the relevant Community law concepts, in full respect of the principle of subsidiarity'.[60] The Commission would examine the suggestion; although a general framework directive could not replace sector-specific regulation and could only set minimum standards, 'a Directive should match the high level of our ambition'.[61] The Commission also referred to the possibility of a new subparagraph being added to Article 3 of the Treaty to include within the activities of the Community 'a contribution to the promotion of services of general interest'.[62]

In 2001 the European Parliament also called for a framework Directive on services of general interest.[63] The most important development in this respect occurred at the Barcelona Summit in the summer of 2002. The French Government made its acceptance of further energy liberalization conditional on an obligation on the Commission to propose by the end of the year a framework Directive on services of general economic interest.[64] This was accepted; the summit asked the Commission to continue its work on consolidating and specifying principles on services of general economic interest, and to present a report by the end of 2002.[65] The Commission decided 'that it would first prepare a consultation document in the form of a Green Paper concerning a possible framework directive, thereby engaging in an exercise to take stock of all the EU's policies in the area of [services of general interest] and reviewing them with regard to their coherence and consistency'.[66] The report was published in May 2003.

The 2003 Green Paper[67]

The Green Paper was intended as the start of a debate and set out thirty questions on which views were sought as part of a consultation process.

---

[60] Para. 51.   [61] Ibid.   [62] Para. 52.

[63] Resolution of 13 November 2001, OJ C140 E, 13 June 2002.

[64] 'L'ouverture des services publics reste un casus belli avec 'Bruxelles', *Le Monde*, 3 juin 2002.

[65] Presidency Conclusions of the Barcelona European Council, 15 and 16 March 2002, para. 42.

[66] European Commission, *Report on Thirty-Second Competition Policy 2002* (2003), point 589.

[67] *Green Paper on Services of General Interest*, COM(2003)270 final.

It is thus no criticism to suggest that it was very 'green' in nature, setting out the existing legal position and suggesting tentative developments for the future. Nevertheless, some elements in it are suggestive of important points of principle. In the paper a strongly positive approach was taken to the role of services of general interest; they are 'essential for increasing quality of life for all citizens and for overcoming social exclusion and isolation'.[68] Moreover, 'these services are a pillar of European citizenship, forming some of the rights enjoyed by European citizens and providing an opportunity for dialogue with public authorities within the context of good governance'.[69] Thus the link with citizenship which had developed more explicitly since the Amsterdam Treaty was further developed here. Indeed, the Amsterdam provisions 'are important elements in the development of the process of European integration: from the economic sphere towards broader issues relating to the European model of society, to the concept of European citizenship and to the relations between every individual in the Union and the public authorities'.[70] The Paper also pointed to the positive outcomes of sectoral liberalization of some services of general economic interest.[71]

The debate launched by the Paper was intended to raise questions in four categories:

- the scope of possible Community action;
- the principles that could be included in a framework directive or other instrument concerning services of general interest;
- the definition of good governance in the area of organization, regulation, financing, and evaluation of services of general interest to ensure both greater competitiveness and efficient and equitable access; and
- measures that could contribute to increasing legal certainty and to 'ensuring a coherent and harmonious link between the objective of maintaining high-quality services of general interest and rigorous application of competition and internal market rules'.[72]

Thus there was an evolving refocussing of the debate to include not only compatibility of services of general interest with the competition rules, but to examine principles of good governance which can be applied to them. The principles were drawn from a number of sources, the most important of which was experience in sectoral liberalization and

---

[68] *Green Paper* (above n. 67), para. 2.   [69] Ibid.   [70] Para. 8.   [71] Paras. 5–6.
[72] Para. 12.

regulation, whilst others included the application of Article 16 and the Commission's own White Paper on governance.[73]

The Paper made the familiar distinction between services of general interest and those of general *economic* interest, now defining the former as covering both market and non-market services which the public authorities classed as being of general interest and subject to specific public service obligations; the latter services of an economic nature subject to specific public service obligations by virtue of a general public interest criterion.[74] Thus there was now a more explicit stress than previously on the necessity of specific public service obligations; these could be applied at Community, national, or local levels.[75] The generic term 'public service' was not used given its imprecision and reference also to the ownership status of an undertaking.

As regards Community competence, in the context of subsidiarity, the Paper noted that '[s]ervices of general interest linked to the function of welfare and social protection are clearly a matter of national, regional, and local responsibilities. Nevertheless, there is a recognized role for the Community in promoting co-operation and co-ordination in these areas.'[76] Thus there was a suggestion of the extension of Community interest into non-economic services of general interest. It was noted that these were anyway covered by other Community rules, such as the principle of non-discrimination.[77] The Paper stressed that the distinction between economic and non-economic services is in any case a difficult one, as the two may exist in the same sector and may even be provided by the same organization; moreover, the range of services which can be provided in a market evolves over time, and more and more activities have become of economic relevance.[78] Thus it would be neither feasible nor desirable to provide a definitive a priori list of all non-economic services of general interest, although it might be possible to specify criteria for deciding more clearly.[79] It was suggested in Chapter 6 above that such criteria are sorely needed.

The Paper also asked whether a Community regulatory framework should also be established for services other than the large network industries (the latter will be discussed in the next chapter), and whether experience from sector-specific regulation, for example in electronic

---

[73] *Commission White Paper on European Governance*, COM(2001)428, 25 July 2001.
[74] Paras. 16–17.   [75] Para. 20.   [76] Para. 31.   [77] Paras. 32, 43.
[78] Paras. 44–5.   [79] Paras. 45–8.

communications and energy, can provide the basis for the development of 'a common European framework...in order to ensure coherent implementation of the principles underlying Article 16 of the Treaty at Community level'.[80] This illustrates an important theme throughout the Green Paper; that experience in the liberalized sectors may provide a basis for the development of general principles applicable to services of general economic interest as a whole; examples given are principles relating to universal service, continuity, quality of service, affordability, and user and consumer protection.[81] These concepts were discussed in considerable detail, aided by an annex to the Paper which described a set of public service obligations that could be derived from existing sector-specific Community legislation and could characterize a Community concept of services of general economic interest.[82] These principles share both elements from French *service public* and the policies of UK regulators. More will be said on this aspect of the Green Paper in the following chapter.

The Paper then considered issues of good governance, discussing the definition and enforcement of obligations and choice of organization to deliver services of general interest, the financing of such services, and their evaluation. On definition, the freedom of Member States was stressed once more, although public service requirements should be properly specified, and the procurement directives or general Community law would apply to the choice of organization, creating the need for a transparent selection process.[83] Various means of financing were open to Member States, including tariff averaging to create a uniform national tariff independent of costs, so long as these did not distort unduly the functioning of the internal market.[84] Interestingly, the Paper stated:

[o]ther relevant criteria for selecting a financing mechanism, such as its efficiency or its redistributive effects, are currently not taken into account in Community legislation. Neither have the effects of the selected mechanism on the long-term investment of providers of services and infrastructure and on security of supply been specifically considered...At this stage, the Commission considers it appropriate to launch a debate on whether these criteria could lead to the conclusion that specific funding mechanisms should be preferred and whether the Community should take measures in favour of specific funding mechanisms.[85]

---

[80] *White Paper* (above n. 73), paras. 36–7.   [81] Para. 49.   [82] Paras. 49–73 and Annex.
[83] Paras. 80–1.   [84] Paras. 86–8.   [85] Paras. 91–2.

The questions for consultation included whether the consequences and criteria of solidarity-based funding should be clarified at Community level.

The section on evaluation of services of general interest built on the earlier work discussed above, stating also that '[a] comprehensive evaluation must be multidisciplinary and multidimensional and include political, economic, social, and environmental aspects, including externalities'.[86] The Paper concluded with a brief discussion of services of general interest in the context of globalization and the World Trade Organization.

Consultation and the White Paper

Comments were sought on the thirty questions set out in the paper; it is interesting to note, incidentally, that national responses show vividly the underlying differences in approach documented in this book. Thus that from the UK Government was strongly opposed to the establishment of a common framework of cross-sectoral public service obligations at EU level, and continually stressed that any change should be made within specific sectors only: '[t]he Green Paper does not make a convincing case for a common concept of services of general economic interest'.[87] By contrast that of the French Government stated that 'the French authorities want the Community framework for the provision of services of general economic interest . . . to be clarified and enriched' whilst also stressing the importance of the principle of subsidiarity and of the need for discretion on the part of Member States in defining public service missions and choosing the means of financing them. It also denied that there was a general principle (as opposed to requirements in specific sectors) that regulation must be independent of government supervision over public operators.[88]

---

[86] Para. 96.

[87] United Kingdom Permanent Representatives to the European Union, *UK Government Response to the Green Paper of Services of General Interest* (2003), available at http://europa.eu.int/comm/secretariat_general/services_general_interest/docs/public_authorities/repress_uk.pdf (consulted 15 July 2004), para. 21; see also paras. 6, 9, 14, 15, 24, 25, 27, and 28.

[88] French Republic, *Memorandum of the French Authorities re Answers to the Questionnaire in the Green Paper on Services of General Interest Presented by the European Commission* (2003), available at http://europa.eu.int/comm/secretariat_general/services_general_interest/docs/public_authorities/pic_en.pdf (consulted 15 July 2004), 1, 3, 4, 7.

There was in fact an overall lack of consensus in the replies to the consultation, including whether it was feasible to establish common principles applicable to all services of general economic interest, and whether a framework Directive was necessary.[89] As a result, it is not surprising that the White Paper that resulted was extremely cautious.[90] It reported a consensus on the importance of services of general interest as one of the pillars of the European model of society, both for citizens as necessary for full enjoyment of fundamental rights, and for enterprises as an indispensable prerequisite for a competitive business environment.[91] Universal service was also seen as essential for social and territorial cohesion. However it was also necessary to respect the diversity of different types of services, for example the difference between social and health services and network industries. Given the lack of consensus on the matter of a framework Directive, the Commission decided to re-examine this issue after the coming into force of the Constitutional Treaty, which would provide a new legal base for such a Directive.[92]

More immediate steps would be taken to clarify the position of compensation for public service obligations, through a decision which would exempt small-scale funding from the need for notification, and to do the same for funding of services of general economic interest provided by hospitals and social housing irrespective of the amounts involved. A framework would be published for the assessment of other compensation for such services, and further clarification would be given on the circumstances in which it constitutes state aid, including the distinction between economic and non-economic activities.[93] A communication would also be issued on social and health services of general interest to identify their special characteristics and to clarify the framework in which they operate.[94] As regards institutional arrangements, the Paper also emphasized the importance of the existence of independent regulators with clearly defined powers and duties to protect user rights, and the need to provide a clearer framework for the selection of undertakings entrusted with a service of general interest, particularly in their provision by means of public–private partnerships.[95]

---

[89] See Commission of the European Communities, *Report on the Public Consultation on the Green Paper on Services of General Interest*, COM(2004)326.

[90] Commission of the European Communities, *Communication from the Commission to the European Parliament, the Council, the European Economic and Social Committee and the Committee of the Regions: White Paper on Services of General Interest*, COM(2004)374.   [91] S. 2.1.

[92] S. 4.1.   [93] S. 4.2.   [94] S. 4.4.   [95] Ss. 3.5, 4.3.

To summarize the two papers of 2003–4, the Green Paper was clearly of very great importance and illustrated some key emerging themes. No longer was the central stress on compatibility of services of general interest with the internal market; rather it was on the essential role of such services for citizenship and, in particular, how their performance could be improved. There is also some suggestion that non-economic factors might be taken into account more fully in Community policy in relation to such services. The White Paper was cautious in its proposals, which consisted almost entirely of soft law rather than a binding framework Directive, but did promise a potentially important clarification of some major issues, especially in relation to health and social services.

The Convention and the Constitutional Treaty

Before concluding this chapter something needs to be said about developments at the constitutional level. The European Convention reported in 2003 with a draft Constitutional Treaty for Europe. Within the Convention there had been calls for further constitutionalization of services of general interest, for example by recognizing their role in the first part of the Treaty as guarantees of fundamental rights, elements of the model of social Europe, and links between citizen and society. It was also proposed by some Members to insert into a modified Article 16 the principles of neutrality, equal access, universality, quality, transparency, and the precautionary principle, and explicitly to recognize the right of public authorities to supply services themselves.[96] The Working Group on Social Europe was in the end unable to reach agreement on this matter; a substantial number of its members had wanted a clause on social values in the Treaty, including as an objective that the Union aim 'to guarantee universal accessibility of services of general interest which are financially viable, of high quality and organized on the basis of solidarity by individual Member States'.[97] Some members wanted a new legal basis for the Union to adopt framework legislation at European level in this area. However, others considered that existing competences were sufficient, including the UK which considered that amendment of Article 16

---

[96] European Convention, *Contribution from Ms Marie Nagy, alternate member, and Mr Johanes Voggenhuber, member, of the Convention: 'Services of general interest'*, Contrib 178, CONV 468/02.
[97] European Convention, *Final Report of Working Group XI on Social Europe*, CG XI 9, CONV 516/1/03, REV 1, para. 20.

would result in a substantial expansion of Community competence in fields such as social security and education 'by the back door'.[98] Thus the question of the amendment of Article 16 was remitted to the Convention itself.[99]

In the Constitutional Treaty produced by the Convention the changes to the relevant articles are minor. Apart from drafting changes, the only one of substance is to the new Article III-6 (the former Article 16), which states that European laws shall define the principles and conditions which will enable services of general economic interest to fulfil their missions, thereby providing clearer competence for the issue of a framework Directive. The Treaty was agreed in June 2004, but considerable uncertainly remains as to the eventual outcome given the need for national ratification before it comes into force.

Conclusion

In this chapter we have seen important and fundamental changes in the Community approach to services of general interest, including those of general economic interest. Initially they were seen as something of an irritant, limiting the creation of a full internal market. Now a much more positive view is taken, despite only cautious substantive proposals in the 2004 White Paper. Such services are confirmed an essential element of European citizenship and, rather than the main question being that of how their operation can be restricted and remodelled to become compatible with the single market, it is of how their operation can be improved and made both more efficient and more responsive to social values such as those underlying universal service. This has provided a means by which the values of public service (although the term is disliked by the Commission) can be brought into the European law relating to services of general interest; as we shall see in the next chapter, the adoption of British ideas of independent regulators as a source of improved service quality has also been important.

This change of emphasis is no doubt partly due to the near-completion of the single market project, thus creating the opportunity to consider other values than those of the market; the Commission can no longer be credibly characterized as a 'liberalization machine'. However, we can also

---

[98] House of Lords European Union Select Committee, *The Future of Europe, 'Social Europe'* HC 93 (2002–3), para. 35.   [99] *Final Report of Working Group XI*, op. cit., para. 35.

identify two other reasons for the shift in emphasis. The first is that of the constitutionalization of the role of services of general interest in Article 16 of the Treaty; although its implications are not yet fully evident, what is clear is that it has led to renewed interest in the role and values of services of general interest both in themselves and as attributes of European citizenship. In this sense it seems that the more radical interpretations of the Article are the correct ones. Secondly, the Community has now acquired considerable experience in the liberalized but regulated sectors such as electronic communications (formerly tele-communications) and energy. In combination with developing interest in good governance within the Community,[100] this has provided a sub-stantial body of experience which can now be generalized to other areas of services of general interest. This experience will be the subject of the next chapter. For the moment, though, I can conclude by suggesting that there has been much fuller debate, and much more developed consideration given, to the relationship between public service and competitive markets at the European than at the UK level. Although we may disagree with their substantive proposals for change, for this we must be grateful to CEEP, ISUPE, and the French and Belgian Governments.

---

[100] See in particular the *White Paper on European Governance.*

8

European Liberalization and Public Service Obligations

Introduction

The previous two chapters have analysed general developments in European Community competition law relating to services of general interest and examined the approach of the Commission to such services. These chapters have suggested that we can see emerging a greater recognition of the value of these services and of the need for its legal restatement. Especially since the incorporation of the new Article 16 of the Treaty, services of general interest have been treated less as an unwelcome hindrance to the completion of the internal market and more as an expression of citizenship rights and so of value in themselves, the emphasis shifting to how they can be delivered more effectively. Alongside these developments, there has been a considerable degree of liberalization of utilities as a result of Community law, and in these the protection of public service goals has assumed particular importance.

The degree of liberalization varies from sector to sector. Thus it is extensive in telecommunications, or electronic communications as they are now referred to in order to reflect their convergence with other media, and is in the process of becoming far-reaching in energy. In postal services competition is less developed but has proved especially controversial given the importance attached by many Member States to the maintenance of universal service at uniform prices. In transport, in the case of most of the sector, such as rail, liberalization has been extremely limited (for reasons both of the nature of the industry and of politics) but currently controversial proposals concern the granting of public service contracts and payment of compensation for public service obligations. In aviation, liberalization has been taken further than in any other of the sectors examined, but still remains subject to limited opportunities for Member States to impose and fund public service obligations.

The aim of this chapter will not be to examine liberalization in general in these sectors; a number of excellent texts already do this and will be referred to where appropriate. Rather it will be to assess the extent to which citizenship rights and collective public service goals are protected within the newly liberalized markets, and to examine the techniques used to achieve these goals. A further aim will be to compare the protection of public service goals in Community liberalization with that in domestic liberalization described in Chapter 4 above. It will be recalled that in most of these areas the UK liberalized before Community law did so; public service goals have been secured by the utility regulators and, although a substantial amount of work has been carried out by them which can be seen as protecting public service values, this has been incoherent and uncoordinated. One question in this chapter will be to ask whether the effects of the more developed Community background discussed in the previous two chapters, and in particular the form of constitutional protection for services of general economic interest now given by Article 16, have provided the basis for a more coherent protection of public service values than we have seen in the UK's domestic law and regulatory policy.

Before considering each of the sectors in turn, it should first be noted that, taking them together, the liberalized sectors do appear to have common techniques and conceptual approaches to the protection of public service goals. This is a theme emphasized in the recent Green Paper on Services of General Interest, discussed in the preceding chapter.[1] Thus the Paper begins by emphasizing that 'these services are a pillar of European citizenship, forming some of the rights enjoyed by European citizens and providing an opportunity for dialogue with public authorities within the context of good governance'.[2] The legal provisions relating to such services 'are important elements in the development of the process of European integration: from the economic sphere towards broader issues relating to the European model of society, to the concept

---

[1] Commission of the European Communities, *Green Paper on Services of General Interest*, COM(2003)270 final (2003).   [2] Ibid., para. 2

of European citizenship and to the relations between every individual in the Union and the public authorities'.[3] Within this context the Green Paper then suggests that the existing Community legislation 'contains a number of common elements which can be drawn on to define a useful Community concept of services of general economic interest',[4] and these elements are then set down in some detail.[5]

The common elements are, firstly, universal service; according to the Green Paper, '[d]uring the last two decades, the concept of universal service has developed into a major and indispensable pillar of the Community's policy on services of general interest'.[6] The second element is continuity requiring that service be operated without interruption (directly reflecting the French concept of *service public* discussed in Chapter 5 above), and the third, quality of service, especially in relation to postal services and electronic communications. The fourth element is affordability, requiring a service of general economic interest to be offered at an affordable price in order to be accessible for everyone. The fifth is user and consumer protection. In addition there are some further specific requirements which are sector-specific; these are safety and security, security of supply (an important concern in the energy industries), network access and interconnectivity (especially in electronic communications) and media pluralism (to be discussed briefly in Chapter 9 below).

Together these common principles and the means for their implementation may be seen as forming part of a Community *acquis* relating to services of general interest; this can be further developed by examining them against concerns for good governance and for evaluating performance, themes in the rest of the Green Paper. However, not all these principles are present in every liberalized sector, and their implementation, and indeed the respective roles of the Community institutions and of the Member States, varies from sector to sector, as is apparent in the more cautious White Paper issued after consultation.[7] Thus in the rest of this chapter I shall examine the protection of public service goals sector by sector, returning to the more general issues in the conclusion.

---

[3] *Green Paper* (above n. 1), para. 8.   [4] Ibid., para. 49.   [5] Ibid., s. 3.1 and Annex.
[6] Ibid., para. 53.
[7] *Communication from the Commission to the European Parliament, the Council, the European Economic and Social Committee and the Committee of the Regions, White Paper on Services of General Interest*, COM(2004)374, ss. 4.1, 4.6.

Telecommunications and Electronic Communications

The Liberalization of Telecommunications Services and Infrastructure

Telecommunications (now, as we shall see, referred to as electronic communications) represent the most developed area of liberalization in European Community utilities policy.[8] Thus, as well as using competition law to abolish monopolies in the telecommunications field, directives were used to open and re-regulate the internal market in telecommunications, notably the Open Network Provision Directive, the Interconnection Directive, and the Voice Telephony Directive.[9] The key date in this process was 1 January 1998 when special and exclusive rights for voice telephony were abolished (subject to limited transition periods for certain Member States) and the new regulatory framework established. More recently a new package of directives has been introduced covering all electronic communications services.

From the outset, the concept of universal service played a major role in this liberalization process. It had its origins in a rather different context, that of the development of a private monopoly system of telecommunications in the United States permitting universal interconnection; that is, that all users could connect to each other using the same system.[10] However, in the European debates it came to mean something different: the principle of universal access. It has been summarized as 'the idea that at the current level of societal development, every person, regardless of his or her geographical location, should have the right to be connected to the public telephone system, at a reasonable (or affordable) price'.[11] This emphasizes geographic universal service, that services should be available in all parts of the Community, even those most isolated where provision of services may be most expensive. More recently, as we shall see later, the concept of social or distributive universal service has become increasingly important, which emphasizes the importance of ensuring that even the most deprived groups in the

---

[8] For detailed accounts of liberalization see Koenig, Bartosch, and Braun (2002) and especially Nihoul and Rodford (2004), ch. 5 of which deals with universal service in exhaustive detail. For a summary introduction see also Hammer (2002). An excellent and detailed account of the development of the principles of universal service is Sauter (1998).

[9] Hammer (2002) 61–2; details will be provided below.

[10] See Sauter (1998) 118–20; Mueller (1993).   [11] Sauter (1998) 120.

population have access to at least a basic telecommunications service as a necessary means for participation in modern life.[12]

Before liberalization, the monopoly providers had not succeeded in meeting the goals of universal service provision:

Quality standards and the concept of affordability were practically unheard of: universal service was not targeted on the basis of need. Further where *de jure* universal service obligations did exist, they were not always honoured in practice. Until a few years ago, it was not unusual for citizens of a number of EC Member States to have to wait a year or more for a connection: for example the OECD average for 1980 was fifteen months...Clearly, in some Member States, universal service was not more than a legal fiction, if that.[13]

Bearing this in mind, an emphasis on universal service had two particular advantages in the early stage of liberalization; it suggested that reform could bring real benefits for domestic consumers, and it could also do something to counter opposition on the part of national governments to the (controversial) introduction of competition.

The first stage of the liberalization of telecommunications commenced with the publication of the 1987 Green Paper.[14] This accepted that exclusive and special rights could be maintained where necessary to guarantee the public service role of telecommunications providers; 'under the compromise of the 1987 Green Paper, universal service as "public service" clearly remained under the competence of individual Member States, and in practice, the obligation to provide universal service was hereby limited to the dominant [telecommunications operators]'.[15] As the initial limited liberalization of services was developed to include voice services a clearer definition of universal service at the Community level became more important, and the potential of liberalization was increased by the Court's upholding of the Commission's right to proceed independently of Member States through the issue of Directives under Article 90(3).[16] In 1993 the Council accepted the principle of full liberalization of voice telephony, whilst also recognizing the need to safeguard universal service, and in the same year the Commission identified the political goal of universal service as 'making available a defined minimum

---

[12] Hammer (2002) 68.   [13] Sauter (1998) 123 (footnote omitted).

[14] *Towards a Dynamic European Economy: Green Paper on the Development of the Common Market for Telecommunications Services and Equipment*, COM (87)290.   [15] Sauter (1998) 131.

[16] Case 202/88 *French Republic v. Commission* [1991] ECR I-1223; Cases C-271/90 C-281/90 and C-289/90, *Spain, France, Belgium and Italy v. Commission* [1992] ECR I-5833.

service of specified quality to all users at an affordable price', and as including taking special account of 'the needs of more vulnerable or disadvantaged subscriber groups'; it proposed a Council Resolution implementing these proposals.[17] Following further work by the Commission on definition of universal service,[18] the Council passed a Resolution on universal service defining it as 'to permit access to a defined minimum service of specified quality for all users everywhere and, in the light of specific national conditions, at an affordable price'. It was also expressed as based on the familiar public service principles of universality, equality, and continuity, and set out the basis for acceptable financing schemes for such provision. Finally, the concept of universal service was a dynamic one which could develop beyond basic access to voice and data services.[19]

The next stage of planning for liberalization concerned telecommunications infrastructure rather than simply the provision of services; once more the relevant Green Paper stressed the role of universal service as one of the two key issues underlying it (alongside interconnection). It set out three tiers of universal service, repeating the definition referred to above, but adding secondary objectives including those relating to access to information about the service, dispute-resolution procedures for users, public payphones, access to emergency services, and specific conditions for disabled users and persons with special needs. Finally, targets or recommendations were proposed for advanced features such as itemized billing. The paper also discussed the means of financing universal service.[20]

The result of these preparations was the successful enactment of Directives which whilst implementing extensive liberalization also emphasized strongly the importance of universal service. The most important of these were initially the Open Network Provision Directive, and later the Interconnection Directive and the Voice Telephony

---

[17] *Developing Universal Service for Telecommunications in a Competitive Environment,* COM(93)159 (final) 4. 6, 9.

[18] *Developing Universal Service for Telecommunications in a Competitive Environment; Proposal for a Council Resolution on Universal Service Principles in the Telecommunications Sector,* COM(93)543.

[19] Council Resolution 94/C48/EC on Universal Service Principles in the Telecommunications Sector (OJ 1994 C48/1) and *Commission Statement Concerning Council Resolution on Universal Service in the Telecommunications Sector* (OJ 194 C48/8); see also Sauter (1998) 136.

[20] *Green Paper on the Liberalisation of Telecommunications Infrastructures and Cable Television Networks, Part One,* COM(94)440, *Part Two,* COM(94)682; Sauter (1998) 137.

Directive.[21] The latter two directives contained identical definitions of the term 'universal service':

'Universal Service' means a defined minimum set of services of specified quality which is available to all users independent of their geographical location and, in the light of specific national conditions, at an affordable price.[22]

The Voice Telephony Directive required that Member States secure access to services for all users, independent of geographical location, at an affordable price and continued:

Taking into account the progressive adjustment of tariffs towards costs, Member States shall in particular maintain the affordability of the services set out in this Chapter for users in rural or high cost areas and for vulnerable groups of users such as the elderly, those with disabilities or those with special social needs.

To this end, Member States shall remove obligations which prevent or restrict the use of special or targeted tariff schemes for the provision of the services specified in this Directive and may, in accordance with Community law, implement price caps or geographical averaging or other similar schemes for some or all of the specified services until such time as competition provides effective price control.[23]

The Directive also dealt with the possible means of financing such provision. Alternatives to direct public finance permitted by the Directive were the use of a universal service fund to which market participants all contribute, or the provision of universal service by several organizations, which could then reduce their contributions to such a fund or even receive support from it.[24] In fact the financing of universal service has proved a controversial issue, particularly as there is considerable debate on whether it imposes an overall cost on operators at all; benefits such as brand recognition for the universal service provider may outweigh the additional costs. Alongside the developments relating to universal service there was also a strong move to improve consumer protection, for example through rights to the provision of information.[25]

---

[21] Council Directive 90/387/EEC on the establishment of the internal market for telecommunications services through the implementation of open network provision, [1990] OJ L192/1; Directive 97/33/EC on interconnection in telecommunications with regard to ensuring universal service and interoperability through application of the principles of open network provision, [1997] OJ L199/32; Directive 98/10/EC on the application of open network provision to voice telephony and on universal service for telecommunications in a competitive environment, [1998] OJ L101/24.

[22] Interconnection Directive, Art. 2(1)(g); Voice Telephony Directive, Art. 2(2)(f).

[23] Voice Telephony Directive, Art. 3(1).   [24] Hammer (2002) 69; Sauter (1998) 138–9.

[25] Hammer (2002) 70–2.

This development of a more clearly defined and enforceable concept of universal service was extremely important; as Sauter prophetically put it:

The paradoxical result may well turn out to be that true universal service will for the first time be available throughout the European Union after liberalization has been completed. This may well provide an example for public service in other sectors which have so far resisted liberalization.[26]

Electronic Communications and the 2002 Regulatory Package

The successful liberalization of telecommunications services from 1998 was not the end of the process, for a major review was carried out by the Commission in 1999 which highlighted the convergence of telecommunications with other forms of electronic communications, such as the Internet, and proposed the setting out of clearer defined regulatory principles which would be technologically neutral.[27] This was to be accomplished through a framework Directive identifying general and specific policy objectives, and four specific Directives on licensing, access and interconnection, universal service, and privacy and data protection. They would cover all communications infrastructure and associated services. There was a strong emphasis once more on the central role for the protection of universal service; '[a] major priority for the Commission is to ensure that all consumers have the opportunity to reap the benefits of the Information Society'.[28] Thus the Review emphasized the dynamic and evolving nature of universal service, and considered arguments for and against including within it broadband offering rapid Internet access. It concluded that such an extension of the coverage of universal service would not currently be appropriate, but that the Commission should be obliged to undertake a review of universal service periodically. The Commission also decided to keep under review funding schemes adopted by Member States, and to develop pricing principles at EU level to ensure the affordability of universal service. Once more, developments in universal service were to be accompanied by other changes to improve quality of service and consumer protection.

The proposals were implemented in Directives agreed in March 2002. The framework Directive itself specifies as amongst the tasks of national regulatory authorities 'ensuring that users, including disabled users,

---

[26] Sauter (1998) 142.

[27] *Towards a New Framework for Electronic Communications Infrastructure and Associated Services: The 1999 Telecommunications Review*, COM(1999)539.   [28] Ibid., 38.

derive maximum benefits in terms of choice, price and quality' from competition; 'ensuring that all citizens have access to a universal service' as defined in the Universal Service Directive; and 'addressing the needs of specific social groups, in particular disabled users'.[29] The Universal Service Directive adapts a similar definition of universal service to the earlier directives and imposes a duty on Member States to ensure its provision.[30] Importantly, this may extend to all electronic communications services rather than only traditional telecommunications, although, for the moment at least, broadband is still excluded from the scope of universal service. The Directive thus requires Member States to ensure that all reasonable requests for connection to the public telephone network and for access to publicly available telephone services at a fixed location are met by at least one undertaking; the connection must permit functional Internet access.[31] Public pay telephones are also to be provided 'to meet the reasonable needs of end-users in terms of the geographical coverage, the number of telephones, the accessibility of such telephones, the accessibility of such telephones to disabled users and the quality of services', though the payphones requirement can be waived if comparable facilities are widely available.[32] Special measures are to be taken in relation to disabled users.[33]

Further provisions apply to the affordability of tariffs, where Member States may require that designated undertakings provide 'tariff options or packages to consumers which depart from those provided under normal commercial conditions, in particular to ensure that those on low incomes or with special social needs are not prevented from accessing or using the publicly available telephone service'. Member States may also require the adoption of common tariffs, including geographical averaging throughout their territories.[34] As regards financing of universal service, the Directive requires Member States, where an undertaking is subject to an unfair burden through the meeting of universal service obligations, to provide compensation from public funds or to share the cost between operators.[35] As proposed in the Communications Review, the scope of universal service is to be reviewed within two years and then every three years.[36]

---

[29] Directive 2002/21/EC on a common regulatory framework for electronic communications networks and services (Framework Directive), [2002] OJ L108/33, Art. 8.

[30] Directive 2002/22/EC on universal service and users' rights relating to electronic communications networks and services (Universal Service Directive), [2002] OJ L108/51, Art. 3.

[31] Ibid., Art. 4.   [32] Ibid., Art. 6.   [33] Ibid., Art. 7.   [34] Ibid., Art. 9.

[35] Ibid., Art. 13.   [36] Ibid., Art. 15

Further provisions are concerned with quality of service and consumer protection, or 'end-users rights' through, for example, providing the right to a contract with the supplier which contains certain specified information.

Implementation

Implementation of the universal service obligation is for Member States through their national regulatory authorities; each year the Commission publishes a review of implementation.[37] In general terms, the report for 2003 found that only eight countries (including the UK and Italy) had taken action to incorporate the new regulatory package into their national law by the deadline of 24 July 2003. In the case of France, there was a concern that the passage of drafts through the legislative process was likely to be lengthy, and infringement proceedings against France and other Member States which had not yet implemented the package were commenced in October 2003.

Nevertheless, considerable progress had been made on the basis of the earlier law both in providing a framework of independent national regulatory authorities and protecting universal service; in the context of the regulatory framework, the Commission 'recognizes the *enormous amount that has been accomplished* by the Member States that have transposed the framework in ensuring that the principles on which it is based are faithfully carried over into national law'.[38] The problems with the national regulatory authorities mainly concerned details of their independence where, for example, there was no explicit requirement that they act impartially or where their objectives did not explicitly reflect those of the regulatory package. As regards universal service, the report for 2002 found that '[a]lthough, in general terms, universal service seems to be provided in all Member States with no major problems, there are still some areas of concern'.[39] This was particularly the case with provision of services for the disabled and those with special social needs and the provision of directory services for all users. In the first example, a few Member States had introduced special tariffs for such users (including Austria, Germany, and Italy) and most had implemented

---

[37] See e.g. European Commission, 8th *Report on the Implementation of the Telecommunications Regulatory Package* (2002); *9th Report on the Implementation of the Telecommunications Regulatory Package* (2003).   [38] *9th Report*, op. cit., 5 (emphasis retained).
[39] *8th Report*, op. cit., 42.

specific provisions to facilitate the use of telephone services by disabled users (the exceptions were France, the Netherlands, and Austria). On the other hand, the universal provision of directory services had proved problematic in many countries. Under the new package, there were still concerns that in some Member States the scope of universal service had not been delineated in accordance with the Directive (for example, by omitting a requirement that it be available throughout the national territory or include functional Internet access), and also in relation to the designation of operators, the calculation of costs, and the protection of end-users' rights.[40]

As regards financing of universal service, the Court of Justice had given criteria to assist in the establishment of a universal service fund and for the contributions to it from market actors.[41] There had been an increase in requests for the funding of universal service provision, but only two Member States had established a universal service fund requiring payments from other operators to the universal service provider (France and Italy), whilst Spain and the UK had concluded that the provision of universal service had not imposed an unfair burden on the designated provider.[42]

Looking in more detail at the three Member States covered in this book, as was described in Chapter 4, the UK had a well-established authority in the form of the Office of Telecommunications (Oftel) established under the Telecommunications Act 1984; its responsibilities have now passed to the new Office of Communications (Ofcom) under the Communications Act 2003 (CA 2003). Implementation of the European requirements on universal service in the UK was briefly considered in Chapter 4 above on the work of Oftel. The most important developments in relation to the new regulatory package are implemented through the 2003 Act. The Act empowers Ofcom to make provision for the designation of universal service providers, and to notify designation to the European Commission.[43] Such providers may then be made subject to universal service conditions; however, these are not simply set at the discretion of Ofcom but are to secure compliance with obligations set out in the universal service order.[44] This must be made by the

---

[40] *9th Report*, op. cit., 34.

[41] Case C-384/99 *Commission v. the Kingdom of Belgium* [2000] ECR I-10633; Case C-146/00 *Commission v. France* [2001] ECR I-9767.

[42] *8th Report*, op. cit., 43. On implementation in France, see also *Commission v. France*, op. cit.

[43] CA 2003, s. 66.   [44] S. 67.

Secretary of State and must specify the extent to which a number of things must be provided to comply with Community obligations. The relevant things are electronic communications networks and services; facilities capable of being made available as part of, or in connection with, such services; billing methods; directories and directory inquiry services. The order may also contain guidance about pricing.[45] The order was issued in 2003, and implements Community obligations on the provision of publicly available telephone services, directories, public payphones, methods of billing (including requiring special tariff options and packages for those on low incomes or who have special needs), and special measures for the disabled.[46] The effect is not likely to be different from that of the universal service policies adopted by Oftel and described in Chapter 4; however, the important difference of principle is that the policies are to be determined by the Secretary of State (after consulting the regulator) rather than by the regulator itself.

Turning to France, a regulatory authority was also well established, having been set up in 1996 in the form of the Autorité de Régulation des Télécommunications (ART) discussed in Chapter 5 above.[47] Its powers include proposing tariffs for universal service and other tariffs where competition had not yet been established; the approval of government is needed for these. The substantive requirements for universal service have also been mentioned in Chapter 5, and these requirements are included in the 2003 law permitting the privatization of France Télécom.[48] They include the provision to all of a service at affordable prices, of a continued service for incoming and emergency service calls for a year in the case of failure to pay a bill, and basic Internet access. Universal service may be provided by any operator which can provide the service throughout the national territory, and such operators are to be designated by the minister after receiving bids relating to technical conditions and the cost of provision. A universal service fund is to cover the costs, with the contributions made to it by telecommunications operators determined by the regulatory authority. This issue of financing had in fact caused legal difficulties. The European Court of Justice had determined that the

---

[45] S. 65.

[46] The Electronic Communications (Universal Service) Order 2003, SI 2003/1904.

[47] Loi no. 96-659 du 26 juillet 1996; see Maisl (1995), Chevallier (1997), and the website at http://www.art-telecom.fr/ (consulted 15 July 2004).

[48] Loi no. 2003-1365 du 31 décembre 2003 relative aux obligations de service public des télécommunications et à France Télécom, JO 1 janvier 2004, 1; see Rapp (2004).

original arrangements for calculating contributions from operators were in breach of Community law.[49] The minister then set fresh contributions (under the old law it fell to him rather than to the Authority to do so) and this was upheld by the Conseil d'Etat, though in a decision which characterized the contributions as a form of tax, which could raise further constitutional problems.[50] Further implementation of the regulatory package took place through legislation passed in July 2004, modifying the code of posts and telecommunications to refer to 'electronic communications', replacing the requirement of authorization to provide services with general conditions, and setting out the powers of the Authority to take action in relation to enterprises exercising significant market power.[51]

In Italy, as discussed in Chapter 5, there has also been an independent regulatory authority for some time in the form of the Autorità per le Garanzie nelle Communicazioni (Agcom).[52] The authority also has the task of ensuring the provision of universal service and assessing contributions to its funding by operators. A fresh law implemented the new regulatory package in 2003.[53] It sets out the Community requirements for universal service and gives the Authority responsibility for implementing them, including calculating the cost of universal provision and compensation for operators from the universal service fund established by the minister, as well as their contributions to it.

Conclusion on Telecommunications

The history of universal service in telecommunications shows quite clearly how a determined legal effort can be made to protect a social goal within the context of liberalization. A number of aspects of this history are immediately striking. Firstly, although universal service may have had origins in the protection of monopoly rights, and indeed in the context of liberalization was used as a means of sugaring the pill of increased competition for those governments that were still attached to their

---

[49] Case C-146/00 *Commission v. France* [2001] ECR I-9767.

[50] *Société Tiscali Télécom*, AJDA 2003 1888.

[51] Loi no. 2004-669 du 9 juillet 2004 relative aux communications électroniques et aux services de communication audiovisuelle, JO 10 juillet 2004, 12483.

[52] Legge n. 481, 14 novembre 1995, *Gazzetta Ufficiale* no. 270, 18.11.1995; legge n. 249, 31 luglio 1997, *Gazzetta Ufficiale*, no. 177, 31.7.1997. See also http://www.agcom.it/eng/eng_intro.htm (consulted 15 July 2004).

[53] Decreto legislativo 1 agosto 20003, n. 259, *Gazzetta Ufficiale* no. 214, 15.9.2003.

monopoly providers, it has moved well beyond this towards more clearly social and redistributive goals. Indeed, and ironically, the closer specification of universal service and of the means of its financing has flushed out the costs of providing a universal service much more clearly and, at least in the UK, this has proved to be considerably less than suppliers had claimed. Alongside this, the concept itself has shown a considerable degree of flexibility, especially given its potential to expand through the periodic reviews of the scope of universal service to be carried out by the Commission, something of particular importance given the rapidly developing role of broadband. Moreover, the concept has also changed, as noted above, from being concerned with geographic universality and the inclusion of remote areas, to social universality and ensuring that all social groups have access to the means of communication essential for participation in modern society. As Hammer has put it, '[i]n the telecommunications market the main development concerns the new universal service concept. In reality, it has all the characteristics of the traditional end user oriented public service concept. The most important development so far lies in the new emphasis on disadvantaged customers; universal service is developing as an instrument for social welfare.'[54]

Secondly, the law relating to universal service is subject to well-established institutional arrangements for its implementation. These include the annual reports by the Commission on the implementation of the telecommunications regulatory package and also the work of the national regulatory authorities responsible for implementing the package within Member States. It is now clearly settled that the appropriate means of implementing universal service within a liberalized market is through such an independent authority, although, as we have seen in the case of the UK as well as the Continental countries discussed, the basic responsibility lies with the Minister for determining the overall parameters of what is required for universal service and funding methods, all of course within the framework of Community law. Thus we seem to see a division of responsibilities closer to that adopted for the British utilities in the more recent legislative model such as that under the Utilities Act 2000 discussed in Chapter 4; decisions on principles of social regulation are for the minister and implementation for the authority. The new element here is of course that the Community law framework provides a major constraint on ministerial discretion.

---

[54] Hammer (2002) 74.

Most clearly, however, we see here the translation of social obligations into a well-established and well-developed body of law. This is of course in marked contrast to the earlier UK approach of leaving the protection of such values to the political process, and provides a much clearer set of public service obligations for this area of utility services.

Our next concern is whether this process is mirrored in other areas of Community law relating to public utilities where competition has been slower to develop; the first area for examination will be that of energy.

The Energy Sector

The Liberalization of Electricity and Gas

In the energy sector liberalization has been slower to take root than in telecommunications, largely because of the strong opposition of some Member States (notably France) which are still wedded to the concept of a monopoly, or dominant, unified utility serving as producer, transporter, and supplier. However, recently it has made much greater progress and full liberalization on the telecommunications model has now been agreed by 2007.[55] As we shall see, although universal service has played an important role here, somewhat different methods have been employed to secure it. In addition, there have been more serious problems of implementation of liberalization than in the case of telecommunications (although not in the UK where full supply liberalization had been achieved by the late 1990s).

The Progress of Liberalization

The first stage of liberalization, from 1989 to the end of 1995, has been described as 'characterized by intense and controversial discussions between the parties on possible compromises'.[56] It included minor moves through Directives to increase transparency and non-discrimination, and two Directives on common rules for an internal market in electricity and gas were proposed, but not adopted until 1996–7 and only then with considerable modification. The proposals envisaged a new, transparent,

---

[55] For the background see the detailed account in Cameron (2002), though note that it includes the recent Directives only in draft form. For an account of recent developments see Hancher (2003).   [56] Cameron (2002) 98.

and non-discriminatory system for the licensing of electricity generation and of the construction of new electricity lines and gas pipelines, 'unbundling' or the internal separation of transmission and distribution activities in vertically integrated companies, and, most importantly, third-party access (TPA) to networks. Thus transport and distribution companies would be obliged to offer such access to other companies, permitting the development of a competitive trading system.[57] Alongside this, measures were taken through infringement proceedings against national import and export monopolies.[58] Most importantly for this book, a further development has been described as the 'rediscovery of public service'.[59] The concept was used as a reason to impose limits on the concept of third-party access, and this was central to the Directives actually adopted; much of the impetus for the concern came from the European Parliament.

A major change in the proposals was the development of 'negotiated access' to transmission and distribution systems rather than the automatic right of access originally envisaged; thus '[u]nder a system of negotiated access, the prospective system users would have no right to require access until at the end of a period of unsuccessful negotiation they could show that the network owner has not complied with the good faith and other obligations, as well as with his obligations under competition law . . . '.[60] An alternative was regulated access, according to which producers and customers could contract with each other directly for supply, with access on the basis of published tariffs and a competent body designated to resolve disputes.[61]

Alongside this, revised proposals for the Directives made explicit the right of Member States to impose public service obligations with respect to the security, regularity, quality, and price of supplies. These obligations were to be clearly defined, and their performance could constitute a reason for refusing access to the network, as well as a reason for refusing a licence for new production and transport capacity.[62] A yet further change was the development of the 'single buyer' concept, which originated with the French Government. This involves retaining a single utility which is subject to public service obligations; the utility is responsible for buying all electricity produced or imported into the state and for selling all electricity exported; thus it has a monopoly of import and export.[63]

---

[57] Ibid., 125–6.   [58] Ibid., 132–5.   [59] Ibid., 135.   [60] Ibid., 136.
[61] Ibid., 152   [62] Ibid., 136–7.   [63] Ibid., 139.

Acceptance that this was compatible with the Treaty led to the necessary agreement for the initial stage of liberalization, and a Directive was agreed for the liberalization of the electricity market in 1996, coming into force in early 1997.[64] A similar Directive for gas was agreed and entered into force in 1998.[65]

The Electricity Directive included the requirement that the Member States designate a system operator (or several for transmission and distribution systems), responsible for managing the electricity flows of the system, taking into account exchanges with interconnected systems.[66] As has been noted, '[t]he purpose of the regulation as regards system operation is dual; it shall safeguard traditional public service interests *and* promote competition'.[67] The promotion of competition included completely opening up the construction of new generating capacity to competition through an authorization or a tendering procedure, and non-discriminatory operation of the transmission and distribution systems by the system operator. Access to the networks was to be granted by negotiated or regulated third-party access or through a single buyer.

It has been noted that 'the emphasis placed on public service was greater than in the original proposal, reflecting the Parliament's views on this'.[68] The Directive allowed Member States to impose five categories of public service obligations on their electricity undertakings: security (including security of supply); regularity of supply; quality of supplies; price of supplies; and environmental protection factors. The obligations also had to be clearly defined, transparent, non-discriminatory, and verifiable, and published and notified to the Commission.[69] Most importantly, Member States were given the right not to apply certain provisions of the Directive insofar as application would obstruct the performance of obligations in the general economic interest and insofar as failure to apply them would not affect trade to an extent contrary to the interests of the Community.[70] The provisions affected were those relating to the authorization of, or competitive tendering for, generating capacity, access to the transmission and distribution systems, and the construction of direct lines.

---

[64] Directive 96/92/EC of the European Parliament and of the Council of 19 December 1996 concerning common rules for the internal market in electricity, OJ [1997] L27/20.

[65] Directive 98/30/EC of the European Parliament and Council of 22 June 1998 concerning common rules for the internal market in natural gas, [1998] OJ L204/2.

[66] Arts. 7(1), 7(3).   [67] Hammer (2002) 51 (emphasis retained).

[68] Cameron (2002) 144.   [69] Art. 3(2).   [70] Art. 3(3).

In the case of the gas Directive, similar provision was made for third-party access to distribution and transmission systems in negotiated or regulated form, and almost identical provision made for public service obligations.[71] A right not to apply the provisions relating to the licensing of distribution systems on public service grounds was given in terms similar to that for electricity, but it should be noted that its scope of application was much more limited than in the latter case, as it did not apply to the general competition provisions. It has been suggested that this 'reflects an important difference between gas and electricity. Gas is a substitutable primary source of energy. It can be replaced by alternative sources such as oil and coal. The dependence of final consumers on it is thus therefore less acute than on electricity supply, which is used by virtually all households.'[72]

The approach to the protection of public service goals in energy was thus fundamentally different to that taken in relation to tele-communications in two respects. Firstly, much less was done to specify positive public service obligations which had to be respected, such as those relating to universal service. A much looser framework with a short list of obligations which the Member States could decide to impose was used instead. Secondly, rather than the public service obligations forming an integral part of the new design, they were expressed, especially in the case of electricity, as exceptions to the general policy of liberalization, thus permitting Member States to opt out of this to a limited degree on public service grounds. This reflects the older view of public service goals described in the previous chapter, seeing them as limits to the achievement of a single market and as largely dependent on the discretion of Member States themselves. It contrasts with the more recent view in telecommunications of public service goals, especially the achievement of universal service, as positive attributes of citizenship which Community law requires as part of the liberalization process. This was to change to some degree with the next stage of energy liberalization.

Progress to Full Liberalization and the Directives of June 2003

The Directives discussed above incurred difficulties in implementation, especially in the case of France and Belgium. The Lisbon European Council in 2000 expressed its concern at the slow pace of development of

---

[71] Art. 3(2).   [72] Cameron (2002) 185.

liberalization, and instructed the Commission to prepare a report on liberalization and to make proposals on it. This emerged in the form of a Communication in March 2001.[73] The proposal aimed to amend the Electricity and Gas Directives to ensure full liberalization for non-household customers by the beginning of 2003, and for all customers by the beginning of 2005 for electricity, and 2004 and 2005 for gas. Member States would also be required to establish independent national regulatory bodies with the responsibility of fixing or approving terms and conditions relating to access.

A major concern in the new proposals was that of public service objectives and obligations. Thus the Communication stated that '[t]he attainment of the highest possible standards of public service ... is a primary objective of Community energy policy ... In particular, it is vital that all Community citizens have a universal right to be supplied at reasonable prices and that a minimum set of consumer protection standards is maintained.'[74] It noted that so far no Member State had found it necessary to derogate from the provisions of the earlier Directives to meet their public service objectives and the liberalization accomplished so far had not prevented the maintenance of high standards of public service: '[i]ndeed, as market opening progresses, increasing public service levels have been attained through the imposition of licence requirements or conditions'. This has enabled Member States 'to increase public service standards gradually and continually in a liberalized market'.[75]

The Communication thus proposed that the basic public service objective of the right for household consumers to be supplied with electricity on reasonable conditions be viewed as an underlying objective of the internal market, and that Member States be required to take the necessary measures to ensure that this was achieved. The States should be obliged to ensure the attainment of essential public service objectives relating to the protection of vulnerable customers, the protection of final customers (for example through set contractual conditions, transparency of information, and dispute resolution machinery), social and economic cohesion (for example through ensuring supplies and connection to peripheral areas), environmental protection, and security of supply. The earlier Directives had required notification of

---

[73] *Communication from the Commission to the Council and the European Parliament, Completing the Internal Energy Market*, COM(2001)125 final.   [74] Ibid., 19.
[75] Ibid.

public service obligations to the Commission only where they involved derogation from a Directive's provisions, but, to assist benchmarking and monitoring, henceforth all measures taken to implement public service objectives would need notification.[76]

The proposed package met opposition from France and Germany on the ground that it would imply a move away from public service and would create unemployment, and in the latter because of reluctance to set up an independent regulatory body. However, progress was gradually made; the Barcelona Council in March 2002 accepted the principle of full liberalization for non-domestic consumers by 2004, and the Energy Council meeting in November 2002 agreed to full market opening for household customers by 2007. Draft Directives were revised to incorporate further public service obligations, and in February 2003 the Council adopted proposals for full liberalization by 1 July 2004 and 1 July 2007. These proposals were finally implemented as new Directives (repealing and replacing, not amending, their predecessors) in June 2003.[77]

The Electricity Directive now commences its substantive provisions with a set of articles on public service obligations and consumer protection. They permit Member States to impose on undertakings operating in the electricity sector, in the general economic interest, public service obligations which may relate to security (including security of supply), regularity, quality, and price of supplies, and environmental protection, including energy efficiency and climate protection.[78] This remains permissive, but there is an obligation on Member States to ensure that all household customers (and if the state deems it appropriate, small businesses) enjoy universal service, defined as the right to be supplied with electricity of a specified quality within their territory at reasonable, easily and clearly comparable, and transparent prices (in this case the term 'affordable' is not used). An obligation is to be placed on distribution companies to connect customers to the grid on terms set by independent regulatory authorities.[79] Measures must also be taken to protect final customers, in particular vulnerable customers, including measures to help them avoid disconnection.[80] Member States are also

---

[76] Ibid., 20.

[77] Directive 2003/54/EC of the European Parliament and of the Council of 26 June 2003 concerning common rules for the internal market in electricity, [2003] OJ L176/37; Directive 2003/55/EC of the European Parliament and of the Council of 26 June 2003 concerning common rules for the internal market in natural gas, [2003] OJ L176/57.   [78] Art. 3(2).

[79] Art. 3(3).   [80] Art. 3(5); see also Annex A to the Directive.

obliged to implement appropriate measures to achieve the objectives of social and economic cohesion, environmental protection, and security of supply.[81]

In addition to these requirements, Member States may decide not to apply provisions relating to authorizing or tendering for new generating capacity, third-party access and supply through a direct line where they would obstruct the performance of the obligations imposed on electricity undertakings in the general economic interest, so far as the development of trade would not be affected to such an extent as would be contrary to the interests of the Community, thereby retaining from the earlier Directive the possibility of such an 'opt-out'.[82] Finally, all measures adopted to fulfil universal service and public service obligations must be notified to the Commission.[83]

The provisions of the Gas Directive are similar to those of that for electricity, with the important difference that there is no duty to ensure the provision of universal service. This reflects the fact that, as mentioned above, there are greater possibilities for substitution between gas and other fuels, and the fact that the infrastructure for gas supply is not fully developed, especially in rural areas. In relation to both gas and electricity, further work is continuing in relation to other aspects of public service objectives, for example security of supply.[84]

The continued existence of the limited opportunities for Member States to derogate from market liberalization on public service grounds has led one commentator to suggest that this means that '[t]he approach taken here to universal service and PSOs relating to energy security is therefore markedly different from that adopted, for example, in respect of market liberalisation in the telecommunications and, to a certain extent, postal sectors'.[85] The retention of such opportunities reflects the fraught politics of European energy liberalization, in particular the symbolic importance of public service obligations and the emphasis placed by some Member States on the role of their dominant undertakings in implementing the obligations. However, in the case of electricity this is now supplemented by a strong public service *obligation* similar to that in telecommunications, and even in the case of gas consumer protection

---

[81] Art. 3(7).   [82] Art. 3(8).   [83] Art. 3(9).

[84] See e.g. *Communication from the Commission to the Council and the European Parliament: Final Report on the Green Paper 'Towards a European Strategy for the Security of Energy Supply'*, COM(2002)321 final.   [85] Hancher (2003) 263.

measures are required, including those to protect vulnerable consumers and to help to avoid disconnections. Once more this reflects the general development outlined in the previous chapter away from public service as a hindrance to the internal market and towards the implementation of rights of citizenship through it.

Implementation

As has been mentioned above, implementation of the original Directives proved extremely difficult in some Member States, largely because of their attachment to the achievement of public service goals through large integrated energy enterprises. The UK was the exception, of course, having extensively liberalized electricity and gas since the 1980s, with the final liberalization of supply implemented in 1998–9. However, in the case of electricity, the relevant French legislation was not enacted until one year after the deadline of February 1999.[86] It began with a broad definition of the concept of public service in electricity, characterizing it as having the objectives of supplying electricity to the whole of the national territory and of respecting the general interest; amongst other things, it was to contribute to social cohesion, the right of electricity for all, and the struggle against social exclusion. The law also made explicit that it was to be managed in a way which respected the principles of equality, continuity, and adaptability.[87] This provision of the law remains in force. Other provisions provided for the principle of *péréquation*, or geographically uniform charges, and for the creation of an electricity public service fund with contributions from all operators, producers, suppliers, and end-users importing electricity.[88] It also required, in the interests of public service, that all contracts for the supply of electricity be for a minimum period of three years.[89]

Infringement proceedings were in fact launched against France and (later) Belgium for failure to meet the deadline. In the case of gas, similar proceedings were commenced against France, Luxembourg, and Germany, and the Court of Justice ruled that France was in breach of its obligations.[90] A further law was passed in France at the beginning of 2003

---

[86] Loi no. 2000-108 du 10 février 2000, Loi relative à la modernisation et au développement du service public de l'électricité, JO 11 février 2000, 2143; see also Hancher (2003) 261.

[87] Art. 1.   [88] Arts. 2, 5.   [89] Art. 22.

[90] See generally on problems of implementation Cameron (2002) 253–69; Case C-259/01 *Commission v. France* [2002] ECR I-11093.

(before the second set of Directives) to complete implementation for both electricity and gas.[91] Despite these difficulties, however, important steps had been taken towards liberalization through the establishment of an independent regulatory authority by the law passed in 2000, the Commission de la Régulation de l'Énergie mentioned in Chapter 5; its powers were extended to cover gas as well under the 2003 legislation.[92] Its tasks include analysing the costs of carrying out public service missions and making recommendations to the minister on the compensation to be paid to enterprises incurring such costs. Similarly, the setting of tariffs remains ultimately for the minister and the Commission may only give an opinion or propose them. The Commission considered that the necessary steps had been taken for the opening of the competitive market to industrial consumers by the deadline of 1 July 2004; further legislation was passed by the French Parliament in July 2004 to change the status of Eléctricité de France and Gaz de France and permit the sale of minority stakes in them by the government. It also implements the 2003 Directives and provides for the legal and functional separation of the transmission and distribution enterprises from electricity and gas production and supply.[93]

In the case of Italy, extensive liberalization of energy markets had already taken place through the 'Decreto Bersani' in 1999, and an independent regulatory authority had been established under legislation passed in 1995, the Autorità per l'Energia Elettrica e il Gas.[94] It sets tariffs autonomously in the regulated sectors, notably supply to household consumers, and these provide special protection and guarantees for customers in socially or economically disadvantaged circumstances. Despite the delays in implementing the first set of Directives, the European Commission was able to conclude in relation to universal service that by 2003 all Member States had adopted a framework for ensuring that there was at least one supplier with an obligation to serve

---

[91] Loi no. 2003-8 du 3 janvier 2003, Loi relative aux marchés du gaz et de l'électricité et au service public de l'énergie, JO 4 janvier 2003, 265.

[92] See Titre VI of the loi and the website at http://www.cre.fr (consulted 15 July 2004).

[93] Loi no. 2004-803 relative au service public de l'éléctricité et du gaz et aux entreprises éléctriques et gazières, Jo 27 août 2004, 14256.

[94] Decreto Legge n. 79 del 16 marzo 1999, *Gazzetta Ufficiale* n. 292, 14.12.1999; Legge n. 481, 14 novembre 1995, *Gazzetta Ufficiale* no. 270, 18.11.1995. The Authority's website is at http://www.autorita.energia.it/inglese/about/eng_index.htm (consulted 15 July 2004).

all customers at final prices which could be regulated, even where the market was fully open to competition.[95] It remains to be seen what difference the new Directives will make with their more extensive public service obligations. The UK has of course fully liberalized gas and electricity since the late 1990s, and the Department of Trade and Industry consulted on a number of minor changes to implement the Directives in 2004;[96] means to protect public service were discussed in Chapter 4 above.

Conclusions on Energy

We have seen a somewhat different story here from that in telecommunications with the implementation of public service obligations being left much more in the hands of the Member States, and with greater reluctance to impose a common basic pattern for universal service, largely because of the difficulty in getting agreement on liberalization from Member States with very different political and legal traditions in relation to the energy industries. Nevertheless, as in the case of telecommunications, independent regulation through specially established authorities has become the norm for implementing public service obligations, sometimes in conjunction with the role of the minister (in fact the main opposition to this model in the liberalization process came from Germany, not from the countries studied here). Moreover, the new Electricity Directive, and to a lesser extent that for gas, seems to represent a major move once more in creating a set of positive obligations, derived from citizenship rights, which will be legally obligatory and more effectively monitored by the Commission. As implementation for household consumers will not be until 2007, it will be some time before it will be possible to establish how effective these protections will be. I shall now examine the sector of postal services to establish if similar developments can be found there also.

---

[95] *Commission Staff Working Paper: Second Benchmarking Report on the Implementation of the Internal Gas and Electricity Market*, SEC(2003)448, 30 and Annex A, s. 12.

[96] *Consultation: Implementation of EU Directive 2003/54 Concerning Common Rules for the Internal Market in Electricity* (2004); *Consultation: Implementation of EU Directive 2003/55 Concerning Common Rules for the Internal Market in Gas* (2004).

Postal Services

The Development of Universal Service and Liberalization

The liberalization of postal services has been even more controversial than that of energy, and for similar reasons; the effect of liberalized markets on universal service at uniform prices, and the strong attachment on the part of some Member States to their dominant, publicly owned postal enterprises. Progress has been slow in liberalization, although once more there has recently been a breakthrough paving the way for eventual full liberalization. In this case, from the beginning universal service has played a central role not merely as a means to legitimate liberalization and to ease its political agreement, but as its prerequisite.

As long ago as 1991 the Commission produced a Green Paper on liberalizing postal services.[97] A draft Directive was produced in 1995 which defined a reserved area which would continue to be the monopoly preserve of the national postal administrations whilst opening up other areas to competition. Collection, sorting, transport, and delivery of letter post could be reserved 'to the extent necessary to maintain universal service', and a combined weight and price ceiling was placed on the reserved sector. The draft Directive was accompanied by an Article 90(3) notice setting out the approach the Commission intended to take in applying the competition law rules in the Treaty. This was however not wholly consistent with the draft Directive and the European Parliament asked for its withdrawal.[98] An amended draft was published in 1996, and the Directive became law in 1997.[99] It is noticeable that the title of the Directive does not refer to liberalization but to common rules and the improvement of service quality, thus indicating the sensitivity of this area.[100]

The recitals of the Directive emphasize the importance of universal service; thus 'it is essential to guarantee at Community level a universal postal service encompassing a minimum range of services of specified quality to be provided in all Member States at an affordable price for the

---

[97] *Green Paper on the Development of the Single Market for Postal Services (Communication from the Commission)*, COM(91)476.

[98] For coverage of these early developments see Hancher (1996) 126–31; Pelkmans (1997) 122–4.

[99] Directive 97/67/EC of the European Parliament and of the Council of 15 December 1997 on common rules for the development of the internal market of Community postal services and the improvement of quality of service, [1998] OJ L015/0014.   [100] Pelkmans (1997) 123.

benefit of all users, irrespective of their geographical location in the Community' and:

[w]hereas the aim of the universal service is to offer all users easy access to the postal network through the provision, in particular, of a sufficient number of access points and by ensuring satisfactory conditions with regard to the frequency of collections and deliveries; whereas the provision of the universal service must meet the fundamental need to ensure continuity of operation, whilst at the same time remaining adaptable to the needs of users as well as guaranteeing them fair and non-discriminatory treatment...[101]

This theme is continued in the actual articles of the Directive. Thus the substantive articles commence with a requirement that the Member States ensure that users enjoy the right to a universal service, involving the permanent provision of a postal service of specified quality at all points in their territory at affordable prices for all users. The universal service is further defined as at least one collection and one delivery each working day.[102] It applies to postal items up to 2 kilograms, parcels up to 10 kilograms, and services for registered and insured items, covering both national and cross-border services.[103] Further requirements include non-discrimination and continuity in the provision of the universal service.[104] The Directive then proceeded to harmonize '[t]o the extent necessary to ensure the maintenance of universal service' the services that may be reserved to the universal service provider; in brief, these were those where the price is less than five times the national letter rate and weight less than 350 grams.[105] Further provision was made for non-reserved services within the scope of universal service and for the establishment of a compensation fund for the universal service provider.[106] Quality of service standards were also required.[107] Finally, the Directive also required the establishment of a national regulatory authority legally separate and operationally independent of the postal operators.[108] The Directive was accompanied by a notice on the application of the competition rules.[109]

Further Liberalization and the Second Postal Services Directive

Given the generous definition of the reserved area the degree of liberalization introduced by the Directive was extremely limited; it opened to

---

[101] Directive 97/67/EC (above n. 99), recitals 11–12.   [102] Art. 3(3).   [103] Art. 3(4, 7).
[104] Art. 5.   [105] Art. 7.   [106] Art. 9(20) and (4).   [107] Arts. 16–18.   [108] Art. 22.
[109] Notice from the Commission on the application of competition rules to the postal sector and on the assessment of certain State measures relating to postal services, OJ [1998] C39/2. For a general account of the Directive and Notice see Forbes and Rodriguez (1999) 55–63.

competition only 3% on average of the postal revenues of the public operators. The Directive did require proposals to be brought forward by 1998 on further liberalization; in fact the proposals were not published until 2000.[110] The proposals were for a reduction of the weight threshold for the reserved area from 350 grams to 50 grams and the price threshold from five times the basic rate to one and a half times, and that there be further liberalization from 2007. The effect would be to open around 16% of revenues to competition. No change was proposed in the definition of universal service; the Commission noted its high social importance and that no Member State had notified to the Commission any exception or derogation to the universal service granted to its universal service provider due to circumstances or geographical conditions deemed exceptional.[111] Indeed, the Commission emphasized that there was no contradiction between liberalization and universal service, so long as there was sufficient flexibility for the universal service operator to respond to liberalization, because much universal service provision was already profitable and provision was made for the establishment of a universal service fund if necessary.[112]

Despite this optimism, negotiations on the new proposal proved difficult with strong opposition from the major postal operators on the grounds that the proposed further liberalization would threaten universal service and their own finances. On the other hand, at least some consumer groups were strongly in favour of greater liberalization; for example, the Bureau Européen des Unions de Consommateurs favoured full liberalization as early as possible, accompanied by a clearer definition of 'affordability' in the definition of universal service and a new requirement for a geographically uniform rate in all Member States.[113]

Agreement was eventually reached on a new Directive in 2002.[114] It reduced the maximum for the reserved area to 100 grams or three times the basic tariff from 1 January 2003 and to 50 grams or two and a half times the basic tariff from 1 January 2006. The Commission is also to

---

[110] *Proposal for a European Parliament and Council Directive amending Directive 97/67/EC with regard to the further opening to competition of Community postal services,* COM(2000)319 final.

[111] Ibid., 4–5.   [112] Ibid., 9, 16–19.

[113] Bureau Européen des Unions de Consommateurs, 'BEUC's Comments on the Commission's Proposals for Directive amending Directive 97/67/EC with regard to further opening to competition of Community Postal Services', BEUC/284/2000, 08/09/2000 final.

[114] Directive 2002/39/EC of the European Parliament and of the Council of 10 June 2002 amending Directive 97/67/EC with regard to the further opening to competition of Community postal services, [2002] OJ L176/21.

undertake a study by the end of 2006 on the effect of full liberalization by 2009. No redefinition of universal service was contained in the new Directive, but the existing provisions were of course maintained. Member States are also prohibited from cross-subsidizing universal services outside the reserved sector from revenue derived from services within it.

Implementation

The implementation of the first postal services directive in the UK is of especial interest in that, for the first time, it required a definition of universal service to be included in national law. This was implemented firstly by regulations and then by the Postal Services Act.[115] These are discussed in Chapter 4 above.

Implementation did not prove so smooth in other Member States; in the summer of 2002 the Commission issued a reasoned opinion to the French Government requiring it to reinforce the independence of its regulatory authority, the Minister for Economic Affairs, Finance and Industry. It also commenced similar proceedings against Greece, Italy, and Spain but they responded by taking action to remedy the problem. At the end of 2003 it was decided to refer France to the European Court of Justice because of its failure to establish a regulator independent of the operators; according to the Single Market Commissioner, '[o]nly a regulator separate from the big incumbent former monopolies can ensure that postal services give users the benefits of competition while maintaining the availability of affordable services to all, in line with EU and national laws'. The French Minister was responsible for tasks relating to state property in the postal operator, as well as for its economic and financial performance, and so did not meet the requirement of independence.[116]

In the case of Italy, the national authority was the Minister of Communications, although the Commission was satisfied that this was sufficiently independent from the postal operator.[117] On the general issue of universal service, the Commission was able to conclude in November 2002 that '[t]he *objective* of achieving a minimum Community universal

---

[115] The Postal Services Regulations 1999, SI 1999/2107; the Postal Services Act 2000, s. 4.

[116] 'Postal Services: France Before the Court over the Non-Implementation of Two Postal Directives', European Commission Press Release IP/03/1754, 17 December 2003.

[117] *Report from the Commission to the European Parliament and the Council on the Application of the Postal Directive (97/67/EC Directive)*, COM(2002)632 final, 23.

service has been achieved. The *regulatory impact* of the Postal Directive has been significant. The transposition of the Postal Directive has ensured that essential requirements of the universal service are now established by legislation in all Member States for the first time. Further these requirements are now harmonised in line with the Community requirements.'[118]

In the UK the second Directive was also implemented by statutory instrument.[119] Further steps to implement the Directive were taken through modifications to Royal Mail's licence. Once more, infringement proceedings were commenced against Austria, France, and Greece for failure properly to implement the Directive; except in the case of France they were later dropped, but the proceedings before the European Court of Justice against France also included failure to implement the second Directive. In 2003–4 draft legislation was introduced in the French Parliament to transfer regulatory responsibility to the telecommunications authority, to be renamed the Autorité de Régulation des Télécommunications et des Postes; it will also provide for market liberalization and defines universal service.[120]

Conclusions on Postal Services

In the context of postal services the concept of universal service has assumed an even greater importance than in the other services examined in this chapter. This is apparent even from examining the Directives themselves where it is made quite clear that liberalization is subject to the maintenance of a system of universal service, and from the importance attached to universal service by Member States. Once more we see that the liberalization process in this context has led to a much clearer legal definition of the concept of universal service; this is particularly the case in the UK where it has resulted in such a legal definition for the first time and, as we saw in Chapter 4, ensuring the provision of such a service is the primary duty of the regulatory authority. However, except in the UK, there has been less reliance on specially created regulatory authorities, no doubt reflecting the especial political salience of the universal postal service.

---

[118] *Report from the Commission* (above n. 117), 17 (emphasis retained).
[119] The Postal Services (EC Directive) Regulations 2003, SI 2002/3050.
[120] Projet de loi relatif à la régulation des activités postales.

Transport

Rail

To conclude this chapter I shall say a little about public transport. Transport by rail, road, and inland waterway is subject to a special regime under the Treaty.[121] In particular, Article 73 provides that state aids will be compatible with the Treaty if 'they represent reimbursement for the discharge of certain obligations inherent in the concept of a public service'. Thus here the importance of public service obligations is recognized in a somewhat different form from that in the utility services discussed above. Currently the area is governed by Regulation 1191/69 relating to compensation for fulfilling such obligations.[122] The Regulation enumerates forms of compensation that are compatible with the Treaty and establishes the mechanism of public service contracts as the normal method of securing the fulfilment of such objectives. It does not however say how such contracts should be awarded.

The Commission has now made controversial proposals to replace this Regulation.[123] For the first time, the new Regulation will establish the concept of adequate passenger transport and will require that national authorities should secure it in applying the Regulation. It will also establish as a general rule that authorities' interventions in public transport which involve the provision of state aid should take the form of public service contracts; the only exception being where minimum criteria are specified for all operators, covering only a small proportion of an operator's services. Public service contracts are to be awarded by competitive tendering and must be limited to five years' duration. The proposals have been extensively amended by the European Parliament, most importantly to permit longer contracts, to permit the direct award of contracts without competition in more situations, and to protect local public services from competition if an authority decides to provide the

---

[121] Arts. 70–80.

[122] Regulation (EEC) 1191/69 of the Council of 26 June 1969 on action by Member States concerning the obligations inherent in the concept of a public service in transport by rail, road and inland waterway, [1969] OJ L156/1, as amended by Council Regulation (EEC) No. 1893/91, [1991] OJ L169/1. For a general account of this area see Quigley and Collins (2003) 228–37.

[123] *Proposal for a Regulation of the European Parliament and Council on action by Member States concerning public service requirements and the award of public service contracts in passenger transport by rail, road and inland waterway*, COM 2000/7 final.

services itself.[124] Considerable differences between Commission and Parliament remain, but this dispute, like the *Altmark* decision discussed in Chapter 6 above, illustrates the difficult question of the legitimate role of competitive tendering in relation to public services. This was indeed an area in which the UK Government was highly critical of tendering procedures and requirements for short-term contracts in the related field of maritime transport and the provision of public service ferry operations on the West Coast of Scotland.[125] It is clear from the proposals that public service obligations will continue to be permitted here, but that competitive tendering will be a controversial means of implementing them.

Air Transport

Finally, a little needs to be said about transport by air. This was wholly liberalized within Europe through a regulatory package which became effective in 1993.[126] However, the regulations here permit the recognition of public service obligations on thin routes which are important for the economic development of particular regions. A public service obligation is defined as 'any obligation imposed upon an air carrier to take, in respect of any route which it is licensed to operate by a Member State, all necessary measures to ensure the provision of a service satisfying fixed standards of continuity, regularity, capacity, and pricing, which standards the air carrier would not assume if it were solely considering its commercial interest'.[127]

The process involves competitive tendering followed by exclusive access for only one carrier for up to three years.[128] The procedure has

---

[124] *Amended proposal for a Regulation of the European Parliament and of the Council on action by Member States concerning public service requirements and the award of public service contracts in passenger transport by rail, road and inland waterway,* COM 2000/107 final.

[125] United Kingdom Permanent Representatives to the European Union, *UK Government Response to the Green Paper of Services of General Interest* (2003), available at http://europa.eu.int/comm/secretariat_general/services_general_interest/docs/public_authorities/repres_uk.pdf (consulted 15 July 2004), paras. 17, 37.

[126] Council Regulation 2407/92 on licensing of air carriers, [1992] OJ L240/1; Council Regulation 2408/92 on access for Community air carriers to intra-European services, [1992] OJ L240/8; Council Regulation 2409/92 on fares and rates for air services, [1992] OJ L240/15. For more details see Prosser (1997) 232–7.   [127] Reg. 2408/92, Art. 2(o).

[128] Reg. 2408/92, Art. 4. For further details of the operation of these provisions and the state aid implications, see Quigley and Collins (2003) 235–6.

been used quite extensively by a number of Member States, and the Commission has recently proposed simplification of the rules and the creation of a similar system for routes to third countries.[129] In this area liberalization has proceeded smoothly, despite the less prominent role for universal service in the legislation. This is no doubt due to the less important role of aviation as an essential transport service except in a few peripheral regions; aviation is not really a public utility service.

Conclusions

A number of important conclusions can be drawn from the initiatives described in this chapter. Firstly, it is clear that liberalization has been accompanied by strong protections for public service obligations, in particular universal service, and these have moved such protection from the realm of politics to that of law. In this sense we do see a vivid recognition of the importance of citizenship rights through public service obligations, and such obligations do have a constitutional dimension not only through Article 16 but through their fundamental importance in the process of developing a single market. Once more, public service obligations are no longer a hindrance to such a process but an essential element in its creation. Moreover, there has been a further recognition of citizenship rights in the development of universal service from a geographic to a social concept.

Secondly, there has been an important move towards the establishment of more effective monitoring procedures relating to the implementation of public service obligations, which have largely taken the form of reliance on national independent regulatory authorities. This may seem ironic given the largely British origins of such authorities as part of the privatization process, when Britain has been the nation most reluctant in the past to develop public service law. However, Community liberalization has given a clearer, more coherent, and more legally enforceable basis for the implementation of public service obligations than had been the case in the UK previously, as demonstrated particularly clearly by the transformation of the universal service requirement in postal services from a political to a legal norm. The general approach taken has

---

[129] European Commission, *Consultation Paper with a View to Revisions of Regulations No. 2407/92, 2408/92 and 2409/92 of 23 July 1992* (2003).

not been so much a depoliticization of public service requirements; as we saw with energy and postal services they remain highly politically salient, but a shift towards increased transparency and legal protection for rights to defined aspects of public service.

Finally, the most controversial question appears to be that of the role of competitive tendering for public service contracts as a prerequisite for the award of state aid. This has arisen in transport, and will be examined once more in the following chapter on public service broadcasting, and in the overall conclusion in Chapter 10.

9

Public Service Broadcasting:
A Special Case

Introduction

In earlier chapters I have argued that there are special principles which apply to public services and which may limit the application of competition law to them. These principles can be justified on the ground that, whilst markets enhance efficiency, we do not come to markets as equals but on the basis of radically different resources. As citizens, however, we are equals. The provision of certain services is essential for our participation as citizens in a common standard of life, therefore market allocations have to be adjusted or replaced to reflect our common citizenship. Moreover, the objective of maintaining social solidarity may also justify limiting the application of competitive markets to public services.

In the case of public service broadcasting, there are further considerations which justify special treatment. The first, and most obvious, is that the provision of news, comment, and current affairs programmes has, for democratic reasons, to be provided in an impartial way and where possible by a plurality of sources. This could in part be achieved by the application of competition law to achieve 'external pluralism' through encouraging a large number of market actors. However more is required through 'internal pluralism' requiring internal balance and presentation of different viewpoints.[1] In addition, broadcasting raises cultural concerns; we expect to learn from the output of broadcasters, to come across

---

[1] For further discussion of these themes see Goldberg, Prosser and Verhulst (1998) 15–27.

the unexpected, and to discover preferences we did not know we had, hence requirements for broadcasting a range of different types of programmes. A further, often overlooked, problem is that in fact no market for the purchase of programmes directly by audiences exists where channels are funded by advertising; rather the audiences are 'bought' by advertisers, and this may lead to a neglect of minority interests and of specialist cultural programming. Although we have recently seen a growth of subscription channels, these are not yet sufficiently developed to replace more traditional public service broadcasting, nor do they offer the range of programming associated with public service at its best.

Finally, there are strong linguistic concerns which are linked to the preservation of national cultures; cultural pluralism is to be defended against the dominance of Anglo-Saxon, in particular United States, broadcasters which for economic reasons are able to offer cheap programmes to overseas markets, having recovered their costs on the large home market. The most celebrated expression of the tension between broadcasting seen as essentially a matter of open markets and free trade or as a key element in the expression, and preservation, of national cultures was in the disputes involving the World Trade Organization during the Uruguay Round.[2] Thus '[w]hile the US claimed that cultural identity could not be defined and that film and television products were marketable commodities, subject to the same trade rules as any other goods, opponents interpreted the US position as a challenge to national cultural expression, linguistic diversity, and alterity, in the name of trade liberalization'.[3] The result was a somewhat unstable compromise, in which, whilst it was agreed that audiovisual services were in principle covered by the GATS agreement, neither the EU nor its Member States made any commitments relating to the broadcasting sector. This 'led to a *de facto* exclusion of the sector from the GATS framework'.[4] The reluctance to make such commitments is continued in the current Doha Round of trade negotiations.

The Meaning of Public Service Broadcasting

The above suggests that the role of public service broadcasting is crucial in assessing the limits to markets and to competition law. However, it is

---

[2] See Footer and Beat Graber (2000) and Schlesinger (1997).
[3] Footer and Beat Graber (2000) 119.   [4] Herold (2003) 6.

often difficult clearly to identify what we mean by public service broadcasting. Sometimes it is assumed to be beyond definition; as the Davies Report on the future funding of the BBC put it, 'we may not be able to offer a tight new definition of public service broadcasting, but we nevertheless each felt we knew it when we saw it'.[5] This difficulty is particularly strong in the UK where the courts have not played any role in setting out a constitutional dimension to the concept.[6] However, two rather different models can be identified.

The first we might call the 'market failure' model. To quote once more from the Davies Report, 'it is impossible to argue for a public service broadcaster unless market failure can be shown'.[7] Here the assumption is that we start from accepting the market as the normal means of supplying broadcast services and look for gaps that it does not fill because of the nature of broadcasting as providing public goods or because the costs and benefits of externalities are not fully reflected in the market. A further example would be the tendency by which firms in a competitive broadcasting market move to fill the safe middle ground. Gaps in, for example news, impartial coverage of public affairs, arts coverage, and so on can then be filled by the public service broadcaster. This model may leave a substantial role for public service broadcasting as the gaps may be extensive; it is instructive that the quotations above come from a report headed by a chairman widely perceived to be a friend of the BBC, and who was later made Chairman of its Board of Governors. On the other hand, a market failure model can be used to suggest that the future of public service broadcasting is severely restricted, especially with the development of consumer choice through subscription.[8] The key point about this model is that public service broadcasting is seen as essentially residual; thus it comes under threat with the development of more segmented market provision meeting needs in niche markets such as cultural channels delivered on the basis of subscription. In addition, this model has provided the basis for strong opposition from commercial broadcasters to the expansion of public service broadcasters into new areas which, they have argued, are already adequately catered for by the market.

---

[5] Department for Culture, Media and Sport, *The Future Funding of the BBC: Report of the Independent Review Panel, Chairman Gavin Davies* (1999), 10.

[6] See Craufurd-Smith (1997); Barendt (1993).

[7] *The Future Funding of the BBC*, 137 and see Annex VIII for definitions and implications of market failure.

[8] For examples of such a restrictive view, see Stelzer (nd) and Veljanovski (nd).

Examples are 24-hour news coverage, websites, youth programming, sports and general entertainment, and schools provision. This model of public service broadcasting is thus constantly under threat from technological and commercial development which makes new types of market provision possible.

The other model of public service broadcasting can be called the 'cultural model', and has been developed more fully by Georgina Born and myself elsewhere.[9] We identified the main elements in the model as citizenship, universality, and quality. Citizenship, of course, covers matters such as the provision of impartial news and current affairs information and reporting major national events, but also includes appealing to the various groups which constitute a society in such a way as to bring them together whilst recognizing their differences, for example by constructing common identities and encouraging inter-group communication. Universality means three things. The first is geographical universality so that all members of the society can receive broadcasting services, including those, for example, in rural areas; it is thus a similar concern to universal service discussed in earlier chapters. Secondly, it refers to social and cultural universality through the provision of programmes that reflect the needs of a wide range of different groups. Finally, universality means universality of genre, the opposite of specialized, niche broadcasting. It means the provision of a range of different genres to meet a wide variety of needs and interests, and indeed to permit self-development through the discovery of unanticipated needs and interests. Finally, quality means both the public service broadcaster providing high-quality programmes itself and offering a lead to other broadcasters; it is connected, for example, to originality, to the need to invest in the more expensive types of production, and to support for indigenous programme-making facilities.

What is important about this cultural model is, firstly, unlike the market failure model it does not take consumer preferences as given and simply fill in gaps in meeting them. Rather it sees broadcasting as a means of developing and shaping those preferences and assisting self-development. In that sense it precedes the market rather than merely fills gaps in its provision. As one UK public service broadcaster put it, 'public service broadcasting is about an approach to broadcasting and not simply a requirement imposed on one or two broadcasters to address specific

[9] Born and Prosser (2001a).

issues of market failure'.[10] Secondly, the test for the extent and growth of public service broadcasting is different; rather than simply filling gaps in the market, new services may be justified as bringing new types of audience to the cultural mix provided by the range of public service offerings, or retaining audience there.[11] It thus comes close to the approach to public services outlined in Chapter 2 above which is based on citizenship and social solidarity rather than that underlying competition law.

Whichever model one adopts, there are important tensions and controversies in play around the relations between public service and commercial broadcasting. The most important one has been discussed already; the opposition to the expansion of public service broadcasters into fields in which the market allegedly offers adequate provision.[12] The allegation is that these expansions are unfairly subsidized by cross-subsidy from the privileged sources of funding of public service broadcasters especially if, as in the case of the BBC, that funding takes the form of a licence fee. Moreover, the provision of such funding could amount to an unlawful state aid under European Community law. Indeed, the same criticisms can be applied to existing public service provision; if a competitive market in broadcasting has already developed, how can we justify special treatment for public service broadcasting? This is especially the case if the public service broadcaster, in its eagerness to justify its position by achieving high viewing figures, has entered the mass market vigorously and so can be accused of 'dumbing down' and of neglecting minority and cultural interests, precisely criticisms which have been made recently of UK public service broadcasters including the BBC. I shall now proceed in a different way from that of earlier chapters; I shall first discuss the position of public service broadcasting in European Community law and shall follow this by more detailed description of the position in the UK.

European Law and Public Service Broadcasting

It became clear quite early on that Community law applies to broadcasting; thus in the case of *Italy v. Sacchi*[13] it was held that national

---

[10] Channel 4, *Response to the Invitation to Submit Comments on the Communications Reform White Paper* (2000).   [11] See Born and Prosser (2001b).
[12] For an excellent summary of the background see Currie and Siner (1999).
[13] Case 155/73 [1974] ECR 409.

rules protecting a public service broadcaster from competition by other European broadcasters might fall foul of the Treaty articles on competition and protecting freedom of movement of services. One outcome was the Television without Frontiers Directive of 1989 (later revised in 1997) which guarantees freedom of transmission and re-transmission whilst setting out minimum standards as a common floor; it does not prevent Member States from imposing stricter standards on broadcasters within their own jurisdictions.[14] It is also clear that, although there are no specific Community rules limiting concentration of media ownership, the general competition law rules will apply subject to the normal exceptions discussed in Chapter 6 above, and the state aid rules are also in principle applicable. As we saw in other contexts in earlier chapters, the normal rules on trade and competition are the starting point for assessing the lawfulness of the special treatment of public service broadcasting.

However, we have also seen the development in the Treaty of principles which seem to protect cultural goals.[15] For example, Article 151 introduced by the Treaty on European Union in 1992 commits the Community to 'contributing to the flowering of the cultures of the Member States' and requires the Community to take into account cultural aspects in action taken under other provisions. However, only limited measures are permitted to be taken under this article; notably, only incentive rather than harmonization measures may be used. Similarly, the same Treaty introduced a new discretionary exemption for state aid that promotes culture and conservation, but this has not been interpreted widely enough to cover most public service broadcasting.[16]

More explicit support for public service broadcasting has come from Community institutions, in particular the Parliament.[17] In 1999 representatives of Member State governments, together with the Council, resolved that public service broadcasting is of 'vital significance for

---

[14] Directive 89/552/EEC of 3 October 1989 on the co-ordination of certain provisions laid down by law, regulation or administrative action in Member States concerning the pursuit of television broadcasting activities, [1989] OJ L298/23, as amended by Directive 97/36/EC, [1997] OJ L202/60. For the results of the recent review of the Directive see European Commission, *The Future of European Regulatory Audiovisual Policy*, COM(2003)784 final.   [15] See Craufurd-Smith (2004).

[16] Art. 87(3)(d), but see Case NN-88/98, *Kindercanal and Pheonix* [1999] OJ C238/03.

[17] See notably the 'Tongue Report' appended to the European Parliament Resolution on the Role of Public Service Television in the Multi-Media Society, 19 September 1996, A4-0243/96.

ensuring democracy, pluralism, social cohesion, cultural and linguistic diversity'; moreover, 'public service broadcasting must be able to continue to provide a wide range of programming in accordance with its remit as defined by the Member States in order to address society as a whole; in this context it is legitimate for public service broadcasting to seek to reach wide audiences'.[18] By far the most important development, however, took place under the Treaty of Amsterdam. As well as introducing the new Article 16 on services of general economic interest, as discussed earlier, it introduced a new Protocol on public broadcasting, described in its recitals as comprising 'interpretative provisions'. The Protocol recites that public broadcasting is 'directly related to the democratic, social and cultural needs of each society and to the need to preserve media pluralism', and then provides that:

[t]he provisions of this Treaty . . . shall be without prejudice to the competence of Member States to provide for the funding of public service broadcasting insofar as such funding is granted to broadcasting organizations for the fulfilment of the public service remit as conferred, defined and organized by each Member State, and insofar as such funding does not affect trading conditions and competition in the Community to an extent which would be contrary to the common interest, while the realization of the remit of that public service shall be taken into account.[19]

As we shall see below, this is hardly self-explanatory, though it does reflect the underlying thrust of Article 86(2). However, as we shall see in a moment, it does appear to have influenced the Commission in favour of an approach which affords a considerable degree of discretion to national authorities in conferring a public service broadcasting remit so long as that remit is properly defined. Before considering this in detail, however, we must look at the relevant case law.

European Case Law on Public Service Broadcasting

Though there has been plenty of litigation in this field, judicial decisions establishing principles relating to the public service remit as

---

[18] Resolution of the Council and of the Representatives of the Governments of the Member States, Meeting with the Council, Concerning Public Service Broadcasting, [1999] OJ C30/1.

[19] European Union, *Treaty of Amsterdam*, Protocol on the System of Public Broadcasting in the Member States (1997).

such are few. Probably the most important such decision was taken before the Protocol was added to the Treaty; it was *Métropole Télévision SA and others v. EC Commission*.[20] The Commission had granted the European Broadcasting Union (EBU), comprising European public service broadcasters, exemption from the application of Article 81 of the Treaty for its operation of the Eurovision system for the joint buying of television rights to sporting events. Membership was only open to broadcasters providing a service of national character, producing a substantial proportion of their own programmes, and being required to provide balanced programming catering for minority interests and covering all or most of the population of their states; clearly an attempt to differentiate public service broadcasters from purely commercial concerns. The exemption was successfully challenged by excluded broadcasters in the Court of First Instance on several grounds, notably the wrongful applications of considerations relevant to Article 86(2) in granting an exemption under Article 81(3). The Commission had not applied Article 86(2) directly as it had taken a narrow view of the Article's scope, seeing it as only appropriate where the full application of the competition rules would make the public service task impossible; as we have seen in Chapter 6, this interpretation has been considerably loosened by later case law.

The Court also decided that the Commission was under a duty to examine whether the EBU's membership rules were objective and sufficiently determinate to enable them to be applied uniformly and in a non-discriminatory manner. The Commission had failed to do so, and according to the Court the content of the conditions, in the absence of further specification, could not be applied in a uniform and non-discriminatory way.[21] Nor had there been an adequate explanation of why these obligations made exclusive purchasing indispensable, and so the EBU could not benefit from an exemption under Article 81(3).

The appeal to the European Court of Justice in this case was dropped as the Commission agreed to grant a fresh exemption after the EBU had agreed new licensing rules, though this exemption for the amended licensing conditions was itself later annulled by the court on the basis of a manifest error of assessment by the Commission in determining the extent of third-party access to rights to transmit

---

[20] Cases T-528/93, T-542/93, T-543/93, and T-546/93 [1996] ECR II-649. For discussion see Craufurd-Smith (1998) 151–66.　　　　　　　　　　　　[21] At para. 97.

sporting events.[22] There has been other litigation on the issue, but it does not take further the point of general principle on the public service remit.[23] This point is that, if public service broadcasting is to be accorded exemption from the normal competition rules, there must be a clearly defined conception of such broadcasting. Otherwise, the more concrete and clearly defined concepts of competition law will prevail. This anticipates the later approach of the Commission, as we shall see.

We shall return to this question of definition of the public service remit when we come to consider Commission decisions below. It should be mentioned at this point, however, that there are important decisions relating to state aids which have a particular relevance to public service broadcasters.[24] In one decision, the Court of First Instance annulled a decision by the Commission not to proceed to a full investigation on state aid grounds of compensation paid to a Portuguese broadcaster for its public service obligations; as the Court put it, '[t]he fact that, according to the Decision, the grants were merely intended to offset the additional cost of the public service tasks assumed by RTP cannot prevent them from being classified as aid within the meaning of Article 92 [now Article 87] of the Treaty'.[25] This is of course now questionable given the *Altmark* decision discussed in Chapter 6, concluding that, subject to strict conditions, public service compensation does not constitute state aid.[26] This decision appears in conflict with the earlier decision on Portuguese compensation payments; however, the question remains whether the conditions set out in the *Altmark* decision have been met, a point to which I shall return in discussing Commission decisions below.

The two key issues raised by the case law are thus the need for a definition of the public service remit and the question of whether compensation for delivering the remit constitutes a state aid. My focus now

---

[22] See Commission Decision of 10 May 2000 [2000] OJ L151/18 and Font Galarza (2000). For the annullment, see Cases T-185/00, T-216/00, T-299/00, and T-300/00 *M6 v. Commission* [2002] ECR II-3805.

[23] See Case T-206/99 *Métropole Télévision v. EC Commission* [2001] ECR II-1057 and Case T-354/00, *M6 v. Commission* [2001] ECR II-3177.

[24] For general discussions of the position of public service broadcasters under the law of state aids, see Craufurd-Smith (2001).

[25] Case T-46/97 *SIC v. Commission* [2000] ECR II-2125, at para. 82.

[26] Case C-280/00 *Altmark Trans Gmbh* [2003] ECR I-7747.

moves from the court to the Commission in examining the rules and decisions which it has issued in this area.

The State Aids Communication

In late 2001 the Commission issued a communication on the application of state aids to public service broadcasters.[27] This is extremely important in clarifying the meaning of the Protocol to the Treaty and in stating authoritatively principles already developed in Commission decision-making. It is relevant both to state aids themselves and to the scope of the general competition rules, as, in effect, it makes the legality of state aid dependent on whether the broadcaster is providing a service of general economic interest which qualifies for a derogation from the competition rules under Article 86(2). I shall begin by examining the Communication and then consider the individual decisions taken both before and after it.

The Communication states that a public service mandate which encompasses a wide range of programming can in principle be considered as legitimate.[28] However, it sets out a number of conditions which must be complied with to render state aid for public sector broadcasting lawful. The first is that the service in question must be a service of general economic interest and clearly defined as such by the Member State. The definition falls within the competence of the Member State; in particular

a 'wide' definition, entrusting a given broadcaster with the task of providing balanced and varied programming in accordance with the remit, while preserving a certain level of audience, may be considered, in view of the interpretative provisions of the Protocol, legitimate under Article 86(2). Such a definition would be consistent with the objective of fulfilling the democratic, social and cultural needs of a particular society and guaranteeing pluralism, including cultural and linguistic diversity.[29]

Moreover, the public service remit might include services other than traditional programmes, such as on-line information services.[30] Whenever the scope of the remit is extended to cover new services, the definition and entrustment act (for which see below) should be extended accordingly.

The role of the Commission is limited to checking for manifest error in the definition of the public service remit; the Communication stresses

---

[27] *Communication from the Commission on the Application of State Aid Rules to Public Service Broadcasting*, 2001/C 320/4, [2001] OJ C320/5.   [28] Para. 13.
[29] Para. 33.   [30] Para. 34.

that '[i]t is not for the Commission to decide whether a programme is to be provided as a service of general economic interest, nor to question the nature or the quality of a certain product'.[31] However such a manifest error would be present if the remit included 'activities that could not reasonably be considered to meet – in the wording of the Protocol – the *"democratic, social and cultural needs of each society"'*.[32] The example given of an excluded activity is e-commerce, and where public service broadcasters perform commercial activities such as the sale of advertising space, this cannot normally be viewed as part of the public service remit.[33] It is emphasized that the definition of the public service mandate should be as precise as possible.[34]

The second condition is that the public service remit is entrusted to the broadcaster by means of an official act; examples given are legislation, contract, or terms of reference.[35] This clearly permits flexibility in the choice of national measure, but a further, important, condition is attached. This is that an appropriate authority monitors the application of the remit in practice; the Member State can choose the monitoring mechanism, but '[t]he role of such a body would seem to be effective only if the authority is independent from the entrusted undertaking'.[36] As we shall see below, this may have important implications for the regulation of public service broadcasting in the UK.

Finally, the funding of public service broadcasting must meet a proportionality test. For compensation, public service duties must entail supplementary costs that the broadcaster would not normally have had to meet, but the choice of the scheme of finance, for example through licence fee or a mixture of fee and advertising, falls within the competence of the Member State.[37] To assess whether the support is disproportionate, there must be 'a clear and appropriate separation between public service activities and non-public service activities' through separate accounts.[38] However, in this sector, costs that are entirely attributable to public service activities, whilst also benefiting commercial activities, need not be apportioned between the two and can be entirely allocated to public service. This would include a programme shown as part of the public service remit and later sold to other broadcasters, and also where audience is built up both to fulfil the public service remit and to sell advertising space. However, undercutting prices below stand-alone

---

[31] Para. 36.   [32] Ibid, emphasis retained.   [33] Ibid.   [34] Paras. 37–9.
[35] Para. 40.   [36] Paras. 41–2.   [37] Paras. 44–6.   [38] Para. 49.

costs in the commercial sector would indicate overcompensation for the public service remit and infringe the Protocol by affecting trading conditions and competition to an extent that would be contrary to the common interest.[39]

It should be clear that this Communication is of great importance as an interpretation of the Protocol and in granting Member States considerable freedom of movement in their definition of the public service broadcasting remit. In this sense, the Protocol seems to have had a real effect in broadening the scope for public service in the broadcasting sector, as in the case of Article 16 in other sectors. However, some important questions still remain, in particular the extent of the limitation of the permissible remit to meeting the 'democratic, social and cultural needs of each society'. In particular, to what extent can a mixed service fall within the Protocol, where it includes these themes but also includes subject matter also covered by commercial broadcasters, such as entertainment and sport? To answer these questions and others we need now to turn to some recent decisions from the European Commission.

European Commission Decisions

The first two sets of decisions taken by the Commission and to be discussed here were taken after the coming into effect of the Protocol but before the issue of the Communication. The first was the decision on *Kindercanal and Pheonix*.[40] This concerned a German children's channel with a high information content and a current affairs channel; neither carried advertising. Unsurprisingly, the Commission concluded that these did meet social and democratic objectives and so fell within the Protocol.

The second decision concerned the financing wholly from the licence fee of the new BBC News 24 channel, after a complaint had been received from BSkyB, broadcasters of the competing Sky News.[41] Among other grounds, the complaint argued that there could be no exemption under Article 86(2) as the new service did not form part of the BBC's public service tasks as defined in its Charter. The Commission decided that the funding did constitute state aid as the BBC did not have to compete for the funding in the open market, unlike its competitors. However, it was

---

[39] *Communication* (above n. 27), paras. 56–8.   [40] Case NN-70/98 [1999] OJ C238/3.
[41] Case NN 88/98 [2000] OJ C78/6.

not for the Commission to pronounce on the definition of public service in national legislation and it was for the Member State to define and organize the public service mission in the way that best suits the needs of its citizens. Nor should the Commission assess whether a service is to be provided by the market or as a service of general economic interest. In this case, it was clear that the UK authorities considered the provision of a special-interest news channel carrying no advertising to be a service of general economic interest. The Commission clearly regretted the lack of clarity in the definition of the public service under the BBC Charter in relation to ancillary services such as the new channel, but their provision needed the explicit consent of the UK Government and, notwithstanding the lack of a precisely defined remit in this case, there was a sufficient official entrustment of the task of providing a specific public service. The Commission concluded that the conditions set out in Article 86(2) were satisfied and the state aid was thus lawful.

Once more, this concerned a specialist channel devoted to news. The next decision, taken after the publication of the Communication, related to a wider range of services. It also involved the BBC, this time its highly controversial digital expansion, which has been strongly opposed by commercial broadcasters as representing unfair competition to their own services.[42] The Secretary of State had notified to the Commission her approval of nine new digital services, which she considered to be part of the existing public service remit. The services included both television and radio channels; two of the television channels were aimed at children, one was to create a 'forum of debate' aimed at 'anyone interested in culture, arts and ideas', whilst the radio services were aimed at, amongst others, a young specialist audience and an Asian audience. The Commission decided that, although the licence fee in principle provided the BBC with an economic advantage and so distorted competition, the amount provided did not go beyond the net extra costs of the public service obligation and in the light of the *Ferring* case (discussed in Chapter 6 above), it did not constitute a state aid. However, even if it was to be considered a state aid, the exception in Article 86(2) would apply. The new services could be considered to comply with the conditions in the Protocol as they 'stimulate the diversity of cultural activity in the United Kingdom, contain coverage of news and current affairs in the UK and throughout the world, provide wide-ranging coverage of sporting

---

[42] Case N 631/2001 *BBC Licence Fee.*

and other leisure interest, contain programmes of an educational nature and include a high standard of original programmes for children and young people'.[43] On the question of entrustment, once more the Commission regretted that this had not been clearly defined in relation to the new channels in the relevant legal documents, but independent supervision was secured through the role of the Board of Governors of the BBC, appointed by the Government. The Commission also stressed that the BBC kept separate accounts for public service and commercial activities, and no cross-subsidization took place, therefore the compensation could be shown not to be disproportionate to the public service costs, and so did not represent a real economic advantage to the BBC.

Several points are worthy of note about this decision. First, it relied on the controversial *Ferring* decision to decide that there was no state aid. The *Ferring* approach has been confirmed in the more recent *Altmark* decision, but subject to strict conditions. In particular, the latter suggested that, apart from the now uncontroversial requirement that public service obligations and the method for calculating compensation must be clearly defined, where no competitive tendering process had been adopted (and this had clearly not taken place in the case of the BBC), costs should be compared to those of a notional efficient undertaking performing the same tasks. No attempt to address the general efficiency of the BBC compared to such a notional undertaking has been made by the Commission and indeed it is difficult to see how such an analysis would have been possible given the enormous difference between both the nature and the scope of activities of the Corporation and its potential competitors. Instead, the Commission merely pointed to the requirements for accounting separation, for audit and the existence of the fair trading commitment by the Corporation requiring market charges to be paid by its commercial subsidiaries in acquiring programmes from its public service activities. The Corporation had to act in a similar way to a commercial undertaking in commercially exploiting such programmes, and undercutting a rival efficient operator would indicate overcompensation for public service activities. However, the fair trading commitment, commercial policy guidelines, and external audit were sufficient to show that there was no cross-subsidy from public service to commercial activities. Therefore compensation for the new digital services was not disproportionate to costs and did not constitute state aid.[44] There was no

---

[43] *BBC Licence Fee*, case (above n. 42), para. 31.   [44] Paras. 39–55.

discussion of the point made in the earlier decision relating to News 24 of the advantage given to the BBC through not having to compete in the open market for such funding. Should a similar approach continue after *Altmark*, it seems that the Commission will not require that public service compensation is awarded in future only through a system of competitive tendering but that existing methods of allocation by government will suffice.[45]

Equally importantly, even if the compensation did constitute state aid, separate justification for funding can be found on the basis of the Protocol and Article 86(2); 'the Commission also notes that, even if the measure were to be considered as a state aid, it would be compatible on the basis of Article 86(2) EC'.[46] This is important as the range of programmes included in the new services was not limited to current affairs or children's programmes, as in the earlier decisions, and the quotation above relating to the application of the Protocol suggests that the public service remit could extend to 'wide-ranging coverage of sporting and other leisure interest'. The real test of this final point could have been found in approval of a further digital channel, BBC3, which had been delayed by the Secretary of State and so was not included in the Commission's examination. This provided a service for young adults with strong entertainment content, and was the subject of the most vociferous objections from private broadcasters. However, the decision by the Commission that funding did not represent state aid made notification of this service unnecessary; had it been referred, the Commission would have had to consider whether funding could be justified on the basis of completing the BBC's digital portfolio, of attracting a major audience group to public service broadcasting and of assisting plans for digital switch-over.[47]

Finally, it is worth noting that the Commission has also taken a liberal position in other recent cases relating to funding of public service broadcasters.[48] The Commission here has taken a dual approach; examining ad hoc measures to establish whether they are compatible with state aid requirements, and undertaking so-called 'appropriate measures' proceedings to ensure that continuing support is compatible with the state aid rules, even if the basis for such support pre-dates the Treaty of Rome. It has decided that ad hoc measures taken by Italy, Portugal, and

---

[45] Cf. Santamato and Pesaresi (2004).   [46] *BBC Licence Fee*, case (above n. 42), para. 55.
[47] See Born and Prosser (2001b).
[48] For a detailed discussion see Depypere, Broche, and Tigchelaar (2004).

Spain, which had been the subject of complaints by private broadcasters, constituted state aid on the *Altmark* principles as clear parameters for their calculation had not been established in advance. However, they were saved by the application of Article 86(2) as they fell within the public service remit permitted by the Protocol, and compensation had not been in excess of the cost of meeting the public service obligations. However, issues had been raised concerning continuing support arrangements and proposals were made to increase their transparency and to avoid the possibility of overcompensation.[49] A similar decision was also taken regarding France.[50] In relation to these decisions, the Commission's Director General for Competition has noted 'I should emphasise in this context that the so-called Amsterdam Protocol on Public Service Broadcasting annexed to the EU Treaty allows the Member States *substantial latitude in defining the scope of public service broadcasting*. Nonetheless the costs for running that public service need to be clearly identified.'[51]

In European law it thus seems that the Amsterdam Protocol has made a difference; the Commission is prepared to grant a very considerable degree of latitude to Member States in defining the public service remit of broadcasters, so long as the definition falls within what appears to be a broad concept of meeting the 'democratic, social and cultural needs of each society'. What is crucial is that a clear definition and a supervisory authority are provided by a Member State wishing to take advantage of these provisions.

Public Service Broadcasting in the UK

I shall now consider the arrangements adopted in the UK, dealing first with attempts to define and enforce public service broadcasting

---

[49] *Commission Decides on Public TV Financing in Italy and Portugal*, Commission Press Release IP/03/1399, 15 October 2003.

[50] *Public Financing of Television in France Between 1988 and 1994 Proportional to the Cost of its Public Service Obligations*, Commission Press Release IP/03/1686, 10 December 2003.

[51] P. Lowe, 'Media Concentration and Convergence: Competition in Communications', *Speech to the Oxford Media Convention 2004*, available at http://europa.eu.int/comm/competition/ speeches/text/sp2004_002_en.pdf (consulted 15 July 2004) (emphasis retained). For a less liberal approach to the provision of electronic programme guides see case C2/04, *Ad hoc Measures to Dutch Public Broadcasters and NOB* (2004) OJ C61/8. I am grateful to Rachael Craufurd-Smith for drawing this to my attention.

obligations and then with recent modifications to competition law to reflect the special nature of this area.

The BBC

The primary provider of public service broadcasting in the UK is the BBC. The Corporation is not regulated by statute but under the terms of its Royal Charter and its Agreement with the Secretary of State.[52] The Charter requires the BBC to provide broadcasting services 'as public services' and programmes of information, education, and entertainment. Under the Agreement, the Corporation

undertakes to provide and keep under review the Home Services with a view to the maintenance of high general standards in all respects (and in particular in respect of their content, quality and editorial integrity) and to their offering a wide range of subject matter (having regard both to the programmes as a whole and also to the days of the week on which, and the times of the day at which, the programmes are shown) meeting the needs and interests of audiences...[53]

Other requirements are that programmes 'are provided as a public service for disseminating information, education and entertainment' and that they 'stimulate, support and reflect, in drama, comedy, music and the visual and performing arts, the diversity of cultural activity in the United Kingdom'.[54] The requirement of a wide range of subject matter is re-emphasized later in the Agreement in the context of programme standards, and due accuracy and impartiality are required in relation to controversial subjects, as well as the customary prohibition on offending good taste and decency. The Charter and Agreement are currently being reviewed as they expire in 2006; amendments were also introduced at the time of the establishment of Ofcom to bring the provisions closer into line with those applying to other broadcasters under the Communications Act, for example by requiring the BBC to produce annual statements of programme policy (for which see below) and clarifying its relations with Ofcom.[55]

[52] Department of National Heritage, *Copy of Royal Charter for the Continuance of the British Broadcasting Corporation*, Cm 3248 (1996) and *Copy of the Agreement Dated the 25th Day of January 1996 Between Her Majesty's Secretary of State for National Heritage and the British Broadcasting Corporation*, Cm 3152 (1996).   [53] Cl. 3.1.
[54] Cl. 3.2.
[55] Department for Culture, Media and Sport, *Copy of the Amendment Dated 4th December 2003 to the Agreement of 25th Day of January 1996 Between Her Majesty's Secretary of State for Culture, Media and Sport and the British Broadcasting Corporation*, Cm 6075 (2003). For the review process see http://www.bbccharterreview.org.uk/ (consulted 15 July 2004).

These provisions are supplemented by the controversial Fair Trading Commitment and Commercial Policy Guidelines. Thus the Charter requires that commercial services are funded, operated, and accounted for separately from public services.[56] The requirement is implemented and supplemented by detailed Commercial Policy Guidelines designed both to ensure that commercial activities do not conflict with the values of public service, and that there is no use of public funds to support commercial services resulting in unfair competition.[57] The rules were reviewed by a leading competition lawyer and given a generally clean bill of health; he concluded that '[i]n my view the fair trading policies of the BBC compare favourably with those of other undertakings. Indeed, I am not aware of any organization that is subject to as much scrutiny – internally and externally – to ensure compliance with Competition Law.'[58] Despite this, there has been heavy criticism of the enforcement of the Guidelines (a matter not considered in the review) by commercial operators, and this raises the general question of how the BBC is regulated.

Regulation of both the implementation of the public service remit and fair trading has been a matter for the Board of Governors of the BBC. This has been heavily criticized on the grounds that there is not a sufficiently clear separation between their management and regulatory functions so they cannot offer sufficient guarantees of independent supervision; the criticism has been reinforced by an independent, Government-commissioned review of News 24 which criticized the Governors' 'perfunctory' supervision of the new service and their failure to set targets or to provide a more detailed remit for it.[59] In response to earlier criticisms, the Governors published plans for increasing their internal independence, for example by publishing key objectives through Statements of Programming Policy, allocating to Governors responsibility for monitoring performance against specific objectives, and

---

[56] Cm 3152 (1996), (above n. 52), Art. 7(g).

[57] BBC, *Fair Trading Guidelines* (nd) available at http://www.bbc.co.uk/info/commercial/index.shtml (consulted 15 July 2004). For discussion see Currie and Siner (1999).

[58] R. Whish, *Review of the BBC's Fair Trading Commitment and Commercial Policy Guidelines* (BBC, 2001).

[59] Richard Lambert, *Independent Review of BBC News 24* (Department for Culture, Media and Sport, 2002), 21–3, available at http://www.culture.gov.uk/NR/rdonlyres/egw2mwt2 rbsj5kt4nipejt4ev4g5dpql33baiyqcm3czc3jbtn7gkcdmraiknykqyhizvb3uqkkyiz2oqvou5khhsra/independentreviewnews24.pdf (consulted 15 July 2004).

creating a specialist department of Governance and Accountability to support them.[60] In a further reflection of the criticisms, the Government has attached strict conditions, including the requirement of external review, when new services have been launched such as the new digital portfolio discussed above.[61] Under the Communications Act 2003 (CA 2003), the Governors will retain responsibility for implementing the qualitative public service broadcasting remit even after the new Office of Communications is established for the rest of the broadcasting sector. However, the new Office will have concurrent powers to enforce competition law in relation to the BBC, thus providing a level of external fair trading scrutiny.[62]

This arrangement appears unlikely to survive the Charter review given the strong criticism of governance arrangements in the Hutton Inquiry investigating the circumstances which led to the death of the Government scientist Dr David Kelly after the broadcast of material which the inquiry considered unfounded partly based on an interview with him. The inquiry report criticized the Governors as 'they should have recognized more fully than they did that their duty to protect the independence of the BBC was not incompatible with giving proper consideration to whether there was validity in the Government's complaints...'.[63] As a result, the Chairman of the Board of Governors and the Director General of the BBC resigned. In its contribution to the Charter Review, the BBC has proposed greater separation of the Governors from management within a distinct governance unit, and a 'public value test' for all new services.[64]

Public Service Broadcasting and the Private Sector

An important feature of British broadcasting is that public service obligations are not confined to the BBC, but cover the other terrestrial

---

[60] BBC, *BBC Governance in the Ofcom Age* (BBC, 2002). See also the 2003 amendment to the Agreement (above).

[61] See Department for Culture, Media and Sport, 'Tessa Jowell Announces Decision on Proposed New BBC Digital Services', Press Release 244/01, 13 September 2001; 'Tessa Jowell Gives Approval to BBC3' Press Release 175/02, 17 September 2002; 'Tessa Jowell Gives Approval to BBC Digital Curriculum', Press Release 4/03, 9 January 2003.

[62] CA 2003, s. 371.

[63] Lord Hutton, 'Report of the Inquiry into the Circumstances Surrounding the Death of Dr David Kelly C.M.G.', HC 247, 2003–4, para. 291(5).

[64] BBC, *Building Public Value: Renewing the BBC for a Digital World* (BBC, 2004), available at http://www.bbc.co.uk/thefuture/pdfs/bbc_bpv.pdf (consulted 15 July 2004).

broadcasters as well. This is most striking in relation to Channel 4 which, though financed by advertising, is a statutory non-profit corporation with no shareholders and cannot be taken over. The Broadcasting Act 1990 (BA 1990) required Channel 4 programmes to 'contain a suitable proportion of matter calculated to appeal to tastes and interests not generally catered for by Channel 3' and that 'innovation and experiment in the form and content of those programmes are [to be] encouraged'. The Channel 4 service was also to have a 'distinctive character'.[65] In the case of Channel 3, better known as ITV, there were further public service requirements in the Broadcasting Act, supplemented by the licences under which each of the broadcasters comprising the channel operate. Some took the form of negative 'consumer protection' requirements, for example the statute required in relation to all licensed services that nothing was included in programmes which offended against good taste or decency or that was likely to encourage crime or lead to disorder or be offensive to public feeling, and that news was presented with due accuracy and impartiality, a requirement also applying to the treatment of matters of political controversy or public policy.[66] The Independent Television Commission was also required to draw up a detailed programme code.[67] In addition to these negative requirements, Channel 3 licences could only be awarded if other positive conditions were fulfilled, notably that sufficient time was given to high-quality news and current affairs programmes and a sufficient amount of time was given to other programmes of high quality.[68] Further requirements imposed in the licensing process included that at least 65% of programmes should be originally produced.[69] Channel 5 was subject to less demanding quality requirements, which included a service of high quality and diversity.

Enforcement of these requirements was the responsibility of the Independent Television Commission, which could impose substantial fines for breach of licence conditions. As well as dealing with individual breaches of licensing policies or codes, the Commission undertook annual performance reviews of each licensee, taking an overall

---

[65] BA 1990, s. 25(1) (repealed by the Communications Act 2003).

[66] S. 6(1) (repealed by the Communications Act 2003).

[67] S. 7 (repealed by the Communications Act 2003).

[68] S. 16(2) (repealed by the Communications Act 2003).

[69] For further details of the requirements and the licensing process see Prosser (1997) 255–66.

view of performance during the year and highlighting any deficiencies. In 2001, however, the Commission moved to a system of self-reporting by means of annual statements of programme commitments published by the broadcasters themselves, thus anticipating more recent reforms.

The Communications Act 2003 and the Definition of Public Service Broadcasting

I have only dealt with the regulation of private public service broadcasting under the Broadcasting Act 1990 in the briefest of terms as the system was subject to major reform under the Communications Act 2003. Indeed, this Act, and the debates surrounding its passing, illustrate in microcosm the general theme of this book, being aimed both to increase the competitiveness of the British media industry through lifting restrictions on ownership and concentration, and to redefine the requirements of public service broadcasting; it will be clearer if I deal with these themes in reverse order.

The Act established the new Office of Communications (Ofcom) to regulate private sector broadcasting (along with telecommunications), although, controversially, it has no role in enforcing qualitative public service broadcasting requirements in relation to the BBC. The opportunity has been taken in the Act to spell out more clearly the public service remit applying to public service broadcasters as a whole: the BBC, and Channels 3, 4, and 5. The new regulator must produce a report within its first twelve months, and then at least every five years, on the extent to which all broadcasters, including the BBC, meet the public service remit set out in the new Act.[70] The purposes of public service broadcasting in the UK are characterized as follows;

(a) the provision of relevant television services which secure that programmes dealing with a wide range of subject-matters are made available for viewing;
(b) the provision of relevant television services in a manner which (having regard to the days on which they are shown and the times of day at which they are shown) is likely to meet the needs and satisfy the interests of as many different audiences as practicable;
(c) the provision of relevant television services which (taken together and having regard to the same matters) are properly balanced, so far as their nature and subject-matters are concerned, for meeting the needs and satisfying the interests of the available audiences; and

---

[70] CA 2003, s. 264(1–3).

(d) the provision of relevant television services which (taken together) maintain high general standards with respect to the programmes included in them, and, in particular with respect to –
(i) the contents of the programmes;
(ii) the quality of the programme making; and
(iii) the professional skill and editorial integrity applied in the making of the programmes.[71]

Further requirements for satisfying the overall public service remit are then set out; these include that the services provide a public service for the dissemination of information and for the provision of education and entertainment, that cultural activity is reflected and stimulated, that civic understanding and fair and well-informed debate on public affairs are facilitated, that the services 'satisfy a wide range of different sporting and other leisure interests', and that educational programmes are included, as must be programmes on matters such as social issues and matters of international interest. There must be a suitable range of high-quality and original programmes for children and young people, and programmes that reflect the lives and concerns of different communities within the UK.[72]

For the first time, then, we have a definition of the public service remit applying to all UK public service broadcasters, and one which goes well beyond the market failure model to appeal to a much broader cultural conception of what public service broadcasting requires. In relation to the BBC, as we saw earlier, enforcement is for the Board of Governors. For the other public service broadcasters, their regulatory regime must include a specific public service remit; for Channels 3 and 5 this is for the provision of a range of high-quality and diverse programming; that for Channel 4 includes demonstrating innovation, experiment, and creativity, appealing to the tastes and interests of a culturally diverse society, including educational programmes, and exhibiting a distinctive character.[73] In addition, of course, all services will be subject to negative consumer protection requirements, such as to abide by the standards code to be issued by Ofcom.[74]

Enforcement of the public service remit will be through a form of co-regulation.[75] Each of the broadcasters will be required to publish an annual statement of programme policy, and to monitor its performance

---

[71] CA 2003, s. 264(4).   [72] S. 264(6).   [73] S. 265(1–3).   [74] S. 325.
[75] For the role of co-regulation in broadcasting, see Closs and Nikoltchev (2003).

against the statement; Ofcom will prepare guidance on what should be included.[76] Should Ofcom consider that a public service broadcaster (except the BBC) has either failed to meet its public service remit, or (and this is very important) has failed in any respect to make an adequate contribution towards the achievement of the public service broadcasting purposes set out in the Act, if the failure is serious and not excused by economic or market conditions, Ofcom may give directions to remedy the failure. If the direction is not complied with, the broadcaster's licence may be amended to impose detailed regulation on the broadcaster.[77]

The existence of the new, more developed, definition of public service broadcasting is clearly an important development. However, given the lack of detailed or quantified requirements in it, the approach of the regulator will be crucial in determining what it means in practice. The first stage in the process of applying it is the Ofcom review of public service broadcasting in television.[78] This is to be far-reaching, being conducted in three phases which look firstly at the current position and the extent to which public service broadcasters have fulfilled the purposes set out in the Act, and assess current expectations about, and costs of, public service broadcasting. The second phase will examine prospects for the future, in the context of technological and market changes. Finally, Ofcom will issue a final report at the end of Autumn 2004, covering the extent to which public service broadcasting is being delivered effectively and setting out options for its future provision. In the first phase report, Ofcom considered that the requirements of the Communications Act had only partially been fulfilled. In the changing broadcasting environment, there would no longer be a consumer rationale for public service intervention in the market, but such a rationale based on citizenship would continue to exist. Controversially, it recommended that the obligations of commercial broadcasters should be reviewed and that public service broadcasting funding be shared between broadcasters rather than being directed only at the BBC.[79]

---

[76] CA 2003, s. 266(4–5).   [77] S. 270.

[78] For further details see Ofcom, 'The Ofcom Review of Public Service Broadcasting (PSB) Television', (2003), available at http://www.ofcom.org.uk/codes_guidelines/broadcasting/tv/psb_review/reports/112799/?a=87101 (consulted 15 July 2004).

[79] Ofcom, *Ofcom Review of Public Service Television Broadcasting: Phase 1 – Is Television Special?* (Ofcom, 2004), available at http://www.ofcom.org.uk/consultations/past/psb/psb.pdf?a=87101 (consulted 30 June 2004).

There is thus a very considerable amount of work being conducted about the concept of public service broadcasting which is most appropriate for modern UK conditions. This has to be seen in the context, however, of the simultaneous liberalization of UK media markets and the increased reliance on competitive markets subject only to general competition law even in broadcasting.

Ownership Liberalization and the Plurality Test

The other major change introduced by the Communications Act 2003 in relation to broadcasting was a considerable liberalization of ownership rules. One example was that the Act simply lifted the restriction in previous legislation which prevented persons or companies from outside the European Economic Area from holding broadcasting licences, which had excluded, for example US firms.[80] This proved highly controversial because of fears that UK broadcasters would be bought up by US media conglomerates with limited local links and little understanding of European public service expectations. The UK Government's position was that the controls on the content of the public service channels are sufficient to prevent this, and that the change was necessary to attract the maximum investment into the UK broadcasting industry. Other changes in the Act lift the restrictions on holding several Channel 3 licences, thereby ending its previous status as a network of regional licensees, and permit a concern holding more than 20% of the newspaper market to control Channel 5.[81]

The Government accepted that competition law was not sufficient in itself to guarantee that a significant number of media voices would be heard or to address concerns over editorial freedom or community voice.[82] However, the policy was also to be 'as deregulatory as possible'.[83] The influential joint House of Lords and House of Commons Committee on the draft Bill, chaired by Lord Puttnam, the film producer, took the view that the draft Bill paid insufficient regard to the requirements of media plurality, with control of mergers left to ordinary competition law. It proposed that the new merger regime under the Enterprise Act be amended to include a new plurality test, permitting the Secretary of State

---

[80] CA 2003, s. 348.   [81] S. 350 and sch. 14.

[82] Department for Culture Media and Sport and Department of Trade and Industry, *Consultation on Media Ownership Rules* (2001), para. 1.10, available at http://www.dtg.org.uk/news/archive/ownershi.pdf (consulted 15 July 2004).   [83] Ibid., para. 3.7.

to serve a public interest intervention notice (see Chapter 3 above) where plurality was at issue. The latter was to include the maintenance of a wide range of owners and voices to satisfy a variety of tastes and interests, the maintenance of a plurality of owners with a commitment to impartial news and factual programming, and a balanced and accurate presentation of news and the free expression of opinion.[84] A similar test was to apply to market investigations under the Enterprise Act, and the lifting of nationality restrictions should be delayed until Ofcom had undertaken a review of the programme supply market and had established itself as an authoritative regulator of commercial public service broadcasting.[85]

The Government's initial reaction was to resist these proposals strongly; 'the only way to guarantee sufficient levels of plurality on a cross-media basis is to set clear, specific limits on ownership through a number of key rules. Since these rules, which will apply to all mergers, are directed at the same objectives as a general plurality consideration, we do not believe that there is a need to provide additionally for a general plurality test in the Enterprise [Act] merger control regime.'[86] However, after unease at the potential effect of mergers a successful late amendment introduced a plurality test into the Act.[87] It makes complex amendments to the Enterprise Act 2002 to permit the Secretary of State to intervene in a media merger where she considers that there is a public interest consideration including the need for there to be a sufficient plurality of persons with control of media enterprises, the need for availability throughout the UK of broadcasting of high quality and calculated to appeal to a wide range of tastes and interests, and the need for a genuine commitment to the attainment of the objectives of Ofcom's standards code.[88] In such cases Ofcom will make a report on the public interest consideration, and the minister may then refer the merger to the Competition Commission. After the Commission has reported, the minister may intervene on public interest grounds to block the merger or to permit it only under conditions. No plurality test is introduced for

---

[84] Joint Committee on the Draft Communications Bill, *Draft Communications Bill: Report*, HL 169, HC 876, 2001–2, para. 224.   [85] Ibid., para. 249.

[86] *The Government's Response to the Report of the Joint Committee on the Draft Communications Bill*, Cm 5646 (2002), 25.

[87] CA 2003, ss. 375–89, and see Ofcom, *Ofcom Guidance for the Public Interest Test for Media Mergers* (Ofcom 2004), available at http://www.ofcom.org.uk/codes_guidelines/broadcasting/media_mergers/media_mergers.pdf (consulted 15 July 2004).

[88] Enterprise Act 2002, new s. 58(2C).

market investigations, nor was the liberalization of foreign ownership delayed until after the establishment of Ofcom. Although the new provision in relation to mergers was widely welcomed, it must be doubted whether it will have much importance in practice given the central role of the Secretary of State (the Ofcom report is not binding on her) and the Government's strong commitment to liberalizing media ownership markets. Overall, the Government's commitment to open markets subject to ordinary competition law is more likely to prevail than the special considerations in the plurality test.

Conclusions

A number of issues raised earlier in this book emerge particularly clearly from examination of the position of public service broadcasting in the current competitive broadcasting environment. Clearly, important tensions will remain between increased consumer choice, increased commercialization, and the requirements of public service broadcasting and these will continue to be expressed in challenges by commercial broadcasters brought in relation to the activities (especially the *new* activities) of public service broadcasters. However, dealing firstly with European law, in this context the Amsterdam Protocol does appear to have made a difference; it has been a means of protecting public service provision against successful challenges on the basis of competition and state aids law. Indeed, it goes well beyond protecting the market failure model of public service broadcasting towards accepting the cultural model; the crucial terms in the Protocol are the 'democratic, social and cultural needs of each society' which permit considerable discretion to Member States. The current approach of the Commission seems to be that public service broadcasting, on a broad cultural definition of the concept, is permissible so long as it is subject to a clearly defined remit. A couple of qualifications may be entered at this point; this has not been tested for a wholly entertainment-based service, and, despite *Altmark*, some uncertainty remains as to the conditions on which support for public service broadcasters will or will not be classified as state aid. However, recent Commission decisions suggest that these will not amount to insuperable problems as a wide range of services will fall within Article 86(2).

It could be argued that a further problem is the fact that a definition of the public service remit is needed, for this is to require definition of the

indefinable. However, the provisions in the Communications Act discussed above do go a considerable way to providing a broad cultural
definition which is nevertheless clear enough to comply with Community
law, although much depends on interpretation by Ofcom. This brings us
to the question of the relationship between public service broadcasting
and competitive markets in domestic law. It is worth pointing out at this
stage that the other countries referred to in this book, France and Italy,
have had some form of constitutional protection for public service
broadcasting through the decisions of their constitutional courts. The
effect of these has not been negligible; '[t]he primary achievement of
constitutional courts throughout Europe has been to give a clear signal
that the audiovisual media should not be treated as just another com-
modity: radio and television have become central mechanisms through
which we gain an understanding of ourselves and others'.[89] However,
these decision have had only a limited practical effect in protecting public
service principles in an environment of liberalism and a growing link
between media ownership and political influence; as the same author
notes, even at the time of the initial privatization of the major French
channel TF1, and despite a decision from the Conseil Constitutionnel
requiring continued protection of constitutional principles, the actual
obligations imposed on the privatized broadcaster were limited.[90] In Italy
the weakness of constitutional protection was even more striking; the
network became dominated by 'two national giants, RAI and the private
networks of Silvio Berlusconi'.[91] With the latter's election to the pre-
miership the concentration of interests became even more extreme, with
dire consequences for the content of Italian broadcasting.[92]

The UK experience may suggest a fruitful alternative means for protecting public service values. Rather than relying on abstract constitutional principles, the regulatory authority is given a definition of these
values by statute. This is important as it is unique to public service
broadcasting; no other area in this book has such a definition in UK law.
The regulatory body is then placed under a duty to examine the extent to

---

[89] Craufurd Smith (1997) 241. Her book gives a comprehensive analysis of the role of constitutional principles and public service broadcasting in several European jurisdictions.

[90] Ibid., 240–1.   [91] Ibid., 240.

[92] For an entertaining if horrifying account see Jones (2003) ch. 5; for controversial criticism
see the European Parliament, 'Report on the Risks of Violation, in the EU and Especially in
Italy, of Freedom of Expression and Information (Article 11(2) of the Charter of Fundamental
Rights)', 2003/2237INI.

which public service values are being achieved and to recommend better ways of doing so. However, the problem with this approach is that it sits uneasily with the Government's strong commitment to liberalization of markets and reliance on ordinary competition law, a commitment which also seems to be shared by the new regulator. Despite the cultural values implicit in the concept of public service broadcasting set out in the Competition Act, the danger is that tension may only be resolved by adopting a residual, market failure concept in practice, and that, as competition develops, this could lead to a withering away of public service values. A further problem is likely to be that of enforcement. In the UK, reflecting broader worldwide trends, the tendency has been towards concentration and internationalization of media ownership. This will be exacerbated through the Communication Act's lifting of restrictions on concentration and on cross-media ownership, whilst also opening the broadcasting ownership market to non-EEA ownership for the first time. If, as is quite likely, broadcasters become part of larger international conglomerates, it is likely to become more difficult to enforce the public service remit, especially given the new stress on self-regulation and co-regulation. It is still too early to assess the effect of the Communications Act on public service broadcasting, but it is clear that there are serious tensions between the policies it expresses of defining public service more clearly and opening markets and reliance on competition law. There could be no clearer illustration of the basic themes of this book.

10

Conclusions

Conflicting Values

This book commenced by pointing to the evident tensions between the use of markets policed by competition law and public service values. I hope that it has now documented vividly the importance of such tensions and of the contrasting ways of attempting to resolve them in different nations and in European Community law.

In some ways the tensions reflect broader clashes of vision outside the scope of this book. Thus implicit in them is one of the most fundamental conflicts of modern economic and social life; whether action is primarily determined by incentives, as the market-based model assumes, or by culture, such as the culture built around the values of public service. Similarly, the market and competition law approach can be seen as a postmodern statement of the importance of individual choice and of the undesirability of the state imposing arbitrary values on its citizens. By contrast the public service approach reflects modernist values of *égalité* and *fraternité* in addition to the *liberté* of the postmodern approach; after all, public service values have had a particularly French resonance.[1]

Development of these underlying clashes of vision must be left for elsewhere; however, one implication of them might seem to be that the market and public service approach represent incompatible visions of the world and that attempts to resolve the tension between them would be fruitless. This book has shown that in fact they must be rendered compatible because of the real dilemmas they raise; questions such as the extent to which equal access to public services should be

---

[1] For a discussion of some similar themes in relation to regulation see Moran (2003).

protected, whether pricing policies should reflect principles of affordability and geographic uniformity, and the extent to which competition law is appropriate for application to health services, all need resolution. What is most interesting is the different ways in which law has attempted to do this.

One apparently straightforward solution is to adopt a radical separation between market-based competition law and public service and simply to implement the former fully in relation to public services, whilst leaving other values for implementation by transfer payments via the tax and social security systems. We saw at the outset of this book that the recommended approach of the OECD came close to this. A further example is a recent proposal to change radically the role of the UK utility regulators, either by simply replacing them with a reformed and slimmed-down general competition authority, or by stripping them of their social responsibilities and instead requiring them only to engage in economic regulation to create competitive markets. Thus

[t]oday the regulators . . . no longer have the development of competitive markets as their primary goal. They see themselves as police forces, if not gaolers, with permanent responsibilities to protect consumers and pursue the interests of government.

This is a serious shift of orientation and almost certainly negative for GDP. One might wonder if the regulators have forgotten that free market business profits provide the wealth and the taxes for the country as a whole.[2]

Reasons for rejecting this view have been suggested earlier; in the case of the UK it looks perilously like seeking to re-run the 1997 and 2001 general elections where a commitment to social values in regulation was expressed clearly by the winning party; it is unrealistic to expect government to observe such a simple division of labour and it does not answer the objection to markets and competition law as fragmenting important values of social solidarity.

Anyway, this separation of the economic and the social and the limiting of regulation to the former does not reflect the world described in this book. This world has a complex mixture of competitive markets, competition law, and public service values, each with their own role and importance. Thus it is now almost universally accepted that liberalized markets have resulted in considerable improvements in the efficiency of some areas of public service delivery and have increased consumer choice,

---

[2] Boyfield and Ambler (2004) 3; see also 42–9, 60.

for example in the telecommunications sector. No one in any of the countries studied seriously recommends adopting an all-embracing model of service delivery through state monopolies with exclusive rights. Yet alongside this there is a continuing sense of distinctive public service values, as we can see most clearly in the recent developments in European Community law. It is important to avoid marginalizing these values, for example by adopting a minimal and residual version of universal service as the only limitation on market allocations. As we saw most vividly in the case of broadcasting, we should not conceive of public service only as a response to market failure, as that would give an undue priority to market values as the prime means of organizing public services. Rather we are talking about the rendering compatible of arrangements based on two competing sets of values, one drawn from the market with its advantages of efficiency and choice, the other from public service with its recognition of citizenship rights and egalitarian values.

The Role of Public Service Law

It is clear from the discussion in this book that it is through law that these competing values will need their ultimate resolution. This can occur negatively, through setting limits to the application of normal competition law, limits beyond which politics and social solidarity can play their role. Or it can happen more positively, through developing public service law to protect distinctive values, as in France and Italy, or in Community law (and with considerable qualification) through the role of Article 16 of the Treaty. What can we learn about this law from the evidence of this book?

Public Service Law in the UK

In the UK until recently it has not been necessary to have formal limits for the application of competition law to public services simply because the public interest test and the role of the minister gave so much discretion that such limits were unnecessary. This has now changed with the Competition Act 1998 and the Enterprise Act 2002; however, very little attention has been given to the clarification of such limits by the competition authorities and we are, for example, still awaiting a definitive version of the Office of Fair Trading's guidelines on the services of general economic interest exception. Despite the *BetterCare* decision, some doubt still remains about the extent of the application of competition law in the health and social services sectors.[3]

The more positive promotion of public service values had in the past been left to politics rather than law. We are now beginning to see a body of public service law emerging with its main source the sectoral regulators, but, as we saw in Chapter 5, it remains somewhat piecemeal and uncoordinated. One advantage of the system is, however, that we do have regulators with responsibility for securing the effective implementation of such law, and the combination of general guidance from government and detailed implementation by the specialist regulators is a promising one. This is precisely the model set out in the most recent reforms to utility regulation, although so far the role of the guidance has been relatively modest and has not sought to articulate common values across different utility sectors.

France and Italy

It is in France and (to a lesser extent) Italy that we find the positive statement of public service values enshrined in law. This has occurred at the level of principle, through the 'laws of Roland'; continuity, equality of users, and adaptability, supplemented more recently by quality of service. Moreover, these values are not necessarily incompatible with a substantial role for liberalized markets, as we saw in the recent attempts to redefine public service values as distinct from the institutional means for their realization; publicly owned monopolies are no longer required for public service. These principles are of course at a high level of abstraction, and need much work for their practical elaboration and enforcement, but of course concepts of allocative efficiency and perfect (or even workable) competition underlying competition law are also at a very high level of abstraction.[4] The French experience does suggest that social values are not simply matters for political interventions but may be the subject of more systematic legal restatement. In France, and again to some extent in Italy, these values have had a constitutional status; what is striking here is that the institutional arrangements for implementing

---

[3] *BetterCare Ltd v. Director General of Fair Trading* [2002] CAT 7.

[4] Apart from the economics literature, for discussion of these concepts in the context of competition law see Whish (2001) 2–15.

them have once more been treated flexibly, and despite the wording of the relevant French requirement (national public services 'are to become public property'), it is no longer interpreted as requiring public services to be under public ownership so long as the public authorities ensure that the provision of the services themselves is protected.

Within the context of market liberalization, the role of independent regulatory authorities has become important in Italy and France as well as in the UK. The extent to which they have autonomous powers to define public service values, or to which this is the responsibility of government, varies. Nevertheless they also provide an important means for protecting these values in key sectors, and in Italy in particular this is supplemented through the use of public service charters. It is in the context of independent regulation that we see the greatest degree of institutional convergence of any of the areas discussed in this book, largely as a result of European Community liberalization. The balance of responsibilities between Government and regulatory authorities raises issues of democratic accountability, but these are not limited to social questions, for economic regulation also needs legitimizing. The best balance is probably that described above in the UK, with the Government setting general social policies for implementation by specialist regulators.

European Community Law

It is to European Community law that we must turn for a degree of synthesis of substantive principles. For a considerable period, public service law was a poor relation to the programme for completing the single internal market, but we have now seen that this is changing, both as regards the negative restrictions on competition law's applicability and the positive statement of public service values. As regards the former, Chapter 6 documented the more generous approach being adopted by the Community courts in their interpretation of Article 86(2) and the clarification of the position of compensation for the undertaking of public service obligations in state aid law by the *Altmark* decision.[5]

For the positive statement of public service values we have Article 16 of the Treaty and Article 36 of the Charter of Fundamental Rights. There are also important provisions performing a similar role in relation to

---

[5] Case C-280/00 *Altmark Trans GmbH* [2003] ECR I-7747.

public service broadcasting. All these statements of constitutional values are of course highly qualified, extremely ambiguous and leave the initiative in promoting public service values to Member States. Nevertheless, they are important, as has been suggested, in amounting to a recognition of the importance of citizenship rights within the single market and do seem to have had a real effect in promoting a more positive attitude to public service values by the Community courts and the Commission. Fuller recognition of particular aspects of public service, in particular universal service, can be found in the liberalized sectors, especially telecommunications or electronic communications as they are now termed. The 2003 Green Paper on Services of General Interest went further by suggesting common elements which could provide the basis for a Community concept of general economic interest. These include universal service, continuity, quality of service, affordability, and user and consumer protection, and were not simply stated at an abstract level. Thus the Paper discussed in some detail their potential application in practice in various sectors.[6]

The resulting White Paper was more cautious, at least until the new Constitutional Treaty provides a firmer basis for a framework Directive.[7] It did however promise clarification of a number of key questions and, whatever doubts may exist as a matter of practical politics, the various Community initiatives have illustrated once more that there is a common core of principle which is to be found lying behind particular limits to the full application of competition law to public services. Moreover, the Green and White Papers also stressed the importance of independent regulatory authorities as a means of implementing public service values; for example, '[i]mplementation of the principle of universal service is a complex and demanding task for national regulators' and 'implementation of these principles generally requires the existence of independent regulators with clearly defined powers and duties'.[8] This both reflects the growth of such regulatory authorities referred to above, and also encourages it as an essential part of liberalization. The role of the

---

[6] Commission of the European Communities, *Green Paper on Services of General Interest*, COM(2003)270 final, paras. 49–75 and Annex.

[7] Commission of the European Communities, *Communication from the Commission to the European Parliament, the Council, the European Economic and Social Committee and the Committee of the Regions, White Paper on Services of General Interest*, COM(2004)374.

[8] *Green Paper on Services of General Interest*, para. 54; *White Paper on Services of General Interest*, s. 3.5.

regulatory authorities provides a further common element in the developing European concept of public service.

Choosing the Public Service Provider and Supervisory Institutions

If we accept that there are legitimate limits to the use of competitive markets in the provision of public services, how do we than secure accountability other than through the use of competition law? One possible means of doing so remains especially controversial and merits special discussion here. This is the extent to which public services should be delivered only after a choice of the operator carried out by a process of competitive tendering.[9] As we established in Chapter 6, this is now particularly important as a result of the *Altmark* decision, and the fourth, and most demanding, condition in that case for the classification of public service compensation as outside the scope of notifiable state aid. The condition was that either the compensation was awarded through a public procurement procedure based on the lowest cost, or that the compensation was no greater than that which a notional efficient undertaking would require.[10] Similarly, in the area of transport draft legislation to require an extended use of competitive tendering in the award of public service contracts is proving highly controversial.

Clearly, there may in some circumstances be advantages in the use of competitive tendering. The procurement Directives have had an important role in making purchasing by public authorities throughout the Union more transparent, though even these have been subject to criticism as overformalized and restrictive, preventing the building up of long-term co-operative relationships with suppliers.[11] Contracting out some services may also have advantages in increasing the diversity of modes of delivery; a striking example is the very successful history of the British Channel 4 broadcaster which commissions work from

---

[9] See Cox (2003).

[10] Case C-280/00 *Altmark Trans GmbH* [2003] ECR I-7747, at para 93.

[11] Arrowsmith (1997) 401–10. Provision is made in the new Directive for a new procedure of 'competitive dialogue' in the case of particularly complex contracts, as a partial solution to this problem; Directive 2004/18/EC of the European Parliament and of the Council of 31 March 2004 relating to the co-ordination of procedures for the award of public works, supply and services contracts [2004] OJ L134/114, 30/4/04, Art. 29.

independent producers. However, a process of competitive tendering may also have serious disadvantages. These may include high transaction costs due to complex tendering requirements, possible disadvantages to public authorities compared with the private sector, for example due to wage levels and limitations of their work to particular local areas, and a potential 'race to the bottom' lowering standards.[12] Frequent tendering may also contradict the important principle of the continuity of public service. Most fundamentally, the UK experience of compulsory competitive tendering in local government has suggested that it has undermined some of the central values associated with the provision of public services. Thus, to repeat a point made in my introduction, ' "[h]ard" quasi-market structures have tended to undermine the trusting, co-operative relationships necessary for efficient contracting. Excessive separation of interests is accompanied by communication and information flow problems, and by increased risk of opportunism by one or both sides ... The result has been a tendency to relatively high levels of conflict expressed in defaults, penalties and disputes.'[13] If public service is ultimately a cultural commitment, it may prove difficult to express fully that culture in the words of a contract.

Moreover, there will be situations in which it will simply be impossible to create proper competitive tendering because there are overwhelming reasons to favour a particular incumbent because of its critical mass of skills and of established expertise. A striking example is that of the BBC in British public service broadcasting.[14] Although there is currently debate about the extent to which some competitive bidding should be permitted by other broadcasters for a share of the BBC's license fee, putting the entire range of BBC activity out to periodic tender is not on any serious political agenda. Even the UK Government has noted the difficulties of using competitive tendering in relation to the award of ferry services off the West Coast of Scotland where, given the long life of harbour facilities and vessels, a short-term contract allocated by competitive tendering would represent a strong disincentive to investment.[15]

---

[12] Cox (2003) 18–24.   [13] Vincent-Jones (1997) 154.

[14] See Craufurd-Smith (2001).

[15] United Kingdom Permanent Representatives to the European Union, *UK Government Response to the Green Paper of Services of General Interest* (2003), available at http://europa.eu.int/comm/secretariat_general/services_general_interest/docs/public_authorities/repres_uk.pdf (consulted 16 July 2004), para. 37.

The problem is compounded by the fact that there is also difficulty with the other alternative approach suggested in *Altmark*, that of assessing public service compensation on the basis of what a notional efficient undertaking would require. This was already recognized in the slightly earlier *Chronopost* decision, where it was held that such an approach was not appropriate where no market for the provision of universal service existed.[16] This may appear partially to alleviate the problem that where there are a limited number of providers, 'a tender or even a survey of typical costs would not prove very useful, but skipping those procedures leads to a finding of aid'.[17] Nevertheless, the effect of the *Altmark* decision could well be to encourage further use of competitive tendering to avoid the uncertainty connected with alternative means of assessment.

It is useful to compare this approach with that adopted by the Commission in its examination of the BBC's new digital services.[18] Here there had been no competitive tendering for the supply of services, and the Commission made no attempt to compare the BBC with a notional efficient competitor. Instead, it concentrated on the institutional arrangements to secure transparency in the relationship between publicly funded and commercial services. Thus it pointed to the requirements for accounting separation between the two, to the existence of the Corporation's Fair Trading Commitment and Commercial Policy Guidelines, the audit of compliance and the requirement that market charges be paid by commercial subsidiaries in acquiring programmes from the public service side of operations. Such an examination of other institutional means of transparency without requiring competitive tendering or the often impossible task of devising a notional efficient competitor is more in keeping with the spirit of the Public Broadcasting Protocol and Article 16 than a near-general requirement for such tendering. Of course, as we saw in the preceding chapter, there is controversy about the effectiveness of the policing of these obligations and the arrangements for the BBC's governance, but these specific problems of enforcement do not invalidate the overall point that such institutional arrangements may secure transparency if properly implemented; indeed, in the form of accounting separation and independent regulation they form a key plank in Community liberalization policies. Thus an

---

[16] Cases C-83/01, C-93/01, and C-94/01 *Chronopost and Others* [2003] ECR I-6993, and see Bartosch (2003).   [17] Santamato and Pesaresi (2004) 19.
[18] Case N 631/2001 *BBC Licence Fee*, esp. paras. 39–55, discussed in Chapter 9 above.

appropriate balance between competition and public service values may be implemented through 'proceduralization' and appropriate institutional arrangements, especially independent regulation, and this provides the best solution to the accountability problem.[19] Competitive tendering is neither a necessary nor a sufficient condition for transparency in achieving this balance.

Concluding Remarks

In Chapter 2 of this book I examined the justifications for different approaches to the delivery and regulation of public services; the competition law-based model, that based on social and economic rights, and that based on social solidarity. In Chapters 5 and 7 we saw that the different approaches are embedded in diverse national legal traditions around the relationship between competition law and public service law. We are, however, seeing some convergence between the different traditions, especially in Community law. What is important for the future is that none of the models should be ignored. Thus it is clear that the use of markets has brought some important benefits in some areas of public services, especially in the utilities such as telecommunications and energy supply. However, rights-based concerns and the importance of social solidarity also play a major role in the legitimacy of public services. This is why a market failure approach is too narrow; it treats the primary value as that of competitive markets, to which other values are secondary and only come into play as a means of mopping up residual problems which the market cannot resolve. What I have suggested instead is that each of the different approaches has a legitimacy of its own, and that resolving particular difficulties should depend on which we wish to prioritize in the particular situation. Thus, in a type of public service which is required for basic well-being (for example water) we might wish to prioritize social rights and, for example, prohibit disconnection of supply because we regard the service as truly essential. In other situations we might wish to prioritize social solidarity, for example in public service broadcasting with its close links to citizenship. Public service should not be reduced to a minimum, such as only basic universal service requirements, applicable merely in cases of market failure.

---

[19] See Schepel (2002).

How should law implement these values? It is not necessary to give the concept of public service formal constitutional status. Doing so provides a useful starting point for debate about the meaning of public service, and prevents the loss of public service concerns in enthusiasm for competitive markets, as has clearly been illustrated by the role of Article 16 in Community law. Yet in those countries which have given it such status, the concept has had to be interpreted very flexibly to reflect the development of liberalization, and anyway such a constitutionalization is hardly feasible in the UK. However, we should not leave the protection of public service values only to politics (the older UK approach) or to 'soft law' such as codes of practice, guidelines, and social action plans alone. The reason for this is that competition law is now very much a matter of 'hard law', even in the UK as a result of its recent reform, and is clearly applicable to important areas of public service delivery, especially after the *BetterCare* decision. In a conflict between the 'hard law' of competition and 'soft law' of public service, the latter is unlikely to survive as a source of distinctive values.

Fortunately, we do now have a growing body of 'hard law' of public service in the form of the amendments to the Treaty made by the Treaty of Amsterdam, especially Article 16, some of the more recent decisions of the Court of Justice (including, for all its ambiguity in relation to competitive tendering, *Altmark*), and in the law which has accompanied sectoral liberalization, notably universal service in telecommunications. The European Court of Justice and, in particular, the Commission are making progress in their attempts to resolve the tensions between different values relating to public services described in this book. This is particular so in the finding of common principles, largely drawn from the liberalized sectors, which can potentially be applied elsewhere. This was a central theme of the 2003 Green Paper, as we saw in Chapter 7, although the later White Paper takes a cautious approach, at least until the Constitutional Treaty becomes effective. The approach in the Green Paper is far ahead of anything in domestic law, where the extreme delay in finalizing the guidance on the services of general economic interest exclusion suggests that clarifying these issues is hardly a priority for the domestic competition authorities.

This might seem naturally to lead to the development of a framework Directive on services of general interest which can clarify and render consistent the basic common values and principles applicable to such services; and indeed there is an urgent need for such clarification, for example of the application of competition law to health and social services. However, there is no consensus on the need for a Directive and uncertainty remains over the national ratification of the Constitutional Treaty, which might make the likelihood of agreement of such a Directive seem remote. Moreover, given the lack of consensus, the adoption of a framework Directive in this form might lead to the statement of common principles at such a high level that they are difficult to translate into concrete obligations. Nevertheless, the draft Constitutional Treaty does envisage such a framework Directive, and clarification of other issues is promised by the Commission's White Paper, mainly through soft law.

Whatever the outcome, this debate illustrates an important theme which has provided the basic subject matter of this book. Public service, like competition, is too important to be left only to markets and politics and not to law. We are now seeing a greater acceptance of the central role of law in protecting public service values, especially in European Community law. The different national traditions and the contending values, so strongly documented in this book, now show a degree of convergence. It is essential that we continue to protect the distinctive values of public service within our growing body of economic law.

BIBLIOGRAPHY

Abbamonte, G. (1998) 'Cross-Subsidisation and Community Competition Rules: Efficient Pricing versus Equity', 23 *European Law Review* 414–33.

Allison, J. W. F. (2000) *A Continental Distinction in the Common Law*, revised edn (Oxford: Oxford University Press).

Amato, G. (1997) *Antitrust and the Bounds of Power* (Oxford: Hart Publishing).

——(1998) 'Citizenship and Public Services – Some General Reflexions', in M. Freedland and S. Sciarra (eds) *Public Services and Citizenship in European Law* (Oxford: Clarendon Press) 145–56.

Armstrong, K. and Bulmer, S. (1998) *The Governance of the Single European Market* (Manchester: Manchester University Press).

Arrowsmith, S. (1997) 'The Way Forward or a Wrong Turning? An Assessment of European Community Policy on Public Procurement in the Light of the Commission's Green Paper', 3 *European Public Law* 389–411.

Barendt, E. (1993) *Broadcasting Law: A Comparative Study* (Oxford: Clarendon Press).

Bartosch, A. (2001) 'Joined Cases C-147–148/97 *Deutsche Post AG*', 38 *Common Market Law Review* 195–210.

——(2003) 'Clarification or Confusion? How to Reconcile the ECJ's Rulings in *Altmark* and *Chronopost*', CLASF Working Paper 2, at http://www.clasf.org/assets/CLaSF%20Working%20Paper%2002.pdf (consulted 16 July 2004).

Battini, S. (1998) 'La tutela dell'utente e la carta dei servizi pubblici', *Rivista Trimestrale di Diritto Pubblico* 185–95.

Bazex, M. (1998) 'Le droit public de la concurrence', 14 *Revue Française de Droit Administratif* 781–800.

Bell, J. (1995) *French Constitutional Law* (Oxford: Clarendon Press).

——(1999) 'The Concept of Public Service under Threat from Europe? An Illustration from Energy Law', 5 *European Public Law* 189–98.

Beyleveld, D. (1995) 'The Concept of a Human Right and Incorporation of the European Convention of Human Rights' *Public Law* 577–98.

Beyleveld, D. and Villiers, C. (1997) 'A General Right to a Minimum Wage in English Law: An Argument from Generic Consistency', 17 *Legal Studies* 234–57.

Bonadio, G. (2003) 'Il servizio universale', *Cahiers Européens*, at http://www.cahiers.org/new/HTM/ARTICOLI/bonadio_serviziouniversale.htm (consulted 16 July 2004).

Bork, R. H. (1993) *The Antitrust Paradox*, revised edn (New York: The Free Press).

Born, G. and Prosser, T. (2001a) 'Citizenship, Public Service Broadcasting and the BBC's Fair Trading Obligations', 64 *Modern Law Review* 657–687.

——(2001b) 'A Digital BBC', *Financial Times*, 11 September 2001, 23.

Boyfield, K. and Ambler, T. (2004) *Do the UK Regulatory Agencies Provide Taxpayer Value?* (London: London Business School Centre for Marketing), at http://www.london.edu/news_events/March_2004_Ambler_regulation_report.pdf (consulted 16 July 2004).

Braconnier, S. (2001) 'La régulation des services publics', 17 *Revue Française de Droit Administratif* 43–57.

Bright, C. and Currie, K. (2003) 'Is *BetterCare* a Bitter Pill?', 24(1) *European Competition Law Review* 41–5.

Broussolle, R. (1997) 'La création de Réseau ferré de France', *Actualité Juridique – Droit Administratif* 456–461.

Brown, L. N. and Bell, J. (1998) *French Administrative Law*, 5th edn (Oxford: Oxford University Press).

Buendia Sierra, J. L. (1999) *Exclusive Rights and State Monopolies under EC Law* (Oxford: Oxford University Press).

Burrows, N. and Mair, J. (1996) *European Social Law* (Chichester: John Wiley).

Cameron, P. (2002) *Competition in Energy Markets: Law and Regulation in the European Union* (Oxford: Oxford University Press).

Carty, H. (2001) *An Analysis of the Economic Torts* (Oxford: Oxford University Press).

Cassese, S. (1994) 'Deregulation and Privatization in Italy', in M. Moran and T. Prosser (eds) *Privatization and Regulatory Change in Europe* (Buckingham: Open University Press), 50–65.

——(1995) *The Difficult Profession of Minister of Public Administration* (Florence: European University Institute).

——(1999) 'La retorica del servizio universale', in S. Frova (ed.) *Telecomunicazioni e Servizio Universale* (Milan: Giuffre Editore), 91–3.

——(2004) *La Nuova Constituzione Economica*, 3rd edn (Rome: Editori Laterza).

Centre Européen des Entreprises à Participation Publique (1995) *Europe, Concurrence et Service Public* (Paris: Masson).

Chevallier, J. (1996a) 'La nouvelle réforme des télécommunications: ruptures et continuités', 12 *Revue Française de Droit Administratif* 925–43.

——(1996b) 'La réforme de l'état et la conception française du service public', 77 *Revue Française d'Administration Publique* 189–205.

——(1997) 'La mise en oeuvre de la réforme de la télécommunications', 13 *Revue Française de Droit Administratif* 1115–1128.

Clarich, M. (2003) 'Servizi pubblici e diritto europeo della concorrenza: l'experienza italiana e tedesca a confronto', *Rivista Trimestrale di Diritto Pubblico* 91–125.

Closs, W. and Nikoltchev, S. (eds) (2003) *Iris Special: Co-Regulation of the Media in Europe* (Strasbourg: European Audiovisual Observatory).

Colliard, C. A. (1964) 'L'obscure clarité de l'article 37', *Dalloz*, Ch. XXXVII, 263–272.

Conseil D'Etat (1995) *Etudes et Documents No. 46, Rapport Public 1994* (Paris: La Documentation Française).

Cox, H. (2003) 'Questions about the Initiative of the European Commission Concerning the Awarding and Compulsory Competitive Tendering of Public Service Concessions', 74 *Annals of Public and Cooperative Economics* 7–31.

Craig, P. (1987) 'The Monopolies and Mergers Commission', in R. Baldwin and C. McCrudden (eds) *Regulation and Public Law* (London: Weidenfeld and Nicholson), 201–226.

——(1991) 'Constitutions, Property and Regulation', *Public Law* 538–54.

Craufurd-Smith, R. (1997) *Broadcasting Law and Fundamental Rights* (Oxford: Clarendon Press).

——(1998) 'Getting the Measure of Public Services: Community Competition Rules and Public Service Broadcasting', III 1997/8 *Yearbook of Media and Entertainment Law* 147–75.

——(2001) 'State Support for Public Service Broadcasting: The Position Under European Community Law', 28(1) *Legal Issues of European Integration* 3–22.

——(2004) 'Community Intervention in the Cultural Field: Continuity or Change?', in R. Craufurd-Smith (ed.) *Culture and European Union Law*, (Oxford: Oxford University Press), 19–78.

Curien, N. and Henry, C. (1999) 'Liberalisation and Regulation of Public Services in France', in Centre for the Study of Regulated Industries, *Regulatory Review 1998/9* (Bath: Centre for the Study of Regulated Industries), 113–30.

Currie, D. and Siner, M. (1999) 'The BBC: Balancing Public and Commercial Purpose', in Andrew Graham *et al.* (eds) *Public Purposes in Broadcasting: Funding the BBC* (Luton: University of Luton Press), 73–97.

Daintith, T. (1974) 'The United Kingdom', in W. Friedmann (ed.) *Public and Private Enterprise in Mixed Economies* (New York: Stevens), 195–287.

Daintith, T. and Sah, M. (1993) 'Privatisation and the Economic Neutrality of the Constitution', *Public Law* 465–87.

Davies, A. C. L. (2000) 'Don't Trust Me, I'm a Doctor: Medical Regulation and the 1999 NHS Reforms', 20 *Oxford Journal of Legal Studies* 437–56.

——(2001) *Accountability: A Public Law Analysis of Government by Contract* (Oxford: Oxford University Press).

De Falco, V. (2003) *Il Servizio Pubblico tra Ordinamento Comunitario e Diritti Interni* (Milan: Cedam).

De Lucia, L. (2002) *La Regolazione Amministrativa dei Servizi di Pubblica Utilità* (Turin: G. Giappichelli Editore).

Debène, M. and Raymundie, O. (1996) 'Sur le service universel: renouveau du service public ou nouvelle mystification?', 52(3) *Actualité Juridique – Droit Administratif* 183–91.

Depypere, S., Broche, J., and Tigchelaar, N. (2004) 'State Aid and Broadcasting: State of Play', *Competition Policy Newsletter* 71–3.

Downie, G. and Macgregor, L. (2000) 'Essential Facilities and Utility Networks', in L. Macgregor, T. Prosser, and C. Villiers (eds) *Regulation and Markets Beyond 2000* (Aldershot: Ashgate), 19–41.

Duff, A. (ed.) (1997) *The Treaty of Amsterdam* (London: Federal Trust).

Duguit, L. (1970) *Law in the Modern State*, tr. F. and H. Laski (New York: Howard Fertig) (originally published in English 1919).

Dworkin, R. (1985) *A Matter of Principle* (Oxford: Oxford University Press).

——(1986) *Law's Empire* (London: Fontana).

——(2000) *Sovereign Virtue: The Theory and Practice of Equality* (Cambridge, Mass.: Harvard University Press).

Dyson, K. (1980) *The State Tradition in Western Europe* (Oxford: Martin Robertson).

Egenhofer, C. (1995) 'Utilities Policy and the European Union – An Overview', in Centre for the Study of Regulated Industries, *Regulatory Review 1995* (London: Centre for the Study of Regulated Industries), 155–70.

Eisner, M. A. (1991) *Antitrust and the Triumph of Economics: Institutions, Expertise and Policy Change* (Chapel Hill, N.C.: University of North Carolina Press).

Ernst, J. (1994) *Whose Utility? The Social Impact of Public Utility Privatisation and Regulation in Britain* (Buckingham: Open University Press).

Esplugas, P. (1998) 'Le Conseil Constitutionnel et le service public', in Kovar and Simon (eds) vol. II, 39–47.

Ewing, K. (2001) 'Constitutional Reform and Human Rights: Unfinished Business?', 5 *Edinburgh Law Review* 297–324.

Fabre, C. (2000) *Social Rights under the Constitution: Government and the Decent Life* (Oxford: Clarendon Press).

Faulkner, D. (1998) 'Public Services, Citizenship and the State – the British Experience 1967–97', in M. Freedland and S. Sciarra (eds) *Public Services and Citizenship in European Law* (Oxford: Clarendon Press), 35–48.

Fleischer, H. (2003) 'Case C-367/98 *Commission of the European Communities v. Portuguese Republic* (Golden Shares)', 40 *Common Market Law Review* 493–501.

Flynn, L. (1999) 'Competition Policy and Public Services in EC Law after the Maastricht and Amsterdam Treaties', in D. O'Keefe and P. Twomey (eds) *Legal Issues of the Amsterdam Treaty* (Oxford: Hart Publishing), 185–99.

Font Galarza (2000) 'The Commission's Assessment of the Eurovision System Pursuant to Article 81 EC', 2 *EC Competition Policy Newsletter* 28.

Footer, M.E. and Beat Graber, C. (2000) 'Trade Liberalization and Cultural Policy', *Journal of Economic Law* 115–44.

Forbes, A. and Rodriguez, F. (1999) 'The Postal Sector 1997–8', in Centre for the Study of Regulated Industries, *Regulatory Review 1998–9* (Bath: Centre for Regulated Industries), 45–63.

Foster, C. D. (1992) *Privatization, Public Ownership and the Regulation of Natural Monopoly* (Oxford: Blackwell).

Fournier, J. (2000) 'Il Trasport Ferroviario in Francia', in E. Ferrari (ed.) *I Servizi a Rete in Europa* (Milan: Raffaello Cortina Editore), 271–92.

——(2001) *Les Services Publics*, at http://www.premier-ministre.gouv.fr/fr/p.cfm?ref=23009 (consulted 1 July 2004).

Fredman, S. (2004) 'Social, Economic and Cultural Rights', in D. Feldman (ed.) *English Public Law* (Oxford: Oxford University Press), 529–79.

Freedland, M. (1998) 'Law, Public Services and Citizenship – New Domains, New Regimes?', in M. Freedland and S. Sciarra (eds) *Public Services and Citizenship in European Law* (Oxford: Clarendon Press), 1–34.

Freeman, P. and Whish, R. (1999) *A Guide to the Competition Act 1998* (London: Butterworth).

Furse, M. (2002) *Competition Law of the UK and EC*, 3rd edn (Oxford: Oxford University Press).

Gerber, D. T. (1998) *Law and Competition in Twentieth Century Europe: Protecting Prometheus* (Oxford: Clarendon Press).

Gewirth, A. (1996) *The Community of Rights* (Chicago, Ill.: University of Chicago Press).

Giani, L. (2002) *Attività Amministrativa e Regolazione di Sistema* (Turin: G. Giappichelli Editore).

Goldberg, D., Prosser, T., and Verhulst, S. (eds) (1998) *Regulating the Changing Media: A Comparative Study* (Oxford: Clarendon Press).

Graham, C. and Prosser, T. (1988) 'Golden Shares: Industrial Policy by Stealth?', *Public Law* 413–31.

——(1991) *Privatizing Public Enterprises: Constitutions, the State, and Regulation in Comparative Perspective* (Oxford: Clarendon Press).

Hammer, U. (2002) 'EC Secondary Legislation of Network Markets and Public Service: An Economic and Functional Approach', 3 *Journal of Network Industries* 39–75.

Hancher, L. (1994) 'Case C-320/91 P, *Procureur du Roi v Paul Corbeau*', 31 *Common Market Law Review* 105–22.

——(1996) 'Utilities Policy and the European Union', in Centre for the Study of Regulated Industries, *Regulatory Review 1996* (Bath: Centre for the Study of Regulated Industries), 119–42.

——(1999) 'Community, State and Market', in P. Craig and G. de Búrca (eds) *The Evolution of EU Law* (Oxford: Oxford University Press), 721–43.

——(2003) 'Revising the European Community's Internal Energy Market', in Centre for the Study of Regulated Industries, *Regulatory Review 2002/3* (Bath: Centre for Regulated Industries), 253–77.

Harden, I. (1992) *The Contracting State* (Buckingham: Open University Press).

Hare, I. (2002) 'Social Rights as Fundamental Human Rights', in B. Hepple (ed.) *Social and Labour Rights in a Global Context* (Cambridge: Cambridge University Press), 153–81.

Harlow, C. (1998) 'Public Service, Market Ideology, and Citizenship', in M. Freedland and S. Sciarra (eds) *Public Services and Citizenship in European Law* (Oxford: Clarendon Press), 49–56.

Hepple, B. (ed.) (2002) *Social and Labour Rights in a Global Context* (Cambridge: Cambridge University Press).

Herbert, A. and Kempson, E. (1995) *Water Debt and Disconnection* (London: Policy Studies Institute).

Herold, A. (2003) 'European Public Film Support Within the WTO Framework' *IRIS, IRIS Plus*, 2003–6, 1–8.

Jones, A. and Sufrin, B. (2004) *EC Competition Law: Text, Cases and Materials*, 2nd edn (Oxford: Oxford University Press).

Jones, T. (2003) *The Dark Heart of Italy* (London: Faber and Faber).

Klein, G. (2003) *Life Lines: the NCC's Agenda for Affordable Energy, Water and Telephone Services* (London: National Consumer Council).

Koenig, C., Bartosch, A., and Braun, J.-D. (eds) (2002) *EC Competition and Telecommunications Law* (The Hague: Kluwer).

Kovar, R. (1996) 'Droit communitaire et service public: esprit d'orthodoxie ou pensée laïcisée', 32(3) *Revue Trismestrielle de Droit Européen* 215–42, 493–533.

Kovar, R. and Simon, D. (eds) (1998) *Service Public et Communauté Européene: Entre l'Interêt Général et le Marché* (Paris: La Documentation Française).

Lewis, N. (1996) *Choice and the Legal Order* (London: Butterworth).

Lewis, N. and Seneviratne, M. (1992) 'A Social Charter for Britain', in A. Coote (ed.) *The Welfare of Citizens: Developing New Social Rights* (London: Institute for Public Policy Research), 31–54.

Littlechild, S. (1984) *Regulation of British Telecommunications Profitability* (London: Department of Trade and Industry).

Loughlin, M. (1992) *Public Law and Political Theory* (Oxford: Oxford University Press).

Lyon-Caen, A. (2002) 'The Legal Efficacy and Significance of Fundamental Social Rights: Lessons from the European Experience', in B. Hepple (ed.) *Social and Labour Rights in a Global Context* (Cambridge: Cambridge University Press), 182–91.

Maher, I. (2000) 'Juridification, Codification and Sanction in UK Competition Law', 63 *Modern Law Review* 544–69.

Maisl, H. (1995) 'La régulation des télécommunications, changements et perspectives', 11 *Review Française de Droit Administratif* 449–61.

Malaret Garcia, E. (1998) 'Public Service, Public Services, Public Functions and Guarantees of the Rights of Citizens: Unchanging Needs in a Changed Context', in M. Freedland and S. Sciara (eds) *Public Services and Citizenship in European Law* (Oxford: Clarendon Press), 57–82.

Marchetti, P. (ed.) (1995) *Le Privatizzazioni in Italia* (Milan: Dott A. Giuffrè Editore).

Marconi, P. (1998) 'La carta dei servizi pubblici e la *Citizen's Charter*: La normativa sulla carta dei servizi', *Rivista Trimestrale di Diritto Pubblico* 197–205.

Markus, J.-P. (2001) 'Le principe d'adaptabilité: de la mutabilité au devoir d'adaption des services publics aux besoins des usagers', 17 *Revue Française de Droit Administratif* 589–604.

McAuslan, P. and McEldowney, J. (1988) 'A Legal Framework for Privatised Electricity Supply', 9 *Urban Law and Policy* 165–200.

Melleray, F. (2003a) 'La notion judiciaire de service public', *Actualité Juridique – Droit Administratif*, 114–17.

——(2003b) 'Fonction publique et service public: le cas de France Télécom', *Actualité Juridique – Droit Administratif*, 2078–82.

Moderne, F. (1998) 'Les mutations des services publics en droit français', in Kovar and Simon (eds), vol. I, 3–31.

Monti, G. (2002) 'Article 81 EC and Public Policy', 39 *Common Market Law Review* 1057–99.

Moran, M. (2003) *The British Regulatory State: High Modernism and Hyper-Innovation* (Oxford: Oxford University Press).

Mueller, M. (1993) 'Universal Service in Telephone History: A Reconstruction', 17 *Telecommunications Policy* 352–69.

Napolitano, G. (2000) 'Il servizio universale e i diritti dei cittadini utenti', 11 *Mercato, Concorrenze, Regole* 429–455.

Nelken, D. (ed.) (1997) *Comparing Legal Cultures* (Aldershot: Dartmouth).

Nelken, D. and Feest, J. (eds) (2001) *Adapting Legal Cultures* (Oxford: Hart Publishing).

Nicinski, S. (2004) 'Les évolutions du droit administratif de la concurrence', *Actualité Juridique – Droit Administratif* 751–760.

Nicinski, S. and Pintat, P. (2003) 'La libéralisation du secteur gazier', *Actualité Juridique – Droit Administratif* 223–31.

Nihoul, P. and Rodford, P. (2004) *EU Electronic Communications Law: Competition and Regulation in the European Telecommunications Market* (Oxford: Oxford University Press).

Oberdoff, H. (1998) 'La service public à la française', in Kovar and Simon (eds), vol. II, 89–102.

OECD (1997) *The OECD Report on Regulatory Reform: Synthesis* (Paris: OECD).

——(2002) *Regulatory Policies in OECD Countries: From Interventionism to Regulatory Governance* (Paris: OECD).

Ogus, A. (1994) *Regulation: Legal Form and Economic Theory* (Oxford: Clarendon Press).

Parisio, V. (1998) 'Servizzi pubblici e monopoli', in E. Picozza (ed.) *Dizionario di diritto pubblico dell'economia* (Rimini: Maggioli Editore), 687–733.

Pelkmans, J. (1997) 'Utilities Policy and the European Union', in Centre for the Study of Regulated Industries, *Regulatory Review 1997* (London: Centre for the Study of Regulated Industries), 111–31.

Posner, R. (2001) *Antitrust Law*, 2nd edn (Chicago, Ill.: University of Chicago Press).

Prosser, T. (1986) *Nationalised Industries and Public Control* (Oxford: Basil Blackwell).

——(1997) *Law and the Regulators* (Oxford: Clarendon Press).

Prosser, T. (2000) 'Competition, Regulators and Public Service', in Rodger and MacCulloch (eds), 225–41.

—— (2001) 'Regulating Public Enterprises', *Public Law* 505–26.

Prouvez, N. (1997) 'The European Social Charter: An Instrument for the Protection of Human Rights in the 21st Century', 58–9 *The Review* (International Commission of Jurists) 30–44.

Quigley, C. and Collins, A. M. (2003) *EC State Aid Law and Policy* (Oxford: Hart Publishing).

Rangone, N. (1999) *I Servizi Pubblici* (Bologna: Il Mulino).

Rapp, L. (2004) 'France Télécom entre service public et secteur privé ou la tentation de Madrid', *Actualité Juridique – Droit Administratif* 579–90.

Richer, L. (1997) 'Remarques sur les entreprises privés de service public', *Actualité Juridique – Droit Administratif Spécial* 103–12.

Robson, W. (1962) *Nationalized Industry and Public Ownership*, 2nd edn (London: George Allen and Unwin).

Rodger, B. (2000) 'Competition Policy, Liberalism and Globalization: A European Perspective', 6 *Columbia Journal of European Law* 289–319.

—— (2003) *The Competition Act 1998 and State Entities as Undertakings*, CLASF Working Paper 1, at http://www.clasf.org/assets/CLaSF%20Working%20Paper%2001.pdf (consulted 16 July 2004).

Rodger, B. and MacCulloch, A. (eds) (2000) *The UK Competition Act: A New Era for UK Competition Law* (Oxford: Hart Publishing).

Ross, M. (2000) 'Article 16 EC and Services of General Interest: From Derogation to Obligation?', 25 *European Law Review* 22–38.

Saint Marc, R. D. de (1996) *Mission présidée par Renaud Denoix de Saint Marc, Rapport au Premier Ministre: Le Service Public* (Paris: La Documentation Française).

Santamato, S. and Pesaresi, N. (2004) 'Compensation for Services of General Economic Interest: Some Thoughts on the *Altmark* Ruling', *EC Competition Policy Newsletter*, 17–21.

Sauter, W. (1998) 'Universal Service Obligations and the Emergence of Citizens' Rights in European Telecommunications Liberalization', in M. Freedland and S. Sciarra (eds) *Public Services and Citizenship in European Union Law* (Oxford: Clarendon Press), 117–43.

Schepel, H. (2002) 'Delegation of Regulatory Powers to Private Parties under EC Competition Law: Towards a Procedural Public Interest Test' 39 *Common Market Law Review* 31–51.

Schlesinger, P. (1997) 'From Cultural Defence to Political Culture: Media, Politics and Collective Identity in the European Union', 19 *Media, Culture and Society* 360–91.

Schrameck, O. (1996) 'Décision no 96-380 DC du 23 Juillet 1996', *Actualité Juridique – Droit Administratif* 696.

Sciarra, S. (1998) 'Labour Law and Constitutional Rights', in M. Freedland and S. Sciarra (eds) *Public Services and Citizenship in European Union Law* (Oxford: Clarendon Press), 173–205.

Scott, C. (2000) 'Services of General Interest in EC Law: Matching Values to Regulatory Technique in the Public and Privatised Sectors', 6 *European Law Journal* 310–25.

Scotti, E. (2003) *Il Pubblico Servizio: Tra Tradizione Nazionale e Prospettive Europee* (Milan: Cedam).

Sharpe, T. (1992) 'Undue Price Discrimination and Undue Preference: A Legal Perspective', 2(1) *Consumer Policy Review* 33–5.

Shaw, J. (2001) 'The Treaty of Nice: Legal and Constitutional Implications', 7 *European Public Law* 195–215.

Stelzer, I. (nd) 'The Market and the Diffusion of New Media', in Independent Television Commission, *Culture and Communications: Perspectives on Broadcasting and the Information Society* (London: Independent Television Commission), 36–45.

Sunstein, C. (1997) *Free Markets and Social Justice* (New York: Oxford University Press).

Szyszczak, E. (2001) 'Public Service Provision in Competitive Markets', 20 *Yearbook of European Law* 35–77.

Taggart, M. (1994) 'Public Utilities and Public Law', in P.A. Joseph (ed.) *Essays on the Constitution* (Wellington: Brooker's), 214–64.

—— (2000) *Private Property and Abuse of Rights in Victorian England* (Oxford: Oxford University Press).

Thirion, N. (2002) 'Existe-t-il des limites juridiques à la privatisation des enterprises publiques?', 66 *Revue Internationale de Droit Economique* 627–54.

Veljanovski, C. (nd) 'A Market-Led Information Economy', in Independent Television Commission, *Culture and Communications: Perspectives on Broadcasting and the Information Society* (London: Independent Television Commission), 112–17.

Vesperini, G. (1998) 'L'attuazione della carta dei servizi pubblici in Italia', *Rivista Trimestrale di Diritto Pubblico* 173–84.

Vickers, J. and Yarrow, G. (1988) *Privatization: An Economic Analysis* (Cambridge, Mass.: The MIT Press).

Vincent-Jones, P. (1997) 'Hybrid Organization, Contractual Governance, and Compulsory Competitive Tendering in the Provision of Local Authority Services', in S. Deakin and J. Michie (eds) *Contracts, Co-operation, and Competition: Studies in Economics, Management and Law* (Oxford: Oxford University Press), 143–74.

—— (2000) 'Central–Local Relations under the Local Government Act 1999: A New Consensus?', 63 *Modern Law Review* 84–103.

Voisset, M. (1999) 'La reconnaissance, en France, d'un droit des citoyens à la qualité dans les services publics', 15 *Revue Française de Droit Administratif* 743–9.

Whish, R. (2001) *Competition Law*, 4th edn (London: Butterworth).

Wilks, S. (1996) 'The Prolonged Reform of United Kingdom Competition Policy', in G. B. Doern and S. Wilks (eds) *Comparative Competition Policy: National Institutions in a Global Market* (Oxford: Clarendon Press), 139–84.

—— (1999) *In the Public Interest: Competition Policy and the Monopolies and Mergers Commission* (Manchester: Manchester University Press).

World Development Movement (2002) *Serving (Up) the Nation* (London: World Development Movement), at http://www.wdm.org.uk/cambriefs/Serving%20(up)%20the%20nation.pdf (consulted 1 July 2004).

INDEX